Understanding Art Education

What is distinctive about art and design as a subject in secondary schools?

What contribution does it make to the wider curriculum?

How can art and design develop the agency of young people?

Understanding Art Education examines the theory and practice of helping young people learn in and beyond the secondary classroom. It provides guidance and stimulation for ways of thinking about art and design when preparing to teach and provides a framework within which teachers can locate their own experiences and beliefs.

Designed to complement the core textbook *Learning to Teach Art and Design in the Secondary School*, which offers pragmatic approaches for trainee and newly qualified teachers, this book suggests ways in which art and design teachers can engage reflexively with their continuing practice.

Experts in the field explore:

- the histories of art and design education and their relationship to wider social and cultural developments
- creativity as a foundation for learning
- engaging with contemporary practice in partnership with external agencies
- the role of assessment in evaluating creative and collaborative practices
- interdisciplinary approaches to art and design
- developing dialogue as a means to address citizenship and global issues in art and design education.

Understanding Art Education will be of interest to all students and practising teachers, particularly those studying at M level, as well as teacher educators and researchers who wish to reflect on their identities as artists and teachers and the ways in which the subject can inform and contribute to education and society more widely.

Nicholas Addison is Senior Lecturer in Art, Design & Museology and Course Leader for the MA Art & Design in Education at the Institute of Education, University of

Lesley Burgess is Senior Lecturer in Art, Design & Museology and Course Leader for the PGCE in Art & Design at the Institute of Education, University of London, UK.

John Steers is General Secretary of the National Society for Education in Art and Design, and Visiting Senior Research Fellow at Roehampton University, London, UK.

Jane Trowell is Lecturer on the MA Arts Policy and Management at Birkbeck, University of London, UK, and Co-Director of the London-based interdisciplinary group PLATFORM.

Understanding Art Education

Engaging reflexively with practice

Nicholas Addison, Lesley Burgess, John Steers and Jane Trowell

Routledge
Taylor & Francis Group

LONDON AND NEW YORK

First published 2010
by Routledge
2 Park Square, Milton Park, Abingdon, Oxon OX14 4RN

Simultaneously published in the USA and Canada
by Routledge
270 Madison Avenue, New York, NY 10016

Routledge is an imprint of the Taylor & Francis Group, an informa business

© 2010 Nicholas Addison, Lesley Burgess, John Steers and Jane
Trowell.

Typeset in Galliard by
Pindar NZ, Auckland, New Zealand
Printed and bound in Great Britain by
TJ International Ltd, Padstow, Cornwall

British Library Cataloguing in Publication Data
A catalogue record for this book is available from the British
Library

Library of Congress Cataloging-in-Publication Data
Art and design : teaching school subjects / Nicholas Addison ...
[et al.]. — 1st ed.
    p. cm. — (Teaching school subjects 11–19)
    Includes bibliographical references and index.
    1. Art—Study and teaching (Secondary)—Great Britain. I.
Addison, Nicholas, 1954-
    N365.G7A75 2009
    707.1'2—dc22   2009018071

ISBN 10: (hbk) 0-415-36739-5
ISBN 13: (hbk) 978-0-415-36739-4

ISBN 10: (pbk) 0-415-36740-9
ISBN 13: (pbk) 978-0-415-36740-0

ISBN 10: (ebk) 0-203-01978-4
ISBN 13: (ebk) 978-0-203-01978-8

Contents

List of illustrations   vii
Authors   viii
Acknowledgements   x

Introduction   1
NICHOLAS ADDISON AND LESLEY BURGESS

PART I
Histories and Futures   5

1   Art and design in education: ruptures and continuities   7
    NICHOLAS ADDISON

2   A return to design in art and design: developing creativity and
    innovation   24
    JOHN STEERS

PART II
Reconceptualising Practice   41

3   Developing creative potential: learning through embodied
    practices   43
    NICHOLAS ADDISON

4   Learning as a social practice in art and design   67
    LESLEY BURGESS

5   Assessment and learning   93
    NICHOLAS ADDISON

PART III
Relocating Practice   111

6   Critical pedagogy   113
    NICHOLAS ADDISON

7   Collaborative liberatory practices for global citizenship   134
    JANE TROWELL

    Bibliography   148
    Index   165

List of illustrations

Figures

3.1   *The spiral motion of art making*, Peter Abbs   57
4.1   *Placemaking* Project, IoE, photographer Nicholas
      Addison   75
4.2   *Placemaking* Project, IoE, photographer Lesley Burgess   76
4.3   Enquire exhibition, The Nunnery Gallery, Bow Arts
      2005, photographer Nicholas Addison   80
4.4   Enquire exhibition, The Nunnery Gallery, Bow Arts
      2005, photographer Nicholas Addison   81
4.5   Enquire project 2005: still from video, GCSE students   84
4.6   Rasheed Araeen *Deconstructions: Zero to Infinity* 2005,
      291 Gallery, photographer Lesley Burgess   86
4.7   Rasheed Araeen and public *Deconstructions: Zero to
      Infinity* 2005, 291 Gallery, photographer Lesley Burgess   86
4.8   Rasheed Araeen and public *Deconstructions: Zero to
      Infinity* 2005, Spitalfields Market, photographer artist/teacher   87
6.1   *Installation* 1999, IoE PGCE student, photographer
      Nicholas Addison   122

Authors

Nicholas Addison is a senior lecturer in Art, Design & Museology at the Institute of Education and Course Leader for the MA Art & Design in Education at the University of London, UK. He also supervises doctoral students and coordinates the Primary PGCE Art & Design specialism. For 16 years, he taught art and design and art history at a comprehensive school and a sixth form college in London. With Lesley Burgess, he has co-edited *Issues in Art & Design Teaching* (2003) and *Learning to Teach Art and Design in the Secondary School* (2007), also published by Routledge. His research interests include: critical studies, intercultural education, sexualities and identity politics. He directed the AHRB-funded research project, 'Art Critics and Art Historians in Schools' (2003) and co-directed with Lesley Burgess 'En-quire: Critical Minds' (2005–2006), which investigated the types of learning made possible when working with galleries of contemporary art.

Lesley Burgess is a senior lecturer in Art, Design & Museology and Course Leader for the PGCE in Art & Design at the Institute of Education, University of London, UK. She teaches on both the MA Art & Design in Education and Museums & Galleries in Education courses. Between 1992 and 2001, she was Co-Director of the Artists in Schools Training Programme. Before moving to the Institute in 1990, she taught for 15 years in London comprehensive schools. She was a trustee of Camden Arts Centre. With Nicholas Addison, she has co-edited *Issues in Art & Design Teaching* (2003) and *Learning to Teach Art and Design in the Secondary School* (2007), also published by Routledge. Her main research interests are: curriculum development, issues of gender, and contemporary art and artists in education. She co-directed, with the Victoria & Albert Museum, a DfEE-funded research project called 'Creative Connections' (2002), which investigated the use of galleries and museums as a learning resource. She also co-directed with Nicholas Addison 'En-quire: Critical Minds' (2005–2006), which investigated the types of learning made possible when working with galleries of contemporary art.

John Steers was appointed General Secretary of the National Society for Art Education (now the National Society for Education in Art and Design) in 1981 after 14 years of teaching art and design in secondary schools in London and Bristol, UK. He was the 1993–1996 President of the International Society for Education through Art, and has served on its executive committee in several capacities between 1983 and the present. He has also served on many national committees and as a consultant to government agencies. He has published widely on curriculum, assessment and policy issues. He is a trustee of the Higher Education in Art and Design Trust and the Chair of the Trustees of the National Arts Education Archive, Bretton Hall. He is also a visiting senior research fellow at Roehampton University, London, UK.

Jane Trowell is a part-time lecturer in Art, Design & Museology. She is a PGCE tutor and has worked as an MA tutor on the 'Issues in Art & Design Education' and 'Dissertation' modules. Her specialism is critical and contextual studies in art and design and she has taught at secondary schools, and for sixth form and FE. She worked as an action researcher on the AHRB-funded 'Art Critics and Art Historians in Schools' research project (2003) and as a researcher on the DCMS-funded 'En-Quire: Critical Minds' project (2005–2006). Jane has published a number of articles on engaged pedagogies and the interrelation of art, education and activism, and is a Trustee of The Black Environment Network. She is co-director of PLATFORM, the London-based interdisciplinary group, and also lectures on the MA Arts Policy & Management at Birkbeck, University of London, UK.

Acknowledgements

We would like to thank the students and teachers with whom we have worked at the Institute of Education, University of London, UK, and its partnership schools, for their insights into the relationship between art practice and pedagogy. Nicholas Addison would like to thank Roy Prentice for his thoughts on creativity and Anton Franks for furthering his understanding of Vygotskian theory. We wish to acknowledge the contributions made by gallery educators and artists to our teaching and research, particularly those involved in the *Enquire* research project: Bow Arts, Chisenhale, Space and the Whitechapel Art Gallery. Lesley Burgess wishes to thank Catherine Williamson and The Prince's Foundation for the collaboration, *Place Making*. She also wishes to thank Rasheed Araeen and Vivien Ashley for the work they contributed to the research project *Reconstructions* in which artist teachers worked with Araeen on the collaborative piece *Deconstruction Zero to Infinity*.

Nicholas Addison and Lesley Burgess

Introduction

Nicholas Addison and Lesley Burgess

In choosing to become a teacher of art and design in secondary school, you have moved from one field of practice (art, craft and design) to another (that of pedagogy). By making this choice, you have signalled a wish to help young people learn in and through a range of valued practices. These practices gain their value because they provide people with the means to shape the made environment, the world in which we all live, and to explore and celebrate beliefs and identities, thereby extending what it is to be human through imaginative and creative transformations. The fact that you have been immersed in this field, that you may have a 'passionate attachment' to it, is significant. This attachment is likely to inform the type of teacher you will, or have, become. In this sense, your understanding of the field is central to your personal history and identity and is something that you may be intent on sustaining throughout your career as a teacher; indeed, you may see yourself as an artist teacher or a teaching artist, someone who moves across and between fields. As this identity has been so significant for you, it is important that you communicate this to students and that you encourage them to recognise the vital contribution of art, craft and design to the making and remaking of culture. We therefore pose a series of questions to help you look at the specificity of art, craft and design both in education and within society more widely.

What is distinctive about art and design as a subject in secondary schools?

What contribution does it make to the wider curriculum?

How does learning in and through art, craft and design allow students to construct forms of knowledge that are marginalised in other areas of the curriculum?

Can the subject provide ways of thinking and doing that enable students to navigate the rapid changes in contemporary society, both local and global?

How can art and design develop the agency of young people, enabling them to participate, collaborate and contribute to these transformations?

In our earlier edited book *Learning to Teach Art and Design in the Secondary School* (2007), we offered a pragmatic approach to learning how to teach. This book is intended as a complement to the earlier one, a way to incite you to engage reflexively with your continuing practice. We therefore conceive it as a tool to help you question the insularity and sedimented orthodoxies in the subject in order to move art and design forward in response to contemporary realities. However, this process should not only be one of critique, a negation of past practices. On the contrary, it should involve a dialogue between past and developing practices.

In order to facilitate this dialogue, the two chapters in section 1, *Histories and Futures*, examine the histories of art education, providing a genealogy within which you can start to locate your own experiences and beliefs. You may find that your pedagogic practice resonates with some earlier tradition or, in contradistinction, you may sense that any such retrospection is a form of retreat. These two chapters demonstrate that art education has a rich past, one that provides a resource that can still be mined. But it is also important to understand that this past has not necessarily been comfortable; indeed, factions within it have jostled for dominance, very often on class and gendered, as well as philosophical lines. And yet, by the 1950s, Herbert Read's notion of creative learning through art was perceived as an answer to the restrictive practices of traditional pedagogies; indeed, it could be argued that by the 1960s it provided a model for other progressive educators. This centrality was not to last for long. An understanding of the histories and shifting positions of art education will therefore make you more aware of why art and design is now located outside the centre of the secondary curriculum. Nonetheless, creativity is once again being promoted as the panacea to educational reform. This renewed interest provides an opportunity for the subject in secondary schools, something that Steers explores in Chapter 2 on the position of design within the curriculum.

Steers' advocacy leads into the second section, *Reconceptualising Practice*, where, in Chapter 3, Addison revisits definitions of creativity to arrive at an understanding of its democratic potential. He asks you, as a person with experience and knowledge of creative processes, to consider the conditions for creative action rather than creative outcomes or personalities. Burgess, in Chapter 4, focuses on art, craft and design as social practices. She responds to government initiatives to develop creative practices through partnerships, exploring a built environment project in which students worked co-operatively to conceptualise the nature of community. In addition, she makes reference to the findings of a research project 'Critical Minds', and a collaboration with the artist Rasheed Araeen, to look at the way in which art and design teachers can work with others in the field to develop their professional practice. In Chapter 5, on assessment and learning, Addison looks at the ways in which assessment can be used productively to inform and evaluate creative and collaborative practices. This chapter draws on Vygotskian theory to reinforce an understanding of learning as a social activity.

In the final section, *Relocating Practice*, Addison argues in Chapter 6 that critical pedagogy is not antithetical to creative approaches to learning and teaching in art and design. He asks: Why does it appear that the cultural and educational policies of a succession of governments seem incapable of alleviating years of sedimented privilege and alienation both in the arts and in education? He invites you to engage with the notion of an education for democracy by offering strategies for the investigation and interpretation of material and visual culture through both making and discursive practices. He ends by looking at the potential of dialogue to help resolve dichotomies in the field. In the last chapter, Trowell extends notions of dialogue and partnership to look at what interdisciplinarity looks like in practice. She draws on her experience as a member of PLATFORM, an interdisciplinary, activist group, to consider how you might address the National Curriculum's emphasis on cross-curricular collaboration, particularly in respect of citizenship and global issues.

In the book, we argue for a type of reflexivity in which, rather than reflecting on your pedagogic actions as if you were their sole author, you think of them as interactions with others, as co-constructed events through which all participants learn. This is not always a comfortable position to be in. But we think it is important for you to question the rhetorical turn towards forms of 'soft pedagogy' that have become fashionable in recent years because their 'feel-good' aims tend to camouflage the tensions you are likely to experience in your everyday interactions in schools. Tolerance and comfort are all well and good, but understanding and democratic action are more likely to effect change.

Part I

Histories and Futures

Chapter 1

Art and design in education
Ruptures and continuities

Nicholas Addison

Introduction

> I wonder if I've been changed in the night? Let me think. Was I the same when I got up this morning? I almost think I can remember feeling a little different. But if I'm not the same, the next question is 'Who in the world am I?' Ah, *that's* the great puzzle!
>
> (Alice in Carroll 1962: 36)

Education at its most fulfilling is recognised as a transformative process, one in which people come to understandings of the world that help them to live their lives more richly and rationally. In this sense, education changes people; like Alice, on one day they can be one thing, on the next, another. Art education, and the subject in schools, art and design, is frequently spoken of in this way, whether change occurs gradually through modifications to learning dispositions, pleasure in making something worthwhile or, more radically, through an 'illuminating experience' (Taylor 1986: 18–34) or a 'traumatic conversive experience' (Hargreaves 1983). In this sense, the products of art, craft and design activity not only transform people's material and visual environment but also the way they think about themselves and others.

The aim of this chapter is to show you that this transformative potential has not always been central to the aims of art education; indeed, at times, it has been used for explicitly instrumental ends. I try to tell the history of art education as a sort of narrative, one in which different aims and values are proposed, put into practice, pitted one against the other, move to resolution then further conflict, are revisited, reconceptualised and sometimes reformed. In this way, I intend to look at what the subject has become; that is, what it signals within the curriculum as a whole, and how and why it has turned out that way. In effect, this chapter is an analysis of the discourses that have helped to shape a subject that was once central to modernist beliefs about the purpose of progressive education but that has since become more peripheral.

It is important that, as teachers of art and design, you are able to advocate your subject from an informed position, not only in relation to your practice as an artist, craftsperson and designer, but also as a teacher who understands the possibilities for art education in schools. This chapter is therefore designed to help you position and evaluate your beliefs within a specific, educational history and to encourage you to follow up reading that can support your developing pedagogy by placing it within the discourses that, as you enter the profession, dominate it (Moore 2004). In this way, and like Alice, you can engage with the question: 'Who in the world am I?' and, further, 'what might I become?' It is therefore also designed to help you defend and promote what you teach as an instance of wider philosophical concerns and social practices. This is particularly important after the introduction of a new curriculum in 2008 (designed to supplant the old one by 2011). This reconceived curriculum not only encourages teachers to look at local resources and situations, it also foregrounds the contribution that different subjects can offer to ways of learning and how they can work together to equip 'learners with the personal, learning and thinking skills that they will need to succeed in education, life and work' (QCA 2007a).

Art and design teachers often pride themselves on the difference of their subject from others within a school curriculum that many progressive educators have characterised as over-prescribed and information-led (Eisner 1998). This difference revolves around a belief that practices in the subject are, of essence, creative and thus foster creativity in all students. An array of attendant ideas and aspirations is called upon to bolster this unique position and claims are made that qualities and aptitudes – such as individuality, self-expression, autonomy and spiritual well-being – may result from an immersion in its practices. As the foundational document for art and design, the National Curriculum itself is not shy of this perception (QCA 2007a) and there is undoubtedly a degree of credibility in its claims, for art and design does offer the potential for students to develop creative attitudes and practices that increase their ability to make informed choices in shaping the environment in which they live. However, many of the hyberbolic claims extolling the relationship between art and freedom (see the earlier NC order, DfEE 1999) echo and rehearse myths that have accrued to the practice of fine artists in the west since the Romantic period (craftspeople and designers rarely figure in this pantheon) and were initially injected into art education at the turn of the nineteenth/twentieth century (Cunliffe 1999). These myths have coalesced in the popular imagination around the figure of the outsider, frequently tragic, artist; consider Hollywood and British films as indicative of this stereotype, from Kirk Douglas as Van Gogh in 'Lust for Life' (1956), Tony Hancock in 'The Rebel' (1961) to 'Basquiat' (1996), Bacon in 'Love is the Devil' (1998), Pollock (2000) and 'Frida' Kahlo (2002).

In this chapter, I wish to show how this mythology distorts the social and cultural practices of contemporary artists, craftspeople and designers; that is, a distortion of the way in which the majority of artists live their lives and practice their art. I also intend to question the way that these myths have affected the school subject both in terms of practices in the classroom and its wider reception within the school community.

Although this book is primarily concerned to help you contribute to moving art and design forward, for the moment it is nevertheless necessary to look back.

Art and art education in modernism

Some philosophers, artists and art educators have believed that art and aesthetics can change the world (Nietzsche 1872/86; Dewey 1916, 1934; Read 1943, 1950; Beuys 1973). In the first half of the twentieth century, attempts to put this utopian claim into practice took diverging political paths, from the rural sanctuaries and small urban collectives of the early avant-garde, the activist networks of Dada and Surrealism, the design experiments of the early Soviet, De Stijl and Bauhaus, and on to the manic excesses of the Nazi regime (Taylor and van der Will 1990). What all these attempts had in common was that they offered an alternative to the bourgeois norms of the consolidating capitalist nation states of the west, whether in the form of a retreat, critique, intervention or wholesale revolution. It was during this time that many artists had re-educated themselves in opposition to the conservative principles of the nineteenth-century academy and, embodied in the forms of modernist art, craft and design, proffered their beliefs to the people. Often, these beliefs were antagonistic to prevailing norms and were thus received as alien and alienating and, as such, summarily dismissed. However, in those circumstances in which artists were in alliance or collusion with the state, these beliefs were sometimes imposed on urban populations, especially in the form of architecture and design. But newly imposed beliefs and practices tend to last only as long as the regime that imposes them, so, in the second half of the century, the preferred strategy of modernist thinkers in Europe was to parallel urban and environmental change with programmes of education in an attempt to alter the beliefs of the people for the good. Read (1943), for example, echoing Dewey (1934), argued that by educating young people in and through art they could be led away from the conformity and competition fostered by traditional pedagogies towards collective and creative action. More recently, Joseph Beuys (1973) claimed 'Only art is capable of dismantling a senile social system that continues to totter along the deathline: dismantle in order to build A SOCIAL ORGANISM AS A WORK OF ART' (p. 125).

During the 1970s, such claims and practices were increasingly developed in social situations through community and public art, a development that has since come to be known as 'New Genre Public Art' (Lacy 1995), 'relational aesthetics' (Bourriaud 1998) and/or 'dialogical aesthetics' (Kester 2004). This is not so much a movement as a set of common strategies deployed by artists to organise collaborative, temporal and socially situated events. Typically, a small group of artists work with people who are perceived as marginal to the dominant discourses and practices in the field (Paley 1994; Lacy 1995). Although such artists draw on the strategies of the early avant-garde, they are more concerned with changing attitudes and social practices through participation than with critiquing practices within the art world. In relation to school art, they offer real opportunities to develop inclusive, socially engaged and critical practices (greater attention is given to this approach in Chapters 4 and 7).

Counters to modernist beliefs

In contrast to the positive view of the arts as a transformative force, a number of intellectuals have argued that the western concept of art is a primary means for reinforcing and consolidating existing power relations. For Bourdieu (1984), it is a mark of distinction, a way to separate those with knowledge and taste from those with none, a social process that secures and perpetuates class privileges. For Baudrillard (2005), art is (more brutally) an accomplice of power, the most immediate way to construct spectacle and propagate myths and untruths. Power, in its contemporary manifestation as global capital, is sustained through corporate, media practices and disseminated through a multimedia network that is constructed and coordinated by designers. It should be remembered that your students, in terms of numbers, are far more likely to enter this field as a profession than that of fine art or craft. In a post-industrial, service economy, it is also likely to dominate the visual landscape of their lives and is therefore productive of their tastes and desires. The practices of socially engaged artists tend to critique the urgency and hegemony of this field, but many fine artists, despite the resistance of their work to normative taste and morality, are happy to belong to an international system in which the exchange value of a single work may exceed the annual GDP of the smallest and/or poorest nation states (taking Damien Hirst's diamond-encrusted skull '*For the Love of God*' (2007), selling for fifty million pounds, as a benchmark). Such works can be bought and sold as a sign of wealth and accumulated as investments; in this way, the productive work of artists may be just as much a part of the network of global capital as product design and advertising. Nevertheless, these realities and perceptions are rarely encountered in the art room because they do not conform to the Romantic myths of freedom that are so central to art's symbolic role, especially in the context of an education for democracy, nor do these facts reaffirm the sense of intrinsic goodness afforded central tenets of art education such as imagination and creativity. So why has the subject in schools become dominated by a fine art ethos rooted in a mythology, the truth of which is only partial?

Before looking at the changes within English art education in an attempt to map the continuities and discontinuities of the various discourses that in common make it an object of study, it is worth spending time considering how the term 'art' has fared in the same national context and within the time-span of modern history. The radical changes in art practice brought about by modernism are crucial to understanding why art and design has a unique and somewhat wayward position in the secondary curriculum.

Art in England

In England, it is the 'fine' or 'high' (brow) arts that tend to constitute most people's definition of Art with a capital 'A' (Bourdieu's 'field of restricted production', 1993). Williams (1988: 41) argues that this usage was not general until the nineteenth century, although it had already been established institutionally with the foundation of the Royal Academy of Arts in 1768. What differentiated the fine artist from the skilled artisan was the ability of the former to work with imagination and from within a tradition of representation that was afforded intellectual credibility. Together, these faculties came to constitute 'creative' work which, in the proselytising hands of the Romantic poets, was extended to include literary and musical as well as visual work, thus the concept of the arts (Williams 1965: 27–29). Although similar distinctions between the 'ars mechanica' and the 'ars intellectualis' had been formulated since the Middle Ages, and from the sixteenth century had been institutionalised in Renaissance Italy (Pevsner 1940), Williams (1988) associates the distinction in England with the process of industrialisation in the eighteenth and nineteenth centuries. In the context of 'capitalist commodity production', the hierarchical necessity to redefine the 'purposes of the exercise of skill' (p. 42) was a prerequisite for the maintenance of developing power relations between the bourgeoisie (owners) and the aristocracy, and the bourgeoisie (professionals) and the emergent urban working class. Williams argues that, because capitalism reduces 'use values to exchange values':

> There was a consequent defensive specialization of certain skills and purposes to the arts or the *humanities* where forms of general use and intention which were not determined by immediate exchange could be at least conceptually abstracted. This is the formal basis of the distinction between art and *industry*, and between fine arts and useful arts (the latter eventually acquiring a new specialized term, in Technology (q.v.)).
>
> (ibid)

Williams draws on the definition of aesthetic practice provided by Karl Marx (1975) in his 1844 *Economic and Philosophical Manuscripts*, in which a rationale for the separation of art from the utilitarian can be found. Marx suggests that a satisfying and complete life can only be achieved through the cultivation of the aesthetic faculties:

> For not only the five senses, but also the so-called spiritual senses, the practical senses (will, love, etc.), in a word the *human* sense, the humanity of senses – all these come into being only through the existence of *their* objects, through *humanised* nature. The *cultivation* of the five senses is the work of all previous history. *Sense* which is a prisoner of crude practical need has only a *restricted* sense.
>
> (Marx 1975: 353)

The implication here is that within the immediate historical context, the majority of the population are unable to dedicate time to aesthetic cultivation due to the crude necessities of working by selling their labour. It is therefore the social responsibility of artists (in the widest sense; see below) to contribute to this cultivation by disseminating their work and by providing educational opportunities to enable everyone to participate at some level. In the second half of the nineteenth century, the Arts and Crafts movement at its most idealistic, in the late work of Morris and his disciples, attempted to achieve this. However, this group pitted themselves against industrial procedures and were therefore bound in the mid-term to fail. However, it could be argued that their concern with sustainability and the environment will ultimately win the day (Papanek 1994).

The definitions, divisions and uses that Williams identifies (1998) remain current. Therefore, objects whose primary function is representational and/or symbolic (e.g. traditional painting, sculpture: in utilitarian terms, those objects that are 'useless'), and other objects produced by a group of professionals calling themselves artists, are contrasted with two other classes of objects. First, objects manufactured for utility purposes: those produced by a) designers (mass-produced and dependent on industrial technologies) and b) craftspeople (dependent on pre- and post-industrial technologies); second, those objects produced for mass communication: advertising, cinema, television, the Internet (of which the visual component is often dependent on photographic imagery). Given that these uses gained common currency in the nineteenth century, it is not surprising that today traditional forms of fine art are set in opposition to the work of contemporary artists. Much contemporary practice takes the form of explicitly multimodal texts (frequently lens- or screen-based and often produced and disseminated in relation to the mass media tradition – that is, employing its technologies; Pijnappel 1994) – work that is signified as different because it is symbolic, discursive and reflexive rather than explicitly utilitarian (Hapgood 1994; Weintraub 1996; Jones 2003). Additionally, many contemporary artists question the hierarchical structures on which the mythology of traditional art and artists is maintained – in particular, the western, bourgeois notion of individual and originary creativity embodied in the self-expressive realisations of male genius (Parker and Pollock 1981: 1–14). The perpetual challenge to traditional modes, conventions and institutions that such modernist practices signal sits uncomfortably in an education system that aims to acculturate young people within dominant social and cultural practices where art tends to serve celebratory and/or recreational functions. Was it always this way?

Art and industry, art and morality: the Victorian legacy

The dominant form of English art education in the nineteenth century could not be further removed from the rhetoric of inclusivity underpinning the educational philosophy of the early twenty-first century. Swift (1995: 115–127) recounts how, from the 1850s, education at secondary level was unapologetically designed on the basis of class. The 'poor' were instructed in skills that they could apply to future employment but, in addition, received moral guidance as a means to ensure disciplined and conformist behaviour. Middle-class students were instructed in subjects that would provide them with signs of the necessary distinction for management, ownership and rule (e.g. Latin or Greek for boys). The art curriculum, The National Course of Instruction 1852, coordinated by Henry Cole, was likewise divided between a programme in which working-class students (mostly boys) were required to develop proficiency in mechanical drawing so that they could matriculate with the necessary foundational skills for the schools of design (where they had to sign a form agreeing not to pursue fine art), and courses of cultural enrichment where the copying of elevated exemplars inculcated good taste in the middle classes (mostly girls) and potentially enabled candidates to follow a career in fine art (mostly boys). A long, sequenced and assiduous course of drawing was common to both which, although subtly distinguished in terms of exemplars and appropriate mark-making, served a utilitarian function predicated on the principle of accuracy:

> Cole's view was that neat straight lines were the bedrock of all drawing, and from the age of four or so children could be schooled in linear, geometric outlines from flat copies and simple solids until they were ready for more complex solids. This was not a view which gained universal agreement [see the quotation from Ruskin below] but it certainly formed the basis of all children's school drawing until the 1890s, and that of the Art School elementary classes until well into the twentieth century.
>
> (Swift 1995: 120–121)

Because art and design education in Victorian England was inextricably bound to the economy – industrial (for boys), domestic (for girls) – it also served to inculcate and regulate necessary behaviours of production and consumption (Dalton 2001: 34–61), and to produce the 'docile body' (Foucault 1977). This is the morally acquiescent subject that the modern nation state requires.

Moral education

John Ruskin was arguably the most influential and popular Victorian critic on both sides of the Atlantic and he was read avidly by such diverse figures as Morris and Proust. Through his urgent and passionate prose and his principled and holistic vision, he offered an educational alternative to the instrumentalism of Cole – a vision that contributed to the founding of the Arts and Crafts movement. Ruskin argued that art was a particularly significant form of cultural production because, unlike other types of human behaviour, it manifests a moral certitude, not only through its content (a literary quality that was to be anathema to the formalists of modernism) but especially through the necessity for assiduous and loving craftsmanship:

> However mean or inconsiderable the act, there is something in the well
> doing of it which has fellowship of the noblest forms of manly virtue;
> and the truth, decision, and temperance, which we reverently regard as
> honourable conditions of the spiritual being, have a representative or
> derivative influence over the works of the hand, the movements of the
> frame, and the action of the intellect.

> ... For there is no action so slight, nor so mean, but it may be done to a great
> purpose, and ennobled therefore; nor is any purpose so great but that slight
> actions may help it and may be so done as to help it much, most especially
> that chief of all purposes, the pleasing of God.
>
> (Ruskin 1849: 7–8, Ruskin's emphasis)

Ruskin's 'doing acts well' was to take on the force of a prophetic pronounce-
ment in the development of further education at the turn of the century with
the foundation of design schools such as Central, St. Martins in London, and the
Birmingham and Manchester Municipal Schools of Arts and Crafts. However,
Ruskin's quest to develop an English art that could stand both as an emblem and
didactic support for English society was anathema to the new aestheticians and,
in the writings of Roger Fry, Ruskin's advocacy was radically opposed. Indeed, in
1920, Fry dismissed his work as 'a web of ethical questions, distorted by aesthetic
prejudices, which [his] exuberant and ill-regulated mind had spun for the British
public' (in Fernie 1995: 161). If art education was to abandon moral instruction
in this way, the vacuum had nonetheless to be filled.

It was the English language as deployed and elaborated within English literature
that supplanted the narrative image as the critical engine of national morality, a
position that the image had attained only once, and briefly, in England, due in no
mean measure to Ruskin's arguments. In this way, the potential of art to provide
a framework for a moral education, both through an ethics of handiwork and
through the narrative and interpretative potential of pictorial art, was instead taken
up after World War I by Frank Raymond Leavis and his followers; in other words,
the ideological function of moral unification that Ruskin envisaged for visual art
was transferred to literature. Interestingly, a concern for English literature had first
emerged not in the universities but in the Mechanics' institutes and working men's
colleges (see Eagleton 1983: 26) – the very same sites where, at the same time,
Ruskin and Morris had delivered their lectures on the social role of art and craft.

As it turned out, it was not the denial of literary and narrative features within
early modernism that blocked the discursive potential of art from being taken up
in schools, rather it was the emphasis on making in both instrumentalist and craft
education. In some senses, this is surprising given that English Literature has the
same objects of study, 'feeling and experience' as traditional, modernist art history
(although, in schools, Leavis' insistence on 'rigorous critical analysis' provided
English with a sounder methodological basis). But the critical appreciation of art
remained the purview of the adult middle classes, art history and critical studies

only entering the secondary curriculum in the second half of the twentieth century. But the subjects in schools are also different because of the claims made by Leavis and Fry. On the one hand, Leavis advocated a sort of retrospective indoctrination, standards of thought and expression which, had they been replicated, would have returned England to the 'organic' and 'agrarian' moral universe of the seventeenth century – 'a form of living sensibility without which modern industrial society would atrophy and die' (Eagleton 1983: 32). On the other hand, Fry advocated a progressive pedagogy somewhat indebted to Rousseau's belief in the natural and thus innate goodness of children (1762), a goodness contaminated and corrupted by traditional forms of education. But under the influence of 'art for art's sake', Fry purged Rousseau's philosophy of its moral basis so that it was no longer goodness but the imagination that constituted the innate and timeless faculty possessed by all – a faculty that could easily be destroyed or inhibited by moral and didactic teaching methods (see Swift 1992 on the teaching of Fry's associate Marion Richardson). It is true that, in Matthew Arnold (1822–1888) (in particular, *Culture and Anarchy* 1869), Leavis had a forerunner, but the context was very different: 'English as a subject was in part an offshoot of a gradual shift in class tone within English culture: "Englishness" was less a matter of Imperialist flag-waving than of country dancing; rural, populist and provincial rather than metropolitan and aristocratic' (Eagleton 1983: 37). The crafts movement, as it was sustained in art education up to the 1940s, was the equivalent of this tendency, although it was both more divided in terms of gender between practices that were 'appropriate' for girls and boys and more embedded within broader modes of production and consumption (Dalton 2001: 49–52; 91–97).

From the perspective of the progressive educationalists, the Victorian programmes of accurate copying and moral guidance were distortions from a sensory and heuristic education, an inhibiting and stultifying process that produced nothing but a compliant and respectful population alienated from all that is human. Rather, for the progressives, the creativity of every child ought to be a cherished potential that could be cultivated through the free practice of art, a productivity that was a sign both of innocence (untainted by convention) and an indication of healthy growth.

Perhaps surprisingly, a precursor to these beliefs can be found in Ruskin himself, who advised parents and educators to allow children free reign in their early years. However, unlike his Romantic forerunners, he was quick to inculcate disciplinary measures once children were of an age when entry to adult sociality was pressing, realising that cultural conventions do, in fact, allow the individual access to forms of social communication and thus a position within the community:

> I do not think it advisable to engage a child in any but the most voluntary practice of art. If it [sic] has talent for drawing, it will be continually scrawling on what paper it can get; and should be allowed to scrawl at its own free will, due praise being given for every appearance of care, or truth, in its efforts … In later years … [parents] should praise it only for what costs it self-denial,

namely attention and hard work; otherwise they will make it work for vanity's sake, and always badly.

(Ruskin 1857: v–viii)

In the patriarchal society of Victorian England, this induction away from childish things towards a cultivated and moral sensibility was considered to be the role of the mother (Ruskin admitted that his love of literature was entirely due to the affectionate administrations of his mother as she sat with him as a child reading aloud). Indeed, the earlier domestication of women within the philosophy of Rousseau and his followers (see Chadwick 1989: 137–138) produced a feminine discourse of the beautiful, which:

> allowed the expression of tender and subtle emotion, of taste, elegance and smoothness ... It was to be this discourse ... taught by bourgeois women teachers, which was imported into school as a counter-discourse to the dominance of rational models of drawing. Through the benevolence of the bourgeois woman art teacher, the taste and behaviour of working class children could be elevated and improved.

(Dalton 2001: 44–45)

This somewhat limited and patronising discourse, through which the 'primitive' and vulgar were to be excised, was superseded by a discourse from early years teaching (also dominated by women) that was concerned with the affective and spiritual well-being of the child, an 'emotional labour' (Noon and Blyton 1997) that was a direct legacy of Romantic educational philosophy. The transatlantic exchange was significant here, as child-centred European pedagogies infiltrated English education through an American, as well as European, filter in both their progressive and behaviourist forms (Dalton 2001: 65–66).

Creative models of art education, 1900–1980

Art education in late nineteenth-century schools, as opposed to mechanical instruction in drawing, was largely the preserve of women teachers. The Art Teacher's Guild had been founded in 1900 to represent this growing workforce and it enabled women to gain a significant voice in education. Members of the Guild were adamantly opposed to the didactic and instrumental pedagogy of their male counterparts in the National Society of Art Masters, promoting in its place the egalitarian, child-centred pedagogies associated with progressive and liberal education, particularly those of Ebenezer Cooke (c1837–1913) and Franz Cizek (1865–1947) for whom:

> art was more than merely *comparable* to other educational disciplines in the curriculum, but was an aspect of human development whose absence impaired mental growth and diminished social fitness. All perceptible ills of

society ... could be attributed to the suppression of free creativity in children and the encouragement of a substitute, pseudo-creativity in the form of conventional art.

(Thistlewood 1992c: 182)

For the Guild, art education was evidently a historical necessity that could serve to transform the entire nation. This could be achieved because, in childhood, creativity is natural and creativity is the source of all positive change. It was the responsibility of art teachers, and they alone, to develop this natural proclivity rather than suppress it like their erstwhile colleagues. The progressive sequencing of this process, borrowed from psychological models (see Dalton 2001: 62–86) initially emphasised play and the expression of an 'inner life' through the imaginative transformation of traditional pictorial and craft materials. Only slowly, and only when the child was ready, should s/he be introduced to the conventions and social uses of art so that ultimately s/he could contribute to visual culture from a position of organic integrity rather than conventional inculcation. This evolutionary model of the child suggests that each person is a unique and separate being whose inner-self, essentially a 'spiritual essence' or 'mental construct', is separate from, and potentially contaminable by, social interaction. In this sense, it is a model that presents itself as neutral in terms of gender and culture. It has clear affinities with the universal theories of expression being fought over in the field of art production (Croce 1901) in which the artist too was theorised as a unique individual capable of extraordinary feats of the imagination.

Initially, child-centred pedagogies were only loosely connected with those anthropological and colonial discourses (some, supposedly, paternalistically benevolent), simultaneously informing practice in the field of art production. However, through the writings of Fry (1909), progressive art education took on board the continental, universalising discourse of primitivism as well as the potential for formalist interpretation. It was largely due to the pedagogic experiments (1915–1920) of Marion Richardson that a creative model of learning and teaching in art was given lasting credibility in English schools. She met Fry in 1917 at an exhibition of children's drawings shown at his Omega Workshops. He was so persuaded by the work that she brought with her, that he included examples in the same exhibition (Holdsworth 2005). Fry observed that 'all children who had not been taught had got something interesting and personal to say ... with keen and unjaded visual appetite. Further, most educated children infallibly lost much, if not all, of this power when they reached the age of complete self-consciousness' (in Swift 1992: 126). Richardson's methods supposedly allowed the 'unjaded visual appetite' to be healthily directed to personal fruition rather than constrained and contaminated. Field (1970) suggests that the significance of her methods 'in the development of art education in this country cannot be overestimated' (p. 54). After leaving Dudley High School (Birmingham), Richardson's ideas on the creative child were disseminated widely when she became the first person to run a course for specialist art teachers at the London Day Training College and then as a District Inspector of Schools for London under R. R. Tomlinson (see Steers, Chapter 2). By the 1930s, her influence had spread all over the country. This influence was sustained by the publication of her book, *Art and the Child* (Richardson 1948), which she wrote partly to counter the misinterpretation of her methods, 'for her famous "descriptions" were travestied by others who did not really understand' (Field 1970: 54).

If Richardson's methods encouraged art teachers to adopt exercises intended to develop the imaginations of children, it was Herbert Read in his books *Education through Art* (1943) and *Education for Peace* (1950) who developed a modernist ethics of art practice designed to sustain such processes throughout all educational sectors. Yet it should be remembered that his was an ethics informed by his political and theoretical affiliations (initially one of anarchy, see his novel '*The Green Child*' 1935) and Jungian psychoanalysis. Although the didacticists had had their day in the 1918 educational reforms, it was the philosophy of the Guild (by 1940 reconfigured as the Society for Education in Art) that informed the Butler Education Act (1944) and, bolstered by Read as the most prominent member of the society's Consultative Committee, the principle of individual growth for a healthy and unified society permeated the provision for art in legislation, just as Lowenfeld's theories on creativity (1947) were beginning to inform changes in US art education (Efland 1990).

Thistlewood (1984) highlights Read's importance for art education mid-century:

> In *Art and Society* [Read 1937] the artist was still an exceptional individual, an otherwise-neurotic who had chanced upon ways of evading this fate by expressing potentially repressed phantasy in plastic or literary form ... In *Education through Art* everyone – that is, every child – is a potential neurotic who may be saved from this prospect if early, largely inborn, creative abilities are not repressed by conventional education.
>
> (pp. 112–113)

This later book, written at a time of war, proved very influential and persuaded a wide public, but particularly teachers, that art practice provided not only a solace but the means by which society could be transformed towards a non-alienated, organic unity. Influenced by Nietzsche, Read promoted the artist as an 'ideal type' who is capable of overriding conventional prejudices, a process central to his redemptive vision of utopia. This type, replicated and multiplied through creative education, would transform the whole population and, as a counter to totalitarian experiments in social unification, lead to peace.

It is not surprising, given Read's immense stature within the cultural establishment and his ability to communicate to a general audience, that his advocacy provided art education with a compelling rationale and a status that overturned earlier economic and recreational justifications. His advocacy of imaginative processes (rather than his political convictions) was to resurface in the 1970s in the work of Witkin (1974) and later Ross (1978; 1984) and Abbs (1987; 1989; 1994). The work of this group revives the liberal humanism of Leavis, arguing that the arts provide an aesthetic and spiritual counterweight to an instrumentalist, information-driven curriculum. But these appeals to truth in the name of universalism were, and are, profoundly Eurocentric in orientation (see, for example, Hardy's discussion of Ruskin's cultural misunderstandings, 2003; see Cahan and Kocur 1996, and Addison and Dash 2007, for further discussion of working towards a plural curriculum).

For the entrenched traditionalists of the mid-century, Read's advocacy was so much 'tosh' and the split in ideals between progressive and traditional pedagogies was reinforced by the establishment of two professional organisations that perpetuated the old gender divide: the Society for Education in Art (SEA) (formed 1940, previously the Art Teachers' Guild) and the National Society for Art Education (NSAE) (formed 1944, previously the National Society of Art Masters [NSAM]). The SEA remained entirely persuaded by untutored forms of creativity, whereas the NSAE were convinced by the need for a didactic programme. During the war, and immediately after it, the progressives won the argument for art education, albeit that practice remained obdurately traditional in many schools. After the war, the male members of the NSAE found in Basic Design (see below) the potential for a new didacticism that could contribute to the masculine endeavours of industrial reconstruction (Dalton 2001: 102–105). Exercises adapted from Basic Design found their way into schools and, for a short while, transformed the look of school art in some centres. Basic design was therefore the only principled incursion into a pedagogy that upheld a pictorial regime, whether academic or 'untutored' (although this was supplemented by traditional craft activities). This regime could not be further from the reductive formalism of Greenberg (the dominant tendency in the field of art production during the same period, the 1950s and 1960s), suggesting the extreme divergence of school art from mainstream developments in associated cultural fields. Despite the cogent advocacy of the progressives, the traditionalists ensured that, for most school students, drawing from observation remained the bedrock activity right up to (and beyond) the 1950s – a legacy of Victorian pedagogy where drawing was both a moral exercise and technical prerequisite for good design.

Basic Design

Although Basic Design is associated with a tradition stemming from Bauhaus pedagogy, it can be seen as a mode of teaching that reconciles the earlier philosophies of the Victorian Arts and Crafts movement with modern modes of production and theories of perception. The founder of the Bauhaus (1919–1933), Walter Gropius (1883–1969), had been quick to acknowledge his indebtedness to the socialist vision promulgated by English theorists, particularly William Morris (1834–1896). It is therefore not surprising, after the emigration of Bauhaus personnel and principles to the USA during the mid to late 1930s, to encounter in English higher education a variation of Bauhaus practice after World War II (earlier, more local applications are discussed by Thistlewood 1992a). In the Bauhaus experiment, an attempt had been made to ally modernist aesthetics and pedagogy to inform 'building' (Gropius was, after all, an architect); in this sense, it was an attempt to transfer an aesthetic from the restricted field (albeit of design) to the field of mass production. In line with the socialist principles that underpinned its philosophy, the Bauhaus aimed to improve the built environment in order to transform society, an effort that, unlike the Arts and Crafts movement, was not necessarily antagonistic to new technologies and thus potentially applicable to industrial production. In practice this ambition was not fulfilled because, despite the dream of a unified and unifying social art, as the Bauhaus developed, the various artists/pedagogues tended to factionalise and 'the increasing specialisation of architecture in particular … resulted in the separation of the disciplines into "purist camps"' (Meecham and Sheldon 2000: 45). However, in the 1950s and 1960s, its English disciples drew heavily on the pedagogic writings of Paul Klee and Lazlo Moholy-Nagy to initiate post-school courses that collectively became known as the Basic Design movement (see Thistlewood 1992a; Lynton in Thistlewood 1992; Yeomans 2005). The exercises in formal and material experimentation encouraged within this pedagogy were intended to support individual aesthetic experience and originating activity, and thus to inform design for better living. But in their application, the 'abstract' results were sometimes superimposed on structures, both physical and social, that proved antithetical to well-being (for an example, see Passmore's architectural experiments at Peterlee, Walker 2003: 18).

In secondary education, the book *Basic Design: the dynamics of visual form* by Maurice De Sausmarez (1964) encouraged art teachers to move beyond the expressivist model that was so beneficial for young children towards a system in which the interdependence of intuition and intellect was acknowledged as necessary for adult creative action. This move to engage with art practice as an objective and rational entity chimed with attempts in the USA to recognise art as a cognitive mode of enquiry (Efland 1990). In Basic Design, the emphasis shifted from drawing the seen world to an investigation of the underlying mathematical structures that formed the basis of the natural world, an approach influenced by the work of D'Arcy Thompson whose *On Growth and Form* (1917) had been republished and revised in 1942. Acknowledging the material and abstract basis of much contemporary art (Thistlewood 1990a), students were provided with a range of media, often three-dimensional, and set a sequence of experiments in which the formal elements of visual design were presented as a type of proto-grammar and syntax. Proponents argued that the knowledge accruing from investigations into the relationship between form and function could be applied and extended to all forms of visual practice: abstract or figurative, expressive or applied. Process was emphatically foregrounded to the extent that outcomes were often discarded, a tendency that was motivating only for those intent on pursuing art education to higher levels.

Thistlewood (1992b) estimates that Basic Design was a revolutionary period of creative art education; Dalton (2001), however, exposes its masculinist credentials. Field (1970), on the other hand, would rather see it, and the period as a whole, as a nadir in British art education – one that, in combination with various expressivisms, almost ruined art and design's hard-won place in the school curriculum. He notes that it was not until the later 1960s that 'certain art educators [began] to argue that a truer balance must be sought between concern for the integrity of children and concern for the integrity of art' (p. 55) (he cites Manzella 1963; Barkan and Chapman 1967; Eisner 1968). The scene was set for arguing the case for art as a cognitive and critical, as well as creative, field of study.

The critical turn in art education since the 1960s

The move to a critical model of art education was partly a response to criticism levelled at the use of public monies to support a 'useless' activity in Higher Education during the 1950s. Starting with the report directed by Coldstream (1960), attempts were made to ensure that art and design diplomas had parity with degrees in other disciplines, and courses were consequently injected with an 'academic' component. In the new diploma, this took the form of an art history programme that was intended to act as a complement to studio practice; indeed, it was largely due to this insertion that post-school art and design qualifications were finally accredited with degree status. This had a gradual, generational effect in schools when students who had trained under the new regime turned to teaching and brought with them knowledge and attitudes to making informed by historical exemplars. It could be argued that it was this art historical turn that was responsible by the mid-1980s for the degeneration into a curriculum predicated on transcription and pastiche (Hughes 1989, 1999). However, initially, the historical emphasis encouraged teachers to question both the notion of natural, god-given talent and the perceptual model of art education based on assiduous mimetic exercises. It did so by demonstrating that art is not the result of isolated acts of expression, but a form of social and cultural practice with its own traditions and conventions, producers, networks and audiences. These systems, once understood, could be passed on, questioned, undermined, reinforced, hybridised and transformed.

However, before this change could take hold, criticism of the school system was already being produced on both sides of the Atlantic; Dick Field (1970) forcefully attacked the expressivist, laissez-faire attitudes embedded in the secondary art curriculum advising moves toward more cognitive modes of learning in art in line with US thinking (Efland 1990). Brian Allison (1972) advocated the need for school students to develop a specialist art language and discussed the need for multicultural education, a call that moved towards a more politicised, anti-racist education in the 1980s (see, for example, ILEA policy 1983). Eliot Eisner (1972), in the USA, helped to define Discipline-Based Art Education in which studio practice formed just one part of a quartet of studies, the others being aesthetics, criticism and history. John Berger (1972), in both book and televised formats, demonstrated how Marxist analysis could provide insights into art as a social and hierarchical practice, including issues of class and gender. Feminist perspectives took longer to enter the field, despite Linda Nochlin's early provocation (1971). Rozsika Parker and Griselda Pollock (1981) intervened into the histories of art by making women's practice visible both within and as a counter to the traditions of patriarchy, a rewriting that only gradually informed the focus for investigation by art and design students in schools.

Rod Taylor (1986) shifted attention away from critical studies as an academic complement towards a model in which it was integral to studio practice and informed by artists working in schools and galleries. David Thistlewood (1989) suggested the heresy that critical studies would never be taken seriously until it was a separate subject standing to practical work in the way that literature stands alongside language in the English curriculum. The first National Curriculum (DfE 1991) picked up on the term 'visual literacy', acknowledging the historical and contemporary function of art as a form of communication equivalent to the word. Henry Giroux (1992) argued that art could only be studied critically (a necessity in a democracy) if it was placed in the context of visual culture (particularly popular forms of culture) and, drawing on the Frankfurt school, provided critical studies with theoretical credibility (see Chapter 6). Roy Prentice (1995) reminded art and design teachers of the legacy of aesthetic education, exploring the processes of making itself a critical practice through the writings of Schon (1987). Liz Dawtrey *et al.* (1996) provided a round-up of developing thinking, including feminist and multicultural perspectives. Arthur Hughes (1999) pointed out that the moribund, acritical art curriculum was unlikely to survive the new century unless it was radically reformed, and John Swift and John Steers (1999) recognised that the pluralist and inclusive discourses of postmodern theory should inform such change. Pen Dalton (2001) cautioned that there could be no radical change unless the continuing patriarchal bias of art education in schools was recognised and, quoting Julia Kristeva, asked for attention to be given to the 'unsatisfied, repressed, new, eccentric, incomprehensible, disturbing to the status quo' (p. 153). Kerry Freedman (2003) formulated seven strategies to support learning in which the experiential focus of art and design acknowledges students' own lives as a ground for enquiry. At the same time, she recognises that their subjectivities, or sense of self, are formed within the context of an expanding, pervasive and conditioning visual culture. Dennis Atkinson (2006) also recognises changing contexts and counselled art and design teachers to let go of the past by finding ways to mourn its passing. More recently (2008), Atkinson calls on art teachers to resist the audit culture that constrains and limits practice by creating 'a new vision, a new myth … which evolves from local practices driven by a sense of social responsibility that have a universal potential for learning' (p. 240).

Where to go from here?

This is where art and design has got to and you will have noted that there is a diversity of philosophical and political positions from which to develop the subject.

You will also have seen that this history has shifted in different and sometimes opposing directions, directions motivated by clear class and gender interests (issues of race are given more attention in Chapter 6). This suggests that you need to navigate and mine this complexity if you wish to negotiate a pedagogy that recognises and draws on what is nourishing from the past, necessary in the present and which provides hope for the future. This future will undoubtedly be one in which the dialogue between local and global initiatives will frame your practice and will therefore condition rather than determine what you choose. But this book has also been written at a time when intellectual fields are being repositioned in relation to an 'affective turn', a move that recognises that language and discourse do not encompass everything within human experience (Greco and Stenner 2008). This recognition of the emotional dimension of human existence does not have to be at odds with forms of rationality, and the arts (in particular) offer ways of engaging with the world that can inform the direction that this turn takes.

In the following chapter, John Steers looks at the same period of history that I have discussed here (see also Romans 2005), but through the lens of design education. In it, he gives more attention to recent history, particularly around the development of the National Curriculum and the choice of the name 'art and design' for the subject in schools. In respect to the reform of this pedagogical framework (QCA 2007a), he notes a return to creativity – a return that coincides with the affective turn more generally. He therefore argues that this provides art and design with a unique opportunity to inform the educational process more widely.

Chapter 2

A return to design in art and design

Developing creativity and innovation

John Steers

Introduction: A brief history of design education in the UK

It can be argued that formal design education in the United Kingdom can be traced to the Great Exhibition held in London in 1851. This event was intended to raise the level of industrial design and to display products from Britain and the Empire, with the intention of acquiring new and larger markets. In part, it was a competitive response to the highly successful French Industrial Exposition of 1844 and, significantly, both governments' recognition of the importance of design to their respective economies. In the second half of the nineteenth century, one outcome was the further development of municipal schools of art and design in most major British towns and cities.

The art schools had a triple function: they offered training for the professional artist, courses in drawing and painting for polite society (segregated for gentlemen and ladies), and training for the artisans destined to work in the manufacturing industries such as ceramics and textiles. The latter aim was not always enthusiastically embraced and the following example illustrates how there is a tension that continues, to this day, between art and design education seen as a matter of economic necessity and 'art for art's sake'. In 1888, the principal of the Royal College of Art, the designer and illustrator Walter Crane, had recently reorganised the curriculum to face what he saw as the challenges of the approaching twentieth century and to absorb the Arts and Crafts philosophy into teaching. Sir Christopher Frayling, rector until 2009, describes Crane's thinking and curriculum thus:

> The key, [Crane] said, was to engage in a debate with the new world of manu-
> facturing industry – not by stimulating it, as the high Victorians wanted, but
> by *criticising* it through the medium of beautiful one-off pieces or artefacts
> within a craft tradition, which would be seen by the public as criticisms of the
> general shoddiness of mass-produced goods available in the high street. "One
> hour of creative life says 'yes'" he wrote, "but all the others say 'no' ... we are
> gradually impoverishing the soil while we are forcing the crops". It was art
> and design education against the world, and the model of how the College
> studios were to be run was the alternative one of the medieval workshop

with 'masters' and 'apprentices'. So the exhibition of the 1890s was all about calligraphy and lettering (not yet graphic design), embroidery and weaving (not yet fashion), woodcarving (not yet furniture design), stained glasswork (not yet glass and ceramics), modelling (not yet sculpture) and mural painting (not yet painting).

(Frayling 2008: 9)

Early in the twentieth century, the National Society of Art Masters insisted on '... elevating craftwork, and design for industrial applications, to levels of acceptance afforded to those subjects ... [such as] Drawing from Life and the Antique, and Anatomical and Architectural Drawing' (Thistlewood 1988: 53). It is interesting to note that the value of these practical alternatives to traditional art education had been perceived by other governments. Hermann Muthesius reported to the Prussian Board of Trade in 1907 on the work of British Art Schools, his survey initiating the foundation of the Deutscher Werkbund, an organisation dedicated to raising the quality and competitiveness of German design and production. Thistlewood (1988) observed 'This in turn had given rise to the complete revision of German design education, and the formation of regional schools, usually serving the needs of local industries, the most famous of which is now the Weimar Bauhaus' (p. 53).

However, in schools, rather than design education, the predominant influence in the first half of the twentieth century was the Child Art Movement, the philosophy of which can be traced to Jean Jacques Rousseau, and later, the concept of 'Education through Art', which followed the ideas set out by Herbert Read in his eponymous book of 1943. Another influence was the Austrian Franz Cizek, whose declaration that 'Child Art is an art which only the child can produce' – recognition that children's work could be worthy of being seen as 'art' in its own right – was a milestone in the history of art education. Cizek believed that children should be allowed freedom of expression and preserved from adult influences. Yet the work that he exhibited in London in 1908 was sophisticated and highly disciplined, often in the demanding form of woodcuts and paper cuts. 'It was their sheer competence which astonished British and American art teachers, many of whom thought that a well-shaded group of solids was the apogee of child art' (MacDonald 1970: 345).

The 'New Art Teaching', initiated by two London County Council inspectors, Marion Richardson and R R Tomlinson, flourished between 1930 and 1939. Richardson opposed Cizek's ideas, considering the results of his approach most unchildlike. She searched for a more psychologically relevant art education, more suited to the child's individual development stage, and realised that children need positive stimulation by the teacher before they can understand how to express their own ideas. She developed a range of strategies for enabling children to develop their own imagery, including 'mind pictures', where children painted from mental images rather than observation. At this time, the subject was usually referred to as 'Art & Craft' in the curriculum.

By the second half of the twentieth century, the range of the subject continued to broaden and various initiatives designed to develop design education in secondary schools began to appear. Design education generally was seen as an element of two apparently overlapping school subjects – 'Art, Craft and Design' and 'Craft, Design and Technology'. The latter, CDT, developed in the 1960s out of a general dissatisfaction with traditional boys' crafts (woodwork and metalwork) and girls' crafts (needlework, cooking, child care and home economics). The change of mind set required to establish CDT was hampered by a reluctance of many craft teachers to move away from the safe ground of their practical training and long-established workshop practices.

At the same time, although most art teachers were aware that 'art' and 'design' were theoretically interdependent and interrelated, this was not enough to change practices in schools that were essentially fine-art-based with some additional light craft activities such as pottery, textiles (both woven and printed) and, occasionally, jewellery. A further feature of art and design in some schools at this time was an approach derived from the 'Basic Design' movement, with its roots in Bauhaus ideas and introduced into the art schools by Harry Thubron, Victor Pasmore and Tom Hudson. This very formalist approach became popular in secondary schools partly through the influential book *The Dynamics of Visual Form* by Maurice de Sausmarez (1964).

From the 1960s to mid-1980s, 'Design Education' offered a new approach that was to be integrated into the art curriculum in schools. The work of Peter Green (1974) at Hornsey College of Art and of the Royal College of Art's Design Education Unit, under the guidance of Bruce Archer, were particularly important in this respect. School departments that hitherto had been simply known as 'Art' or 'Art and Craft' were often redesignated 'Art, Craft and Design' or even incorporated into broader 'Design Faculties'. Significant interventions came from a government-funded agency, the Design Council (2008), which commissioned influential reports such as *Design Education at Secondary Level* (1980) and *Design and Primary Education* (1987) and the establishment of a 'Schools' Design Prize'. Design was seen as a critical area of experience and learning in the contemporary world that required a strong cross-curricular approach in schools. Baynes' seminal paper *Defining a Design Dimension of the Curriculum* (1985) provided a well-argued rationale for some subtle ideas about the cross-curricular nature of design education that deserve to have flourished much more than they did.

Baynes revisited these ideas at a seminar held at the RCA in 2006, suggesting that changes in society – including the growth of consumerism, the environmental crisis, economic changes, changes in children's culture and how children are perceived – all make design, and design education, more important. Baynes (2006) reminded his audience:

> The arena for design activity is material culture: products, places and images. It is designerly thinking and action that shapes the future of our made world. It happens at every level and is ubiquitous in its impact. The function of a

designed thing always has two complementary aspects – its physical performance and material reality, and its meaning in the lives of those who make and
use it. This meaning can be economic, strictly practical, or deeply spiritual
and aesthetic.

Unfortunately, in the late 1980s, when the first national curriculum in England
was developed, much valuable work was discarded in developing a narrowly
subject-based, closely prescribed curriculum that sought to eliminate the apparent
'overlap' between disciplines. As a consequence, early national curriculum propos-
als referred simply to 'Art' and 'Technology' as foundation subjects. Significantly,
the word 'design' disappeared from both subjects, giving an unintended but,
nevertheless, clear message to teachers. Although art did not regain the title 'Art
& Design' until 2000, technology had an even more troubled genesis.

The then chief executive of the National Curriculum Council later observed:
'When technology first appeared on the agenda of the National Curriculum
Council it is fair to say that nobody was clear what it was and it was left to the working group to invent it' (Graham and Tytler 1993). He suggested that technology
had all-party support from the politicians because it promised to break down the
academic and vocational divide in education and, provocatively, he proposed that
technology could be '... at the beginning of that revolution as, for the first time,
thinkers will be forced to make and the makers will be forced to think'. He also
revealed that both civil servants and politicians '... felt it was time to do something
to remove the grip of woodwork and metalwork for boys and needlework and
domestic science for girls' (Graham and Tytler 1993).

Design education as a clearly defined element of the curriculum seemed to have
been dismissed in official circles in the early 1990s. Successive curriculum reviews
appeared to ignore or be unaware of opportunities to develop design capability.
However, in 1995, technology was renamed 'Design and Technology' (D&T)
following the introduction of information technology as a separate subject, but
it still concentrated on technology rather than the much wider field of designing
and making. Nevertheless, there was a return to a higher proportion of practical
work, rather than paper-based project work, with pupils developing broader D&T
capability. In 2000, further pressure to slim down curriculum requirements, particularly for primary schools, meant that the programme of study was reduced and
a teaching methodology was set in statute with three different types of activities:
product evaluation, focused practical tasks, and design and make assignments. The
programmes were also updated to include modern technologies, such as smart
materials and CAD/CAM.

After 1991, revisions to statutory provision for Art were essentially limited to
a series of précis of earlier versions of the curriculum. The title 'Art' was retained,
although, as before, a footnote stated: 'Art should be taken to include art, craft
and design'. After much lobbying, the subject was redesignated 'Art and Design'
in 2000, but little progress has been made to halt the subject's retrenchment into
a limited fine-art approach. Few remnants can be found in schools today of the

developments in design education within art & design of the 1970s and 1980s. Whatever happened to the crafts in education? More than 10 years ago, Mason and Iwano (1995) reported on the crafts decline in curriculum and now they have all but disappeared from many art and design departments.

The new millennium

Since 2000, some D&T departments have struggled to live up to the vision set out in the curriculum, and inspections have revealed that making skills were better taught than designing skills. The number of 16-year-old students passing GCSE national examinations in D&T fell by approximately 10 per cent in 2005 as a result of the removal of the subject's statutory (i.e. compulsory) nature for this age range. So, although England and Wales were perhaps the first countries to introduce design & technology as a compulsory subject for all pupils from 5–16 years of age more than 15 years ago, and although there has been considerable interest in developments from around the world, design education within D&T, to say the least, has remained variable in quality.

Evidence in a research report by Downing and Watson, *School Art: What's in it?* (NFER 2004), confirmed frequently voiced concerns about the current content of the art and design curriculum in many schools. Various prevalent characteristics of 'school art' were noted, including the use of painting and drawing as the predominant medium, and the emphasis on development of art form practical skills. Sparse evidence was found of effective use of information and communications technology (ICT), a finding earlier confirmed by Arts Council England's report *Keys to imagination: ICT in art education* that concluded:

> Overall, evidence from the whole array of research sources paints a disappointing national picture. It shows little consolidated progress in effective integration of ICT into art and design education in schools, even while there are undoubtedly areas of practice which are effective and occasionally inspirational. Moreover, results from national ICT surveys suggest the situation is getting worse not better.
>
> (ACE 2004)

Significantly, the subject section in successive Annual Reports of Her Majesty's Chief Inspector of Schools have made little specific mention of design education, despite it supposedly being a key element of 'art and design'. Clearly, design education continues to be much neglected, despite HMI noting more recently that the art and design curriculum had narrowed and their suggestion that '... more needs to be done to transform the relationship between art and design in schools, the creative industries and the cultural sector' (Ofsted 2005b). By this time, it was increasingly obvious that many opportunities had been lost because of the failure to embrace and develop the concept of design education both in and *across* the curriculum.

New opportunities

Although this recent history is somewhat depressing, the latest developments are much more encouraging. At first, change was almost imperceptible, but now there is real momentum, and art and design teachers have been presented with considerable opportunities and significant challenges, particularly in relation to creativity and design education.

A shrewd observer would have first noted, even before 1997, that a new Labour government would have an interest in the 'creative industries' and their growing importance to the British economy. A government-commissioned report *All Our Futures: Creativity, Culture and Education* (NACCCE 1999) was published in 1999 and included wide-ranging recommendations for reform of education. In that document, a clear signal of the government's economic agenda came when prime minister Tony Blair asserted 'Our aim must be to create a nation where the creative talents of all the people are used to build a true enterprise economy for the twenty-first century – where we compete on brains, not brawn' (NACCCE 1999: 6).

Nevertheless, this report seemed to have little impact on a review of the national curriculum in 2000 which, by and large, offered little change. Not long afterwards, however, the government invested more than £100 million in 'Creative Partnerships' – a pilot project to investigate the impact of increased creative and cultural opportunities on teaching and learning in schools. In 2003, Clarke, then Secretary of State for Education, declared: 'Creativity isn't an add-on. It must form a vital and integral part of every child's experience of school. Research has shown that, if it does, it can contribute to improved learning and increased standards across the school as a whole'.

About the same time, the Qualifications and Curriculum Authority (QCA) launched a national debate and consultation on the future of the curriculum. Contributions were invited on the basis that there should be 'blue skies thinking' about a curriculum for the twenty-first century. It was recognised that changes in society, the impact of new technology, new understanding about learning, the effects of globalisation and public policy issues all needed to be taken into account. The concerns that arose in the consultation centred on creating more space for personalised learning and personal development; less curriculum prescription; more innovation; greater student engagement and participation and, of course, improved standards and securing essentials skills.

The process of developing the new secondary curriculum was far more collaborative than anything previously experienced. The subject associations had a seat at the table and were closely involved in drafting new programmes of study and attainment targets, as well as examinations for their subject specialisms. What emerged ready to be implemented from September 2008 is a far more coherent vision of the curriculum that has an increased focus on whole curriculum design underpinned by clear aims and values (QCA 2008). It offers much increased flexibility, less prescription and more teacher autonomy. There are greater opportunities for coherence and relevance: linking learning to life outside school, making connections between subjects through consideration of cross-curricular themes and dimensions. Although there is more emphasis on skills, these are not just functional but wider skills for learning and life. It is fair to say that the new curriculum offers a real opportunity for renewal and revitalising schools through locally determined curricula based on a flexible framework. Of particular interest is the way in which creativity permeates the new secondary curriculum, not just the arts subjects within it. Included in the general aims is the development of successful learners who are creative, resourceful, and able to identify and solve problems. Prominent among the cross-curricular dimensions are 'Creativity and critical thinking', 'Problem-solving' and 'Entrepreneurship and Enterprise'.

In a statement that can equally apply to a concept of design across the curriculum, the QCA acknowledges that creativity involves the use of imagination and intellect to generate ideas, insights, and solutions to problems and challenges.

> Coupled with critical thinking, which involves evaluative reasoning, creative activity can produce outcomes that can be original, expressive and have value. Creativity and critical thinking develop young people's capacity for original ideas and purposeful action. Experiencing the wonder and inspiration of human ingenuity and achievement, whether artistic, scientific or technological, can spark individual enthusiasms that contribute to personal fulfilment … Creative activity is essential for the future wellbeing of society and the economy. It can unlock the potential of individuals and communities to solve personal, local and global problems … Creativity and critical thinking are not curriculum subjects, but they are crucial aspects of learning that should permeate the curriculum and the life of the school.
>
> (QCA 2007b)

QCA continues by suggesting that, in order to develop young people's creativity and critical thinking, they should have opportunities *across* the curriculum to:

- use their imagination to explore possibilities
- generate ideas, take risks and learn from their mistakes
- refine, modify and iteratively develop ideas and products
- make connections between ideas
- engage in creative activities in all subjects, exploring links between subjects and wider aspects of learning
- work in relevant contexts, with real audience and purpose
- work with a range of creative individuals, both in and out of the classroom
- encounter the work of others, including theories, literature, art, design, inventions and discoveries, as sources of inspiration
- discover and pursue particular interests and talents.

(QCA 2007b)

Again, all of this is entirely apposite to design education in both art and design, and design technology.

Creativity in schools

Of course, it must be acknowledged that there is *some* excellent creative art and design teaching in the United Kingdom, and there are *some* excellent art and design teachers and their work should be celebrated. But such excellence is not necessarily the norm. Serious concerns have been expressed for several decades about prevailing orthodoxies of approach to teaching the arts and, necessarily, orthodoxy is the antithesis of creativity. Over the last 25 years, many contributors to the pages of the *International Journal of Art & Design Education* have drawn attention to issues that need to be addressed, to the need to rethink art and design education. These calls have reflected wider calls for fundamental curriculum reform and it was apparent early in the new century that critiques from many subjects had much in common (White 2004).

Some recent research (HMI 2006) has shown that teachers' understanding of the term 'creativity' varies enormously. How creativity should be embedded within the school curriculum is also open to different interpretations: some teachers identify creativity with particular areas of the curriculum, others argue that creativity is synonymous with 'problem-solving', 'imagination' and 'lateral thinking skills'. Possibly, you might agree that while creativity is not the sole prerogative of the arts or design, when well taught it should have a particularly significant role in the curriculum.

In England, it is arguable that the decline in interest in creativity coincided with the development of the first national curriculum in the second half of the 1980s and the introduction of ever more detailed examination specifications. These seemed to remove any real incentive to explore innovatory approaches to the curriculum; there was a sense that the problem of what to teach had been finally codified and there was no need to look further. It is likely that it was never a deliberate intention to inhibit rather than promote creativity but, in the wake of closely specified and detailed statutory programmes of study with an emphasis on 'key skills' and an industrial input/output model, that is what happened.

It seems evident that creative pupils need creative teachers with the confidence to take creative risks. Unfortunately, this takes exceptional commitment and vision in a high stakes education system with its pressures to conform created by a standardised curriculum, standard assessment tasks, examination targets, school league tables, constant initiatives to raise standards, intimidating inspection regimes, scarce resources and limited subject-based professional development. Such conditions severely limit the scope for individual teachers to take risks and to avoid becoming mere 'curriculum delivery operatives'. There seem to be few rewards, if any, for creative initiatives; these were not evident on government school inspection checklists that took little, if any, account of creative education and the processes of teaching, learning and assessment involved.

It is often argued that many teachers, especially arts teachers, are, as a matter of course, predisposed to creativity, that they need to be in order to keep the curriculum fresh for themselves and young people. But, as Cropley (2001) reports, teachers who particularly foster creativity are those who emphasise 'flexibility', who accept 'alternative suggestions' and who encourage 'expression of ideas'. Unfortunately, in a closely monitored education system, those who take such risks may be in a minority and there is a strong contrary risk-averse tendency to make teachers adept at finding safe prescriptions for their students to enable them to satisfy examination assessment objectives. Students are coached to replicate safe and reliable projects year after year and the creativity on display is really that of the teacher who devised the project rather than that of the pupils. Such approaches often reliably produce work of a kind on which teachers can depend for the award of good examination grades. This is important because teachers often are held to account by senior management in schools for whom the *only* performance indicator that really matters is the percentage of grades A–C achieved in national examinations. In this situation, assiduous prescription and teacher direction may pay dividends in grades, but with the consequence that work that frequently typifies the orthodoxy of 'school art' is perpetuated. Even the Office for Standards in Education (Ofsted 2005b) eventually noted the danger, evident in some schools, of the curriculum for 11–14-year olds being little more than a preparation for the examinations at age 16 years. They noted the limitations placed on the breadth of study required by the national curriculum in order to perfect a particular style of work associated with examination success.

The following anecdote perhaps illustrates a deep-seated concern about the notion of creativity felt by some in authority. Not so long ago, I was involved in a round table discussion about creativity. Another panellist and I were extolling the importance of creativity and talked about this at some length. A spokesperson for one of the examination boards listened with growing agitation before intervening. He said that the examination boards were very keen on promoting creativity, they wanted to see much more creativity in schools, he emphasised creativity as really important. But, he said, creativity must be *carefully controlled!* And controlled it often is.

Of course, creativity is not an unqualified virtue. It is not just allied with the pursuit of ideas that are inventive, innovative and imaginative, but also with ideas that may be radical, heretical or revolutionary. The innovative and imaginative outcomes of human invention are just as likely to be malignant as beneficent. Although human creativity may be directed to sustainable development, preventing disease, famine and poverty, it may equally be directed at designing weapons of mass destruction, plotting crimes against humanity, exploiting the vulnerable or encouraging the profligate use of scarce natural resources for commercial gain.

What are the limits on creativity in schools? Should there be any boundaries other than those related to common decency and the practicalities of health and safety? Clearly, there are profound ethical and moral issues that teachers need to consider.

Creativity in the classroom

There are issues that have to be faced in the creative classroom or studio that can be in conflict with the ethos of many schools, social institutions that often place a high value on some degree of conformity. Creative individuals are likely to display a range of characteristics, capacities and abilities that some teachers find hard to recognise or accommodate. For example:

- Tolerance for ambiguity – but how often do people strive to make everything clear-cut, eliminating all uncertainty?
- Flexibility and openness to alternative approaches – but how is it that school managers and inspectors place such high value on adherence to schemes of work and detailed, sometimes minute-by-minute, lesson plans?
- Playfulness with ideas, materials or processes – but how often do we insist that pupils stop messing around and get on with the work they have been told to do?
- An ability to concentrate and persist, to keep on teasing and worrying away at a problem rather than seeking premature resolution – but why do we frequently insist that student assignments must be handed in on time to meet our deadlines?
- A willingness to explore unlikely connections and apparently disassociated ideas – but how often do we say 'get back on task, that's not what I told you to do? Stop wasting time'.
- The self-awareness and courage to pursue their ideas in the face of considerable opposition – but how often do we interpret this as stubbornness or insubordination?
- Confidence, the self-belief to take intellectual and intuitive *risks* (perhaps, in essence, creative thinking is simply 'risky thinking') – so why do we often advise that it is best to play safe, stick to established routines, don't take too many chances?

Can art and design teachers honestly say that it is their principal aim to actively foster the creativity of every child? Is there a fear that any relaxation of control will promptly result in anarchy and a total loss of teacher authority?

Creativity cannot be rushed or reduced to a formula: there is often a long incubation period before creative ideas may, once in a while, gel in that elusive 'Eureka!' moment. Serendipity often plays a key role in developing creative outcomes. It requires 'space' – of a kind often in short supply in target-driven schools.

Dewulf and Baillie (1999) identified four elements of the creative process:

- **Preparation** – in which the problem or question is defined, reformulated and redefined, moving from a given to an understanding.
- **Generation** – moving beyond habitual pathways of thinking, purging associative concepts to the problem; brainstorming.

- **Incubation** – a subconscious stimulus, often following a period of relaxation or relaxed attention.
- **Verification** – where ideas are analysed, clustered and evaluated, followed by planning the action and implementation.

It is important to stress that creativity is rarely a simple linear process and usually there is interplay between these elements, with various phases being revisited and reviewed – for example, when dead ends seem apparent. This suggests that adequate *time* is a key component of creative space if the creative spark is to flourish. How can this be accommodated in school timetables where, at best, an hour for one of the arts subjects is sandwiched between the drip feed of an hour of mathematics and an hour of history for week after monotonous week?

There are other preconditions that are equally important for both teachers and pupils, including a strong atmosphere of mutual trust and affective support – what pupil is likely to take creative risks if they think their ideas will be quashed as soon as they begin to form? The constructive use of probing but sensitive questioning is essential to increase the intellectual challenge. Pupils must be allowed to develop a real sense of ownership of the task or problem, and their confidence has to be bolstered by positive feedback if they are to be motivated.

Of course, the neglect of creativity or failure to afford it a proper opportunity in the curriculum is not an entirely recent problem. Well before the advent of the English national curriculum, Perry pointed out that creativity does not provide a universal golden key to successful learning for all pupils. The key, he rightly asserted, is to do with how far knowledge-based curricula are permeated with creativity and how far creativity is permeated with knowledge, habit-forming, and other perfectly reasonable aspects of the curriculum:

> Those who teach knowledge as a matter of memorising forget that it is the product of past creativity and should be presented as such. Those who teach creativity to the neglect of knowledge should remember that past creativity is preserved and brought into continuity with present creativity by knowledge well learnt. Surely, if we espouse creativity come what may, then 'come what may' is not long in arriving: the curriculum loses structure and form and classes have a long tail of apathetic pupils. If it is knowledge come what may, then we have a daily gap between memory and understanding, lack of vitality, and a long tail of apathetic pupils.
>
> (Perry 1987: 287)

There is another key issue about creativity in schools: should it be assessed and can it be assessed? Gardner (1993) has questioned the validity of *tests* for creativity, pointing out that creativity is not the same as intelligence; although these two traits are correlated, an individual may be far more creative than intelligent, or far more intelligent than creative. Much earlier, Torrance (1970) raised similar issues: '... if we were to identify children as gifted on the basis of intelligence tests, we would eliminate from consideration approximately seventy per cent of the most creative' (p. 358). He noted that teachers rated more highly the children with high IQs on most counts, but claimed that highly creative children appear to learn as much as the highly intelligent without seeming to work as hard. Why? He guessed that highly creative children are often learning and thinking when they appear to be just 'playing around'. Such individuals often seem difficult to manage in the classroom situation, because they often want to follow their own agendas, at their own pace, rather than that of the teacher. What happens to them as a consequence?

I have no doubt that creative progress can be assessed as, for example, Lindström (2006) has demonstrated, providing that authentic, wide-ranging and sensitive assessment instruments are used. I also believe the emphasis should be on assessment for learning and we need to ensure that assessment does not lead the curriculum but follows and serves it.

Finally, consider this advice from Simonton, a professor of psychology at the University of California:

> Know your stuff: creativity requires expertise; but don't know it too well: over specialisation puts blinders on. Imagine the impossible: many breakthrough ideas at first thought seem outright crazy; but you have to be able to impose your idea: crazy ideas remain crazy if they cannot survive critical evaluation. Finally be persistent: big problems are seldom solved on the first try, or the second or the third; but remember to take a break: you may be barking up the wrong tree, so incubate a bit and get a fresh start.
>
> (Simonton 2005: 54)

I think it is abundantly clear that the ethos in which creativity can flourish does not always sit easily alongside nationally prescribed requirements such as national curricula, assessment and inspection regimes that are found in most school systems.

The economic imperative

It is important to understand the motivation behind the promotion of creativity in the curriculum. The British Government, perhaps all governments, among its principal concerns, has to ensure social stability and economic growth. In a multi-ethnic, multi-cultural, multi-faith society such as the United Kingdom, social stability and harmony are necessarily high on the political agenda and in a world where there is global migration on an unprecedented scale. Hence, the importance in the new secondary curriculum of cultural identity, civic participation, sustainable development and globalisation as cross-curricular themes.

Just as important is the ever-increasing recognition of the importance of the 'Creative Industries' to the British economy. According to the Department for Culture, Media and Sport, the creative industries are those that are based on individual creativity, skill and talent and those that have the potential to create wealth and jobs through developing intellectual property. They comprise 13 different subsectors, including: advertising, architecture, art and antiques market, computer and video games, crafts, design, designer fashion, film and video, music, performing arts, publishing, software, and television and radio (DCMS, 2008a).

The significance of the creative industries is emphasised in prime minister Gordon Brown's preface to a recent government strategy document *Creative Britain: New Talents for a New Economy*. He writes: 'In the coming years, the creative industries will be important not only for our national prosperity but for Britain's ability to put culture and creativity at the centre of our national life' (DCMS, 2008b, p. 3). The document emphasises that 'The creative industries must *move from the margins to the mainstream of economic and policy thinking*, as we look to create the jobs of the future ...'. It explains:

> Britain is a creative country and our creative industries are increasingly vital to the UK. Two million people are employed in creative jobs and the sector contributes £60 billion a year – 7.3 per cent – to the British economy. Over the past decade, *the creative sector has grown at twice the rate of the economy* as a whole and is well placed for continued growth as demand for creative content – particularly in English – grows.
>
> (DCMS 2008b: 6)

Later, the strategy document states:

> The creative industries start with individual creativity. So, too, does every child's learning experience. There is a growing recognition of the need to find practical ways of nurturing creativity at every stage in the education system: from the nursery through to secondary school; whether in academic or vocational courses; on apprenticeships or at university. In a world of rapid technological and social change, creativity extends well beyond art or drama lessons. It is as much about equipping people with the skills they need to respond creatively and confidently to changing situations and unfamiliar demands; enabling them to solve the problems and challenges they face at home, in education, at work; and making a positive contribution to their communities.
>
> (DCMS 2008b: 13)

In theory, but not always in practice, the English education system already does much to foster the creativity, play-based learning and critical thinking skills that are central to good early years education. Traditionally, in primary schools, creative thinking has been seen as essential to effective learning, with opportunities to teach and learn these skills threaded through the curriculum. However, such approaches have been eroded in recent years by the prescriptions of literacy and numeracy strategies. There is currently (2008) a review of the primary curriculum taking place that may bring it more into line with the new secondary curriculum being phased in from September 2008.

The new secondary curriculum (QCA 2007a) expects schools to give all young people opportunities to develop their creativity and critical thinking. It is significantly different to its predecessors in that it offers far greater flexibility and autonomy for teachers, and encourages local interpretation of a broad framework with an emphasis on the 'big ideas that shaped the world' rather than prescribing detailed content. Specifically, in relation to design education, the general aims include a call for successful learners who are creative, resourceful, and able to identify and solve problems, and responsible citizens who sustain and improve the environment, locally and globally, to take account of the needs of present and future generations in the choices they make, and who can change things for the better. The cross-curricular dimensions include enterprise, the global dimension and sustainable development, technology and the media, and creativity and critical thinking.

The 'Importance Statement' for art and design states:

> In art, craft and design, pupils explore visual, tactile and other sensory experiences to communicate ideas and meanings. They work with traditional and new media, developing confidence, competence, imagination and creativity. They learn to appreciate and value images and artefacts across times and cultures, and to understand the contexts in which they were made. In art, craft and design, pupils reflect critically on their own and other people's work, judging quality, value and meaning. They learn to think and act as artists, craftspeople and designers, working creatively and intelligently. They develop an appreciation of art, craft and design, and its role in the creative and cultural industries that enrich their lives.
>
> (QCA 2007c)

The art and design curriculum is structured around the key concepts of creativity, competence, cultural understanding and critical understanding. The statement outlining the range of the subject refers to:

a) work in, and across, the areas of fine art, craft and design, including both applied and fine art practices
b) exploration of media, processes and techniques in 2D, 3D and new technologies
c) study of a range of artefacts from contemporary, historical, personal and cultural contexts
d) understanding of art, craft and design processes, associated equipment and safe working practices.

(QCA 2007c)

The corresponding statements for Design and Technology emphasise that pupils should '… combine practical and technological skills with creative thinking to design and make products and systems that meet human needs. They learn to use current technologies and consider the impact of future technological developments. They learn to think creatively and intervene to improve the quality of life, solving problems as individuals and members of a team' (QCA 2007d). The key concepts are very similar to those for art and design: creativity, cultural understanding, critical evaluation, and designing and making. The latter concept includes:

- understanding that designing and making has aesthetic, environmental, technical, economic, ethical and social dimensions, and impacts on the world.
- applying knowledge of materials and production processes in order to design products and produce practical solutions that are relevant and fit for purpose.
- understanding that products and systems have an impact on quality of life.
- exploring how products have been designed and made in the past, how they are currently designed and made, and how they may develop in the future.

(QCA 2008d)

Another innovation that should support reinvigoration of design education is the introduction in 2008 of 14–19 Diplomas, all of which are new qualifications for 14–19-year olds. These are intended as an alternative to more traditional education and qualifications and should give young people a broadly based qualification that combines theoretical and practical learning, including functional English, mathematics and ICT. This will equip them with the skills, knowledge and understanding that they need for further or higher education and long-term employability. There will be 17 Diploma disciplines by 2011 but, one of the first, introduced in September 2008, is the 'Creative and Media Diploma'. It is claimed that 'Students of the Diploma will gain knowledge, experience and skills enabling them to master processes common to all creative industries' (Skillset 2008). Time will tell …

More encouragement can be found in the Roberts Review (2006) *Nurturing Creativity in Young People*, which argues that creativity should be central to every child's early learning experience and that prevailing education policy (with its focus on autonomy, commissioning and personalisation) offers real opportunities for embedding it. Roberts' report provides a framework for developing creativity from the early years to the development of adult skills in the creative industries.

In these circumstances, it is easy to understand the creative and design education imperative that permeates the new secondary curriculum, a curriculum that should help to foster more opportunities in the future. However, if design education is not once again to become marginalised, it is vital that art and design and design and technology teachers understand the government's agenda and reconceptualise at least part of their practice to serve these ends. It would be too easy to dismiss this as surrendering educational values to irrelevant government demands and to use this as an excuse to do nothing. This would be a serious mistake. An education that sets out to help young people make sense of, and contribute to, the world in which they live must be concerned with helping them to investigate their own values and those of others, as well as the development of a range of creative qualities and skills with a wide application and value. Inaction is not an option unless we want to jeopardise a continuing place for art and design in the curriculum.

Perhaps the wider message in all of this is that, while maintaining art and design's core values and beliefs, at the same time we need to work to make art and design education much more relevant to the needs and interests of today's young people and society more generally. With this in mind, it is worth revisiting Baynes' key basic assumptions about the need for design education. First:

> The primary aim of design in general education is to develop everybody's design awareness so they can: enjoy with understanding and insight the made world of places, products and places; take part in the personal and public design decisions that affect their lives and the life of the community; design and criticise design at their own level for their own material and spiritual needs; bring an understanding of design into their work.
>
> ... The secondary aim of design in general education is to provide the seed bed from which will come the range of future professional designers – planners, architects, technologists, engineers, and industrial, fashion and graphic designers. If you get the first aim right, the second will follow.
>
> (Baynes 2006)

The government understands that the first challenge is to give all children a creative education because this is fundamental to a good education. The challenge, which should not be underestimated, is for art and design and design and technology teachers to ensure that they really foster creativity in schools and offer genuine opportunities for design education.

Part II

Reconceptualising Practice

Chapter 3

Developing creative potential
Learning through embodied practices

Nicholas Addison

Introduction

Creativity is commonly understood as the human capacity to make something new. In this chapter, it is my intention to argue and hopefully persuade you to recognise that this capacity is not a special gift as is sometimes supposed, but a very ordinary predisposition; indeed, it is so ordinary that many of its manifestations can easily be overlooked and thus summarily dismissed. However, the commonsense belief that certain people are more creative than others, just as some are more athletic or gifted with language, has led to a situation where creativity is understood as the possession of small, elite groups, especially those associated with the arts and sciences. On the contrary, I wish to draw your attention to evidence and arguments that establish creativity not so much as a possession but more of a potential, one that signals a dynamic and dialogical way of relating to others and the environment, which can be developed by most people given suitable social and pedagogic conditions. It is therefore in the construction of these fertile conditions that educators and teachers of the arts and you, in particular, as an art and design specialist, have the knowledge and experience to provide models for creative action.

It is then no surprise to find that the arts are often perceived as the natural home for creativity (Robinson 1982; NACCCE 1999; Roberts 2006). Indeed, within the school environment, you will find that the subject 'Art and Design', with its emphasis on making, is frequently privileged as the pre-eminent site for creative forms of self-expression and the development of individuality. This notion in reinforced in the National Curriculum subject Order, which opens its 'Statement of importance' for the subject with a claim about the practice of art, craft and design as a means to communicate ideas, a role that is evidently made possible through working 'with traditional and new media, developing confidence, competence imagination and creativity' (QCA 2007a). Nonetheless, if you look at QCA's underpinning concepts for each subject, you will discover that creativity is acknowledged in every school subject except for Citizenship, Geography, History, ICT and RE, but only in Art and Design is creativity the first in the list (D&T 3rd, English 2nd, Maths 2nd, Modern Foreign languages 3rd, Music 4th, PE 3rd, and in Science the word is fundamental to QCA's definition of 'application', which is 2nd). Just so, many theorists and commentators argue that creative thought and action can be applied to all spheres of human endeavour (Vygotsky 2004; Arnheim 1962; Maslow 1968; Torrance and Myers 1974; Best 1985; Boden 2004; Gardner 1993). Through these endeavours – whether in the humanities, mathematics, media, sciences (applied, physical and social), sports, or the visual and performing arts (including architecture) – people are concerned not only to express and communicate personal meanings but to construct shared ones. These meanings are often produced through collaborative, just as much as individual, action.

But art and design, and creative work in art, craft and design, does offer up something qualitatively different. By focusing on creativity, I hope to persuade you to revive a lost potential for art, craft and design in schools, a way of thinking about and doing things that offers exciting opportunities for reconceiving art education as an expansive yet socially engaged, heuristic and embodied activity. By expansive, I indicate the way in which art and design opens up to the whole history of cultural production, it broadens students' knowledge of the diversity of human practices, the ways environments have been, are and might be constructed, what people wish to represent about their culture, and how they might reproduce and sustain it. By socially engaged, I infer a series of activities that have implications for the way in which students live their lives, that the things they do in their lessons have real effects in their immediate social situation. The idea of a heuristic activity suggests a process of discovery, of not knowing the outcomes of an activity even though participants may have clear aims and goals; in other words, heurism is a process of finding out and coming to know, not being told. The idea of embodiment is explored later in some depth, but it encapsulates the idea that works of art, craft and design are produced through the reciprocal action of mind and body working with matter (whether substantial, clay or ephemeral, light) so that the art object/event is an inextricable combination of idea and substance: in this sense, the artwork is analogous to the human being who is indivisibly body/mind.

This potential not only empowers students with agency – a process that enables them to understand themselves as people who matter, are listened to and who have something to contribute to the collective by changing the environment in which they live – but is also able to alleviate the alienation that so dogs contemporary societies. Alienation is produced when a person's physical and mental needs are not met or are indeed obstructed by the situation in which they find themselves, even though these needs are themselves partly constructed by the social environment in which they are embedded. In school, it is often the sensuous needs of people, their agency and sense of fulfilment in relation to their bodily and aesthetic potential, which are sidelined in favour of the acquisition of concrete information and abstracted knowledge.

This split between mind and body will be familiar to you as a fundamental schism within much western philosophy. However, since at least Kant in the eighteenth century, it has been theorised that aesthetic experience, particularly as exemplified in art, is one in which the mind and body work reciprocally, and through this working together it has been argued that received divisions can be repaired. For example, the aesthetician Crowther (1993b: 48–60) suggests that, through creative action, the artist is able to heal the alienating effects of urban life and industrial modes of production and bring people to a greater understanding of what it is to be human. These are no small claims, but I believe they should be pursued. Significantly, this approach foregrounds and, to a certain extent, valorises practical and embodied forms of knowledge and I intend to suggest something of this particularity. But in order to understand this particularity, its material practices as well as its historical and conceptual basis, it is important to challenge the acritical appropriation of the term 'creative' and discourage its promiscuous use. Only then can practice in art and design be legitimately recognised as enabling creativity.

Despite this potential, over recent years regimes of inspection and accountability have tended to coerce art and design teachers into adopting a series of examination-safe procedures that have culminated in a set of reproductive practices known as 'school art' (Hughes 1998; Downing and Watson 2004). The reiteration and reinforcement of this orthodoxy no doubt ensures a certain type of 'excellence', but it also militates against the development of creative practice for which enquiry, discovery, and thinking and enacting difference are central. It is therefore surprising that the subject art and design holds on to the label of creativity as if it were some natural attribute, a given possession offering school students the possibility of pure feeling, a 'freedom' from the rational constraints of logocentric thinking or the determining structures of other embodied practices such as music, sports and dance with their rules and exacting traditions. Art and design does work within or in relation to traditions, and some of these traditions are technically demanding, requiring diligence, determination, immersion and an acculturation to and within valued conventions (Best 1985: 78–9). It is therefore inevitable that you will need to underpin creative work by teaching technical procedures and by providing opportunities for students to imitate, rehearse and consolidate practice through repetition and limited variation; creative work does not mean that technical competence can be ignored or overruled in the name of 'freedom', as is sometimes supposed. In this sense, not all work in art and design is, or needs to be, creative. However, if creativity is the goal, then you will need to encourage students to consider extending the potential uses of, for example, a material by questioning a rule or assumption, or by making connections between or across traditions and representational conventions in ways that set up new possibilities.

As well as attempting to define creativity and differentiate it from other ways of working, it is also important that you consider its purposes, not only as a means towards personal expression, development and actualisation (Maslow 1962/63) (the psychological paradigm for art education, see Dalton [2001] for a critique) but as a form of social and cultural practice. After all, it is through art practices that people are able to represent their worlds, representations that they display and disseminate in order to persuade others of the authenticity and legitimacy of that position. In this way, works of art represent 'what is' or what is believed to be true or necessary for specific groups of people, not as some reflection of those beliefs but as a process through which those beliefs are formed; in this sense, art is a productive process through which beliefs and identities are created. As such, art can also be a vehicle for imagining possible worlds, not representing how things are but envisaging how they might be. This persuasive power of representation, its rhetoric, requires makers to imagine how other people will receive their products and thus immediately sets up a relational, interactive basis for practice that requires making connections and negotiating solutions in fictive, virtual or face-to-face dialogue with others. Educationalists often stress the primary significance of the imagination for creativity (Dewey 1934; Read 1943; Warnock 1976; Egan 1992; Greene 1995) and I aim to show you how some pedagogic regimes may inhibit it while others afford opportunities to use it for thinking about difference and possibility, as well as thinking differently.

In more direct ways, creative practices in craft and design, rather than necessarily reproducing existing traditions, enable people to negotiate ways to transform the environment in which they live to meet the differing needs of new or overlooked circumstances. This ensures that the available technologies, the ways in which people engage with both their environment and with one another, condition what they do and how they do it. At this point in the twenty-first century, it is therefore important for you to consider digital and other electronic media within art education, particularly as they dominate the visual landscape of global communications. After all, as Craft (2006) argues:

> The students in our schools will help to shape the world in which they grow up and in which we grow old. Their ability to find solutions to the problems they inherit from us, and to grow beyond the restrictions we have placed upon our world view will – more than any other generation – define the future of our species and our planet ... The discourse then, which surrounds creativity in education is shifting to include dissidence and critique.
>
> (p. 23)

In this sense, you need to be wary of technological determinism and should recognise the way in which art, craft and design, as embodied practices, enable learners to use the body, both in itself and in conjunction with its material extensions, as a fundamental and potentially inexhaustible technological resource.

Creativity and ordinariness

From the 1970s up to the advent of the National Curriculum in the 1990s, there was a concerted effort by a number of arts educationalists to highlight the importance of the aesthetic domain for a rounded and holistic education. Smith (1970), Eisner (1972) and Greene (2001) in the USA, and Witkin (1974), Ross (1984), Best (1985) and Abbs (1987) in the UK, argued that instrumental forms of schooling, where students are trained in skills for work, dehumanises the process of education and leaves no room for creative expression. They were also at pains to counter the growing use of the term 'creative' as somehow synonymous with all that is effective and good, and thus attempted to define its range of activities and within which domains or conventions it could be most suitably housed. For example, Best (1985) observes that 'the term "creative" and its cognates are often used very loosely, so that anything one does is sometimes regarded as creative' (p. 76). He singles out originality and imagination as the key to creativity, special attributes that somehow make the act itself 'inexplicable'. Although you may find it easy to agree with the necessity of these attributes for doing things creatively, you do not necessarily have to concur with the special and unknowable status that Best, among many others, affords them. It comes as no surprise to witness him exemplifying creativity in relation to the work of a series of extraordinary 'geniuses': Elgar, Mozart, Gauss, Picasso and Haydn, a Eurocentric and hierarchical sampling that typifies the way in which a generation of aestheticians (most recently, Gingell 2006) have tried to divorce cultural excellence from everyday actions. I do not wish to belittle these extraordinary achievements. Creativity with a capital 'C' is used merely to remind you that Creativity and creativity are neither exclusive to western culture nor limited to unknowable instances.

In contradistinction, Csikszentmihalyi (1996) argues that it *is* possible to know what constitutes creativity and, in his collected testimony of the thoughts of creative individuals, constructs a theory of 'flow' based on psychological principles and an acceptance of established domains of practice. From the point of view of teaching young people, however, he too proves a sceptic: 'Children can show enormous talent, but they cannot be creative because creativity involves changing a way of doing things, or a way of thinking, and that in turn requires having mastered the old way of thinking. No matter how precocious a child is, this he or she cannot do' (p. 155). The problem for educators when facing the literature on creativity in the arts is the overwhelming emphasis by writers on the progressive notion of Creativity as a historical process.

Williams (1965) helpfully examines this historical dimension by tracing the changing meanings of 'creativity' within the western tradition. He provides evidence to locate its association with artistic endeavour in Renaissance thought, where it takes on a 'C' connotation. He determines the novelty of this usage by pointing out the distinction between the classical, Greek term for producing a representation, 'mimesis' ('imitation', for Plato 'illusion') and Renaissance 'creativity', which takes on the meaning of invention. In this sense, through creative acts, the poet/artist is able to transcend nature by 'revealing' an alternative reality, at the time a notion close to blasphemy (pp. 19–24). If originality is implicit within this formulation, the imagination becomes the primary faculty only once the Romantic philosophers and poets of the eighteenth and early nineteenth century contribute their reflections on creativity as a process. But here, as Williams demonstrates, imagination is a general property of the human mind and the poet only the most extreme instance of its application, an extraordinary person who is thus able to produce insights beyond the reach of the majority (pp. 24–29). Williams goes on to uncover further shifts and refinements of meaning, arguing that the imaginative process of envisioning the world extolled by the Romantics was re-examined in the twentieth century and shown to have much in common with the basic process of perception itself. These new understandings of perception make it clear that seeing is not just a matter of transmission (like a camera), but a cognitive and creative process through which people come to learn to see – that is, to interpret sensory data in relation to their social, cultural and historical specificity. The phenomenological philosopher Merleau-Ponty (1974) puts it thus: perception is 'subtended by an "intentional arc" which projects round about us our past, our future, our human setting, our physical, ideological or moral situation, or rather which results in our being situated in all these respects' (p. 136).

In the context of education, the US philosopher Dewey, prefiguring Merleau-Ponty, claimed that: 'experience is a matter of the interactions of organism with its environment that is human as well as physical, that includes the material of tradition and institutions, as well as local surroundings' (Dewey 1980: 246). Education should therefore engage fully, productively and reflexively in the whole fabric of society, including its cultural resources. In this way: 'instruction in the arts of life is something other than conveying information about them. It is a matter of communication and participation in the *values of ordinary life* by means of the imagination, and works of art are the most intimate and energetic means of aiding individuals to share in the arts of living' (Dewey 1980: 336). This more inclusive understanding of creativity therefore stresses its ordinariness, for, as Boden (1990) argues, creative processes 'involve special purposes for familiar mental operations and the more efficient use of our ordinary abilities, not "something profoundly different"' (p. 259); in this sense, creativity is extra/ordinary, what Prentice (2008) refers to as 'an extraordinary ordinary function of general intelligence'.

Nonetheless, it should be emphasised that this ordinariness does not signal an 'anything-goes' policy, 'the child-knows-best' approach for which the Plowden Report (1967) is sometimes misguidedly seen as responsible. Rather, the definition of creativity I wish you to consider refers to those many instances of human activity where something is made anew – for example, where something is learned. Thus, the term learning is also ordinary. Drawing on constructivist theory, elsewhere Burgess and I have discussed learning as:

> a social and transformative process. This understanding posits learning as something constructed by individuals in interaction with others and their environment; put simply, learning is a social process through which people make meaning from experience (Vygotsky 1978a). This understanding contrasts with traditional definitions of learning where it is theorised as a process of the acquisition, assimilation and application of knowledge. In this latter definition knowledge is something objective, something that experts (teachers) can pass on to novices (students) ... In contrast, when learning is theorised as a constructive process the learner is recognised as the maker of meaning and the teacher as the person who constructs learning situations to make this process possible. This is not just a facilitative role but a creative and collaborative one.
>
> (Addison and Burgess 2006: 46)

In this way, at some level, you can see that learning is creative in and of itself and, in terms of teaching, you can build on this ordinary process to develop affective and purposeful pedagogic experiences in which students work in relation to given, emerging and potential traditions (see Burgess and Gee 2007 and Burgess 2007 for ways to plan, resource and implement such learning experiences).

In order to take on board new knowledge (not information, but ways of thinking and doing), you need to design a learning environment that both provides opportunities and encourages students to think and behave differently to the ways they have done before. Therefore, learning and other forms of creative action require imagination, a term that includes: visualisation (thinking and 'shaping' through images); ingenuity, invention and the world of possibility; ordering or synthesising and syncretising (seeing as totalities), as well as acknowledging difference and thinking other, a process that leads to empathy. Greene (1970) eloquently proposes this idea of imaginative possibility as the basis for education:

> In a sense, a student stands against a world of possibilities, a world of possible forms. In a sense it is imagination that puts him [sic] in relationship to these possibilities, just as it is imagination which enables him to order the indeterminate situations in which his inquiries begin. As in the case of works of art, possibilities signify richer and richer orders, more and more complex relationships. And this means, perhaps paradoxically, that a proper regard for imagination may intensify the sense of reality.
>
> (p. 326)

It is therefore through the imagination that people are able to intensify habitual ways of perceiving the world to transcend the limitations of their current situation. Through the application of the imagination, people reorganise existing cultural resources to reconceive that which is. They do so both as a means to propose that which might be and as a process of transformation through which they realise the new. As Vygotsky (1994) puts it, '... imagination and creativity are linked to a free reworking of various elements of experience, freely combined, and which, as a precondition, without fail, require the level of inner freedom of thought, action and cognizing which only he [sic] who thinks in concepts can achieve' (p. 269). In this sense, the workings of the imagination are dependent on the depth and breadth of students' experience and the ways that you find to intensify and broaden them.

Egan (1992) argues that imagination is a faculty that is most active, perhaps most real, in humans during childhood and thus critiques traditional pedagogies for suppressing it. This commonly held perception is, however, questioned by Vygotsky (1994) who suggests rather that imagination dominates children's thinking and is therefore more apparent during this period. For him, the imagination is not an add-on faculty enabling people to escape the difficulties of reality, it is pre-eminent within most thinking and action:

In everyday life, fantasy or imagination refer to what is actually not true, what does not correspond to reality, and what, thus, could have no practical significance. But in actuality, imagination, as the basis of all creativity, is an important component of absolutely all aspects of cultural life, enabling artistic, scientific, and technical creation alike.

(Vygotsky 2004: 3)

Vygotsky suggests that, from the earliest years, creativity is fundamental to children's approach to the world, 'A child's play is not simply a reproduction of what he [sic] experienced, but a creative reworking of the impressions he has acquired. He combines them and uses them to construct a new reality, one that conforms to his own needs and desires' (pp. 11–12). This reworking process only leaves people when they become habituated or inured to their situations for, as Vygotsky insists, the propensity for people to rework their environment in relation to their desires presupposes a creative imperative: 'It is precisely human creative activity that makes the human being a creature oriented toward the future, creating the future and thus altering his [sic] own present' (p. 9).

Whatever aspect of imagination is brought into play by a specific activity, the process always implies a sense of originality at some level, a sense of something not yet known or understood from a particular subject position. Even in the everyday act of learning, learners make knowledge, knowledge that for the learners themselves is original (although it may not be for others). As Vygotsky asserts: 'Any human act that gives rise to something new is referred to as a creative act, regardless of whether what is created is a physical object or some mental or emotional construct that lives within the person who created it and is known only to him' (2004: 7). The different locations of originality therefore make it necessary to differentiate between types, something that the report into creativity 'All Our Futures' (NACCE 1999) achieves in the following way:

- *Individual*
  A person's work may be original in relation to their own previous work and output.

- *Relative*
  It may be original in relation to their peer group: to other young people of the same age, for example.

- *Historic*
  The work may be original in terms of anyone's previous output in a particular field: that is, it may be uniquely individual.

(p. 30)

It is unlikely that work of school students will gain recognition of historic significance, although it may well offer you insights into their personal and social experiences which are unique to them and may well inform the writing of educational and social history and theory and thus inform policy. But if you teach an art curriculum centred on prescribed exercises divorced from the life experiences of students, you are likely to deny this potential.

You may have noticed how the term creative is often used by teachers to signify positive and enthusiastic production of any kind in any context, or even just good attitudes to work. The useful survey of the current literature on creativity (Banaji *et al.* 2006) commissioned as a part of the Creative Partnerships initiative (an Arts Council learning programme that started in 2002, see: www.creative-partnerships.com/) examines this phenomenon as well as addressing many of the definitions of creativity focused on here and more besides, and you will find it instructive to refer to its findings. As with Craft (2006), the authors gravitate towards understandings posited on people's general propensity to be creative in both informal and formal situations where creativity is valued and fostered. However, I wish to stress at this juncture that the commonality of creativity is not to suggest that all creative action is of equal value (see NACCE 1999; a point discussed further in Chapter 6). This appropriation and generalisation has come about because of the assumption that creative processes and their outcomes are, in and of themselves, good, even where the term is being used to describe particular skills such as problem-solving, lateral thinking and so on. However, if you reduce creativity to such skills it is easy to identify creative acts that, in human terms, have negative consequences. Imagine how different the texts on creativity would be if exploitative acts replaced the usual litany: what of the imagination required to bully, the collaborative planning necessary to design a major heist or the invention deployed by advertisers to dupe consumers into buying some unnecessary, ecologically unsound artefact. But authors from Koestler (1965) to Csikszentmihalyi (1996) focus on fields such as art and science that carry positive profiles within the history of modern thought. Thus, as with all human action, it is important that you do not divorce creative practice from ethical considerations (an issue discussed more fully in Chapter 6).

Sensory exploration, aesthetic experience and embodiment

Sensory experience and the aesthetic domain

If you accept that creativity is a common property that is central to such ordinary processes as learning, then you must assume that it is a phenomenon hard-wired into the human body and activated through social relations and environmental interactions. Consider, for instance, the way in which an infant comes to know the world through sensory exploration, a process through which they make their first bold attempts to understand and control their environment. These perceptions of their world, received as distasteful or pleasurable, constitute a relatively unmediated aesthetic experience. The simple oppositions produced from these early experiences become less polarised as children are enculturated within tradition so that their aesthetic sensibility is channelled and enriched to develop a particular aesthetic disposition. The tastes or preferences resulting from such sensibilities are profoundly conditioned by the affordances of each person's somatic, social and cultural situation, their 'habitus' (Bourdieu's useful term for the embodied, habituated practices and values inculcated through a person's formative social environments, 1990). Schools can extend students' knowledge and experience of art, craft and design towards both an expansive and focused understanding of aesthetic practices, while acknowledging the dispositions and tastes that a particular habitus presupposes (for example, those based on class identifications).

During the process of enculturation in the home, you may recall how as a child, and given the chance, you ordinarily explored your immediate environment as a sensory playground seeking out and relishing, in and for itself, contact with a certain type of matter: food, hair, mud, water. During such motivated exploration, the combination of the intentional and arbitrary activities of balancing, hearing, seeing, smelling, tasting and touching resulted in other less motivated sensations such as falling, clapping, darkness, bitterness and viscosity. In later and adult life, such sensory activities tend to be channelled into culturally determined forms: dancing, singing, fashion, cooking and sex, so that the immediacy of the experience is lost in expectation, custom, assumption and the mediation of language. In his examination of Derrida's concept of différance, Crowther (1993a) explains how, in infancy, children's explorations enable them to co-ordinate the body and the mind to meet motivated desires. This coordination enables them to differentiate between what is present and what is absent, and to experience the body as both productive of desire but also as the tool for its realisation:

> It is, of course, this learned dimension of sensory fulfilment, and bodily effort as the means to such fulfilment, which enables the child to learn spatialization and temporalization, in all, 'deferall' in its most basic sense. Before the child can speak, therefore, the co-ordination of its sensory-motor capacities into a unified field serves to articulate a proto-world. Things are concretely present as items for inspection or consumption, but they have this character only in so far as they emerge from a background determined by the scope of the body's developing co-ordination. Language grows from this matrix of achieved co-ordination, at once articulating it and rendering it more complex and abstract. The child, in other words, learns a language only because it has already learned the vectors of *différence* through its achieved co-ordination with a world of things.
>
> (Crowther 1993a: 28–29)

This engagement with the environment as beings immersed in a world of matter, space and time allows children to develop a sense of themselves as active agents able to use these resources creatively to get at what they want. As they discover that other people want different things and that these others have more power than they do and may wish them to do other than that which they had wanted, they enter the symbolic world, the world of boundaries, rules, expected behaviours, right and wrong, a complex network of symbolic relations and conventions that cohere as tradition.

Artists work within these traditions, but some also report that they attempt to attain or return to an earlier state of being where, like a child, a lack of knowledge leads to curiosity, to trying things out, to using a resource in a way that for others is unexpected but to the creative agent is a motivated risk because either the normal use of the resource is not known (as may be the case with children) or because s/he purposively suspends knowledge of habituated uses. Occasionally artists, craftspeople and designers have discussed the retention of the earlier faculty, an openness to the sensory properties of a material that fuels a desire to work with, and sometimes against, its affordances: that is the material's physical, formal and symbolic properties, its constraints and potentialities. (For examples of the ways in which artists and craftspeople think about the relationship between materials and meaning-making, see the artists' statements in Burgess and Schofield 2007: 183–184). This dialogue with materials is the primary ground out of which all making practices emerge, practices that take shape in relation to the cultural forms within which the maker is immersed (even for children where available resources signal valued practices, e.g. graphic materials). In this sense, the dialogue is profoundly intertextual, and it conjoins historical practices with the phenomonological event (the maker's actions) to inform future uses – utilitarian, discursive, symbolic.

As you observe lessons in schools, you may well find that this dialogue with materials can be overlooked, especially when the primary objective is to develop technical competency in the service of reproducing a given prototype or to master a formal convention for the purpose of making a conventional representation. Both these outcomes are potentially perfectly acceptable exercises. However, where they dominate the curriculum at the expense of processes in which the optical, tactile and sound properties and the spatial and temporal potential of a range of materials can be explored, they limit possibilities; you have only to recall Boccioni's 1912 'Technical Manifesto of Futurist Sculpture' to consider how varied these might be: 'Deny the exclusiveness of one material for the entire construction of a sculptural ensemble. Affirm that even twenty different materials can compete in a single work to effect plastic emotion. Let us enumerate some: glass, wood, cardboard, iron, cement, horsehair, leather, cloth, mirrors, electric lights etc. etc.' (in Chipp 1968: 304). There needs to be a balance: mastery of conventions provides satisfaction, confidence and self-esteem, and confidence is a prerequisite for risk-taking; conventions and rules need to be understood before they can be questioned, tested or broken, and within the western tradition, such a pushing at boundaries is a prerequisite for creativity.

Alternatively, as some artists are happy to work within tradition and may well be content with the physical resources and their conventional patterns of use, it is also important to consider the way that it can be a regime of representation, rather than its material expression, that forms the locus of creative questioning. For example, Paula Rego has increasingly developed her painting along traditional lines, using pastel in a way that does homage to eighteenth- and nineteenth-century artists. But she deploys these resources on a different scale and with imagery that is at once familiar and strange as she delineates the dysfunctional and disavowed desires at play within contemporary human relations (Addison 2006).

Aesthetic experience and embodiment

So far, although I have been arguing for the ordinariness of creativity and its ubiquity across domains, given the role of this book, I have exemplified it in relation to art and design practice. At this stage, it becomes important to elaborate further on the ways in which art, craft and design offer something distinctive that can complement the approaches of other domains.

Increasingly, art practices draw on other disciplines as a part of the move towards interdisciplinarity in research, and cross-curricularity in schools. Most art forms require time as a principle mode not only for their production but also for their immediate reception. A dance, a novel, a film, a song, all require viewers to attend to their changing forms within a period defined by the work itself as a linear, unfolding sequence of events. Works of art, craft and design may likewise use temporal elements – they may incorporate video, performance, depend on the movement of a viewer through a succession of spaces, the prolonged use of tools through a series of applications and so on – but they may also depend on simultaneity. In other words, the richness and complexity of a vessel, chair, painting or sculpture, with their spatial relationships and formal and semantic possibilities, can be perceived in a comparatively short time. This provides such works with an extraordinary immediacy and potency, which only subsequently invites viewers to attend to particularities. This is not to suggest that time should not be spent in savouring, exploring and investigating them; but immediate aesthetic appreciation can be almost instantaneous as the mind takes in and is able to understand an artefact's organisational principles. This means that when a person looks at an artwork, they can oscillate between aesthetic contemplation or reverie and a more deliberate reflective investigation, analysis or evaluation (this process is given more attention in Chapter 5). For temporal works, particularly those performed in real-time, sustained reflection is always mid- or post-event because such reflection tends to interrupt their continuity.

School students, like anyone, come to artworks with expectations, assumptions and some prior knowledge of the field. It is in a work's resistance to these expectations and norms that the possibility for the transformation of ideas and values lies. By mediating their encounters with artworks, you can help students to construct understandings by structuring discussion, for example around: what appears self-evident and why, what requires cultural investigation and translation, where a work's semiotic potential might lead (Addison 2007). Students can acknowledge the affective potency of immediate responses but go on to seek intentions and possible meanings and then come to some informed judgement about its rightness and authenticity. Crowther (1993b) explains the process thus:

In the specific field of academic inquiry, this movement is described as the 'hermeneutic circle'. It involves proceeding from some foreknowledge of the object, to a consideration of it in the light of those aspects of tradition which are relevant to its interpretation. On the basis of this, we are able to deepen our original understanding. The truth of the object is not reified in some putative notion of definitively achieved absolute correspondence. Rather, it emerges in a gradual unfolding and clarification of its aspects, as the hermeneutic circle constellates around it. Truth is seen as a continuing process of refinement, enrichment, and clarification. It is a dynamic of *interpretation*.

(pp. 10–11)

As you will see later, this cyclic dynamic, when applied to the process of making and using art, is more like a helix as the circle spirals out towards new understandings and potential uses (see Vygotsky at the end of the next section, 'Creativity as a process').

At the same time as being things in themselves, works of art (but also craft and design) may be a representation of something: say, a painting of a landscape, a carved lion's foot, a photograph of a commercial product, and this representational meaning may well dominate the attention of viewers who are not themselves makers. Now a maker's interest is rarely limited to a representation's denotative and connotative potential but rather to the perceptual means through which it becomes known (see Merleau-Ponty [1964] on Cézanne) and in how the material and formal resources of a specific modality and tradition are deployed to make it. Such a concern to retrace the making process, to understand a work's finality as a resolution of almost infinite possibilities, allows makers to investigate artworks as a map of material and formal decisions. As such, craft knowledge, knowledge of materials and their use within tradition, is a necessary ground for all embodied expressions.

In dance, drama, music and other performances, embodiment is more obviously rooted in the body itself as a resource for expression. In traditional types of art, craft and design, the body is less obviously but no less significantly present in the way that it is inscribed in the object through the traces of its actions as the maker transforms materials into some concretisation or crystalisation of an idea. But this is not to suggest that the idea necessarily precedes the reformation of materials; indeed, ideas may emerge and converge within the act of making itself. For example, Matthews (2003) closely examines the relationship between bodily movement and representation in children's drawing, demonstrating how intimately connected the experience of movement is to its shaping as graphic expression. This bodily involvement is also highlighted by Elkins in his exploration of the act of painting by artists:

Paint records the most delicate gesture and the most tense. It tells whether the painter sat or stood or crouched ... Paint is a cast made of the painter's movements, a portrait of the painter's body and thoughts ... Painting is an unspoken and largely uncognized dialogue ... Painters can sense those motions in the paint even before they notice what the paintings are about.

(Elkins 2000: 5)

Is this process of embodiment suddenly of no interest in the work of secondary school students?

The body acts on or with materials to give concrete expression to ideas, to create (as it were) an alternative body, that of the artwork as a phenomenal presence. Like a human being, this artefact is indivisibly matter and ideas. It is therefore important that you retain practices in schools in which the physicality of materials can be explored so that the current obsession with lens-based representation communicated through the screen can be complemented by the inescapable truth of the fully sensory nature of what it is to be human, what it is to be simultaneously of and in the world. As Kearney (1998) notes: 'it is precisely in cyber-culture where the image reigns supreme that the notion of a creative human imagination appears most imperilled' (pp. 7–8). With a mind to futures, it is only by working with concrete materials that students can harness creative processes so as to affect and transform the physical environment and landscape of images and their cultural uses.

Creativity as a process

Abbs (1989; 1994) has been particularly concerned to map the experience of creative activity writing about the combination of emotional and intellectual energy required for creative production. In much of his writing, he is at pains to stress the embodied nature of art-making but also what he sees as its instinctual basis:

Its blossom may open out in consciousness but its roots are down deep in affective impulse, in muscular and nervous rhythms, the beat of the heart, the intake and release of breath, patterns of perception, unconscious coordination of the limbs, the obscure, fluctuating, dimly sensed movements of the organism, in the preconceptual play of the psyche.

(1989: 200)

However evocative such emotive language may be, in the context of art and design in secondary schools it is difficult to conceive of learning situations in which all students might simultaneously engage in such absorbed or potentially rapturous activity. When planning learning situations designed to facilitate creative approaches with large groups, particularly at Key Stage 3, it is perhaps more useful to look at how Abbs describes the way creative practitioners need to be embedded within a tradition. Such a tradition acts as a rich repository and resource for endless reconfiguration, whether that tradition is legitimated within the fields of fine art and design or located in more demotic, craft-based home practices (Mason 2005).

Abbs suggests that during the first stage of the creative process, the initial impulse may often be expressed through such predictable and clichéd form (this is particularly so in schools because students are so often required to replicate 'correct' outcomes that they inevitably gravitate towards ubiquitous and popularly valued metaphors). Towards the close of this stage, the art-maker reflects on the emerging product and deliberates on the relation between it and the initial impulse; s/he:

> begins to discard, to select, to consider, to evaluate … This coincides with a subtle but distinct shift in attention from a preoccupation with immediate approximate expression to a preoccupation with final representative form. As the work moves towards completion the art-maker will frequently consult with an imagined audience, constantly seeking its advice. 'How does this bit look?' 'Should it be this way round?' 'Is this reference too obscure?'
>
> (Abbs 1989: 201)

Clearly, Abbs is imagining the artist working in isolation. But the school environment is a social one and this collectivity can be used to advantage. You therefore need to develop a discursive environment in which criticism is received as a productive activity. Rather than closing down and limiting practice, discussion can be channelled towards opening up possibilities, helping students to make choices and to discriminate between what works for purpose and what does not (official criteria should be addressed here, but should not determine practice; see Chapter 6). However, that which does not work may also offer opportunities – say where the outcome is tangential to purpose but opens up a new seam of possibility. These moments of critical reflection must therefore be open to making new connections, revising criteria or considering unforeseen applications.

Abbs formulates a diagram to help define a cyclic conception of the creative process (1989: 204).

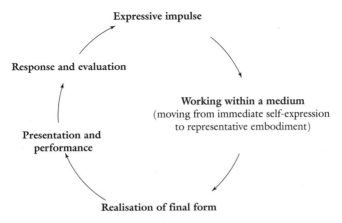

Figure 3.1 *The spiral motion of art making*, Peter Abbs.

Clearly, 'working with the medium' and 'realisation of final form' are the sequences referred to in the quotation above and you might investigate them further by referring to Schon (1987) and his notion of reflection-in-action through which he elaborates the to-and fro between action, reflection and revision/refinement (see also Prentice 2007a). However, Vygotsky (2004) takes this realisation of a final form not as an end but as a beginning – in effect, the construction of a new potential:

> ... once it [a construct] has been externally embodied, that is, has been given material form, this crystallized imagination that has become an object begins to actually exist in the real world, to affect other things.
>
> In this way imagination becomes reality.
>
> ... Finally, once [constructs] have been given material form, they returned to reality, but returned as a new active force with the potential to alter reality. This is the complete cycle followed by the creative operation of the imagination ...
>
> It is a fact that precisely when we confront a full circle completed by the imagination is when we find both factors – the intellectual and the emotional – are equally necessary for an act of creation. Feeling as well as thought drives human creativity.
>
> (2004: 20)

On emotions

Vygotsky (2004) makes it clear throughout his work that the emotions play a significant role in shaping thought, and creative thought in particular. But one way in which artists may differentiate their work from that of scientists is in the recognition that the emotions can underpin or facilitate creative work rather than overlay or possibly impede it. After all, the quest of modern science is to find out what the physical world is like, independent of human mediation. Scientific understandings are then applied to mediate the world by using various technologies to transform natural resources to meet specific (hopefully ethical) ends. In contradistinction, the arts are primarily concerned with the world as perceived and made by the human subject, a world that is of necessity mediated through human consciousness and action. Understandings are then applied, sometimes with the aid of science and technology, to consider how the world might be different and hopefully better. Nonetheless, as Eco argues, 'In every century, the way that artistic forms are structured reflects the way in which science or contemporary culture views reality' (2006: 31). In this way, specific world views determine the nature of representational practices at any one time and place, so that how it is for humans to experience the world as emotional and rational beings is not a universal but a historically and contingent phenomenon; thus the diversity of aesthetic practices.

The emotional core at the centre of aesthetic experience is therefore both fundamental and highly charged, and yet its bodily and involuntary credentials often relegate it to a subsidiary and tainted position within those academic cultures that privilege abstract and conceptual thought. But the visceral arousals (sensations) that aesthetic experiences induce are not the emotion itself (rather sensation is its necessary *condition*), as a visceral arousal can be the same for different emotions: for instance, butterflies in the stomach may anticipate fear or desire. A particular emotion is thus a combination of visceral arousal and cognitive and perceptual evaluations, evaluations that are concerned with the relationship between internal sensation and the external events that have conditioned them (Schachter 1971). In this sense, as Damasio (1994) argues, all experience is infused with emotional feelings so that any consideration of, say, the past or future is inevitably coloured by a particular 'feeling tone' (Getz and Lubart 2000). This background sensation is not necessarily translated into a specific behaviour but provides a condition that informs creative activity – for example: anticipation, excitement, curiosity, uncertainty (when designing a learning situation, you would therefore do well to ensure that you set up *interesting* conditions: a problem, investigation or environment, to act as an initial stimulus). These background feelings are formed through the interrelationship between bodily arousals, which seem entirely factual and demonstrative ('I respond in this way, it's the way I am') and socially regulated and sanctioned behaviours, which may be experienced as inhibiting or enabling ('don't' show yourself up by crying', 'look at the way so and so dances for joy'). The interrelationship between these two produces 'emotional syndromes', a term coined by Averill (2005) to refer to 'organized patterns of response that are symbolized in ordinary language by such terms as *anger, love, grief*' (p. 228). These emotions are a complex of visceral arousals, reflections and actions (physiological, cognitive and motivated experiences) in which subjective experience is channelled into culturally specific, aesthetic forms.

Artists are often called upon to give these emotions socially sanctioned, permanent form as when Rachel Whiteread won the competition in Vienna to commemorate the Holocaust, resulting in the 'Judenplatz Holocaust Memorial' (1996–2000). With the seemingly simple gesture of casting a domestic, if extensive, library, she managed to externalise its many books so that they are displayed as the outer skin of the monument – inverted, their spines, authorship and content hidden. In a sense, this visibility/invisibility is a metaphoric embodiment of the outrage and sense of loss experienced by contemporary societies in response to the way the Nazis exposed, ridiculed, hounded and abjected the Jews while attempting to deny and efface their contribution to the formation of European identity.

When planning for learning it might therefore be useful to think about the feelings, tones and emotional syndromes triggered by the sequencing of events:

- Stimulus – leading to interest, excitement and anticipation.
- Curiosity – leading to investigation, research and exploration (processes that may themselves re-ignite curiosity).

- Immersion – in sustained practice, leading to absorption, pleasure, anticipation, a dynamic between frustration and satisfaction, evaluation/revision – leading to somewhere between vulnerability and confidence, indefiniteness and resolution.
- Dissemination – leading to self-esteem, pride, shared understandings, other interpretations and uses, as the work becomes a new stimulus.

The linear and cyclic progression of this sequence is not a given, it could well be re-sequenced, or orchestrated in different ways. It is also best to remember that stimuli are not necessarily received in the same way by every student: different people receive the same phenomenon differently, somewhere along a continuum between pleasure or distaste.

The simple oppositions that are often used to consider emotions in art and design – that between happiness and sadness, anger and calm – produce a climate in which emotions are considered only as extreme moments of consciousness. In this sense, they hide the constancy of emotionality and reduce its complexity. Although such oppositions are useful hooks with which to engage students, they have the effect of foregrounding dominant ideas about positive and negative behaviours and thus contribute to the attempt to help students 'manage' their emotions (a danger emerging from the way that Goleman's work [1996] is being applied); this initiates a process of self-regulation to produce what Foucault (1977) terms the 'docile body' (as if emotions were somehow pathological). The diversity of art, as crystallisations of others' emotional and intellectual life-worlds, is a rich resource through which students can explore their own and others' feelings in an attempt to understand the significance of emotions and, hopefully, to attain the ability to empathise (for an instance of this approach in relation to desire and sexuality, see Addison 2006). The term empathy encompasses the way in which people are able to imagine what it is to be another person living under different circumstances, to identify with that situation, and to feel for, and with that person; to imagine and feel other. As an emotional goal, it forms the basis for democratic education – it is not antithetical to analytical or critical approaches, which acknowledge just indignation and anger as well as the discomfort of self-knowledge (see Chapter 7), but it is antithetical to those regimes that attempt to contain emotions in the name of appeasement and/or the status quo.

The orientation of my discussion has been primarily western in its focus, but it is also important to recognise that creativity is understood differently across cultures. Ng (2003) has carried out a comparative analysis of 'eastern' and 'western' perceptions of creative practice by questioning students from Singapore and Australia. He found, respectively, notions of conformity and novelty, interdependence and independence surfacing as key descriptors. Pope (2005: 60–62; 149–151) draws your attention to the bases of these differences, discussing the significance of 'fulfilment' rather than 'novelty' as central to an 'eastern' view (although, he points out, that intercultural exchange has meant that this idea has permeated western philosophy for centuries and vice versa). This suggests an affective state of satisfaction rather than excitement, an emotional orientation that refutes the primacy of the new (see also Adorno [1997] for an elaboration of this point in relation to modernism and its problematic identification with that which is novel). Sennet (2008) notices similarly divergent attitudes across cultures between craft and art practitioners, promoting a reconsideration of the workshop environment that is typical of apprenticeships in which novelty for its own sake is rejected in favour of refinement. However, sometimes the leadership of this community of practice by a 'master' contravenes democratic principles so that what you might wish to emulate here is the collective striving for excellence, the absorption of a community towards specific goals and the pre-eminence of practical knowledge (an issue further discussed towards the end of Chapter 5).

Alternatively, you might consider a more critical approach to immersive practices as advocated in the strategies of artists such as Daniel Burin, Adrian Piper or Angela Fraser, who engage in site-specific practices and/or forms of institutional critique. This approach draws on the process of 'distanciation' elaborated by the poet/playwright Bertolt Brecht (see Benjamin 1934) through which an audience is alienated from the spectacle of traditional theatre (art) by interruptions into its regimes of illusion and naturalism – for example, when an actor comes out of role and sings a popular song or talks to the audience as if in conversation. These strategies of defamiliarisation and 'astonishment' (p. 100) disrupt a straightforward reading of narrative and, instead, incite audiences to contextualise the social conditions and relations implied within the dramatic situation but also their own acts of spectatorship. In this way, audiences are drawn away from sentimental identification or empathy towards 'thinking'; Benjamin recounts: 'It sets out, not so much to fill the audience with feelings – albeit possibly feelings of revolt – as to alienate the audience in a lasting manner, through thought, from the conditions in which it lives' (p. 101). Now, although this might be seen to be anti-feeling, and thus anti-emotional, it can be, in consequence, profoundly affecting as hooks explores in her reflections on the process of engaged pedagogy, which, along with Freire, owes something to Brecht's example.

> ... there can be and usually is a degree of pain in giving up old ways of thinking and knowing, and learning new approaches. I respect that pain. I include a recognition of it when I teach, that is to say, I teach about shifting paradigms and talk about the discomfort it can cause.
>
> (hooks 1994: 43)

In the context of art practice, I take an example from the work of Adrian Piper. During the 1980s, Piper initiated a series of lessons and collaborative performances around funk, the Black American musical genre originating in the 1970s, which developed from soul. Among other people, she encouraged participation from middle class and or educated white and black friends, colleagues and acquaintances who, for various reasons which she explores, perceived the genre as 'sexually threatening and culturally intrusive' ... and/or '"mindless" or "monotonous"'

(Piper 2006: 133). Through a combination of carefully sequenced, analytical sessions, and discursive and practical participation, she involved learners in confronting their assumptions and prejudices; she explains in relation to one of the late sessions: 'except for brief pauses for questions, dialogue and my (short) commentaries, everyone was LISTENING by DANCING. We were all engaged in the pleasurable process of transcendence and creative expression within a highly structured and controlled cultural idiom, in a way that attempted to overcome cultural and racial barriers' (p. 131). Her examination of her motivations and aims, and the way in which she planned and organised the activities around the affective responses of participants, might provide a model for recounting the reflective evaluation of your own pedagogic practice.

Conditions for creative work

In this last section, I wish to draw on the discussion so far to provide a framework to help you construct learning environments and conditions conducive to creativity. While recognising Craft's warning that 'it may not be fruitful to consider creativity as something that can be seen as being "triggered" in any direct or simple way' (2006: 25), like her, it is useful at least to provide a structure for action. I therefore end this chapter with a series of recommendations in which I categorise and characterise some of these conditions. I do not propose this as a 'checklist', but as a point of reference to help you to reflect on the learning experiences and creative possibilities that you facilitate through your teaching. (It should be noted that many of these conditions and characteristics could be achieved collectively/collaboratively as well as individually.)

The six key concepts that I have selected as the basis for the framework – motivation, purpose, knowledge construction, environment, imagination, evaluation – are indebted to a number of sources, specifically Arieti (1976), Feldhusen and Treffinger (1980) and Torrance (1981). Additionally, Steers cites other formulations in Chapter 2. Torrance's five factors for creative teaching are particularly succinct – motivation, alertness, curiosity, concentration, achievement – although they focus on psychological dispositions rather than environmental conditions.

Motivation

What is it that serves as the drive or stimulus for creative action? It is evident that many creative practitioners hold great *emotional investment* in the processes and outcomes of their actions; they may feel that what they are doing is necessary and right and directly relevant to themselves and others around them and more widely. For students in schools, it is therefore motivating to engage with practices connected to, or investigations into, their *interests and life worlds*. However, through *curiosity* or excitement in *the unknown*, you can *extend* the interests and life worlds of students through your expertise/interests and those of other artists. Your particular *enthusiasms* may spur students to engage in those same interests or may act as a model to help them realise that choosing something exciting, puzzling, or something that can be explored, expressed or represented through art, craft or design is likely to sustain their own and others' interest. If you can orchestrate moments of *anticipation*, students are likely to look forward to work, and if you can simultaneously demonstrate that there are no easy fixes, thereby *delaying gratification*, then *attention* can be sustained. Once secure in the knowledge that they are working in a secure and respectful environment, students will readily take a *challenge*, through which you can lead them away from predictable and comfortable practices.

Purpose (thinking futures)

Purpose might be seen as a sub-section of motivation in that purposeful activity, such as working towards goals, practical or competitive outcomes, can drive practice. But the way I have expressed the former is largely individualistic, whereas my characterisation of purpose is primarily social.

Students find the idea of *expressing themselves* either as an individual or as part of a specific community particularly engaging as it allows them not only a degree of self-*representation*, or voice, but helps them to actively form an identity, a process of *identification* in which they investigate cultural practices in order to locate themselves within history (potentially rewriting it) and/or conceive possible futures. This might involve combining present forms into hybrids or crystalising emergent ones, as well as elaborating or refining those from the past. To do this, they will need to consider *communications*, how their expressions are received by others – this is a key *relational* factor that is often overlooked in schools: should the artwork be clear, encourage closed or open meanings, invite speculation, argument, relationships across modes (eg. between word and image), *meet the needs* of an audience (possibly by *changing/improving an environment*) or perhaps *challenge* their expectations by questioning norms?

Environments that encourage working for purpose are characterised by: discussion, inquiry, investigation, interpretation; evaluating what works in specific contexts for particular audiences; disseminating, exhibiting, curating; hard work towards realising aims.

Knowledge construction

It is generally agreed that creative action is pursued or emerges from within specific fields or domains of practice. The field of art, craft and design is potentially huge. It is therefore important that students gradually gain knowledge of, and an *immersion* within, not only a generic domain (e.g. fine art), but specific practices (e.g. animation, textiles, painting, sculpture, video). In this way, they can come to know its *material and symbolic affordances*, both in terms of *production* and *reception*. As learners, students will move between the general and particular, theoretical and practical considerations and decisions, using declarative and procedural knowledge to communicate understandings and realise intentions. This will entail engaging in deliberate and *reasoned work* within the field: where work is planned, predetermined and intentional.

At the same time, all knowledge should be open to *enquiry* and *investigation* so that rules can be questioned (a process that first requires an understanding of the rules). This enables naturalised concepts, the givens, assumptions and absolutes that underpin habit and custom to be realised, whether they stem from the school community or vested interests within the field. In this sense, knowledge needs to be understood as a type of constructed truth within co-existing alternatives. Enquiry should therefore be carried out respectfully, with *sensitivity to contexts of practice* (historical, cultural and contemporaneous). To enable this, it is important to provide opportunities to *pose, explore, redefine and solve problems*, encouraging students to *make and share personal meanings*.

The following list characterises different ways to construct knowledge through art and design:

- Exploration/discovery:
  - sensory – treating materials (e.g. paint, plastics, wood, sounds) to physical variation, combination, deconstruction
  - formal – organising and reorganising visual, tactile, spatial and temporal elements
  - observational – recording phenomena (through drawing, photography, modelling)
  - abstract – conceiving structures rather than appearances
- Problem posing/solving: identifying obstacles and exploring ways to overcome them
- Investigation: looking into something, empirically, historically, theoretically
- Reasoning: inductive (observing instances to infer truths), deductive (using theories to explain instances)
- Testing: e.g. a theory in relation to a range of instances and vice versa
- Analysis: categorising, making generalisations from particularities
- Synthesis: drawing ideas together to shape hypotheses, arguments, conclusions
- Lateral thinking: making unexpected connections, thinking in equivalences
- Pattern completion: noticing similarities and differences, completing a line of thought/practice
- Intuition: forming ideas unconsciously so that they appear suddenly, arising as if through inspiration
- Deploying chance: noticing and using serendipity, random procedures

Environment: time, space, matter

Many theorists of creativity talk of a period of *incubation* in which ideas are processed unconsciously, thus the 'Eureka' moment as it surfaces into consciousness (Koestler 1965; Csikszentmihalyi 1996). *Time* is therefore a key resource within creative practice so that it is advisable to allow the possibility for *immersion* or *absorption*: the time, space, environment and resources to enable *concentrated, sustained and extended work*.

Taking students out of familiar surroundings and working with different people also encourages them to *reconsider usual practices*. It is therefore constructive to work with external partnerships, organisations and individuals within the field (see Chapters 4, 6 and 7). Although visiting different environments can ensure this process of *defamiliarisation*, you can also *reorganise* the immediate working environment of the classroom or school grounds to meet specific needs to similar effect. By working in *cross-curricular collaboration*, you can encourage students to consider dialogical, interdisciplinary work, extending and making more permeable the developing 'community of practice' (see Chapter 4).

Such environments are characterised by:

- a range of material, technical and reference resources
- a flexible space
- access: times when resources can be used outside of timetables
- displays of work in progress
- working outside the classroom and school, possibly in partnership
- working across departments within the school.

Imagination

As the imagination is the primary engine of creative action, it is important that you enable students to set up situations, events and investigations in which they can *imagine possibilities* beyond the usual, how difference is understood (*variation and diversity*) and how a sense of the '*other*' is formed and sustained (engaging with knowledge and ideas that fall outside students' own social, cultural and moral frameworks).

Taking risks is also associated with the imagination in that it revolves around the *not-yet-known*, and is thus seen as central to creative thinking. By taking risks, students realise that some things can fail to meet objectives and that they can learn from mistakes. It is also an approach to experimentation and exploration that can help students to *tolerate ambiguity*. In order to encourage risk-taking, you might provide opportunities for students to *work spontaneously* (without premeditation), to *make or break rules, revise* plans (change their minds), *test boundaries* and recognise that ideas can *emerge* through practical activity rather than necessarily preceding it.

Imaginative activity is characterised by:

- making associations/connections
- inventing rules
- combining materials to make new forms
- combining elements from past experiences

- risk-taking
- seeking alternatives
- empathising with others, imagining how others feel
- discussing and representing pasts, presents, futures.

Evaluation

Finally, a creative environment needs to offer up the possibility of *dialogue*, a place where diverse thoughts and practices can be discussed critically so as to establish their value (see Chapter 6). You are likely to work with some students over a number of years; in that time, you can attempt to develop a *common language* to help form a *community of practice*. Within the strength and security that such communities can engender, it is important to develop individual potential, to encourage students to develop *metacognitive skills* and *self-efficacy* (an understanding of how s/he best learns; see Chapter 5). You might begin by *interpreting and translating* official criteria – for example, examination criteria. You might then consider *negotiating critical procedures* to evaluate practice: can you use traditional criteria for creativity – novelty (contribution), effectiveness (use value) and authenticity (emotional sincerity) – as the basis for evaluation, or do you need to construct criteria specific to the project? To enable this environment, you will need to foreground the *ethical implications* of the culture of the classroom and take into consideration how students might wish to disseminate or apply their work.

The question I leave you with is: How do you intend to make these activities and ways of thinking possible?

Chapter 4

Learning as a social practice in art and design

Lesley Burgess

Introduction

The focus of this chapter is on learning and the way in which the process of learning happens within social situations. You have seen that in order to establish conditions for developing creative practice, you have to draw on many of the principles of progressive education: fostering young people's curiosity, their willingness to try out and discover things, to express and share meanings (see Chapter 3). One of the difficulties in discussing creative practice in the visual arts is the way in which the isolated, studio artist is taken as the model for education, a model that sits uncomfortably with the realities of schooling where learning takes place in a collective, social environment. Rather than the artist's studio, you might consider other models of artistic practice in which social interaction is foregrounded – specifically, collaborative, socially engaged, reflexive and dialogical practices (Lacy 1995; Bourriaud 2002; Kester 2004; Bishop 2006). These social situations do not necessarily conform to the comfortable sites of tolerance and consensus that are sometimes promoted within education. On the contrary, they are often sites of contestation, where differences are acknowledged, discussed and negotiated, and where conflict does not always have to be reconciled.

In order to demonstrate how these ideas work in practice, I intend to refer to a project on the built environment in which schools worked in partnership with the Prince's Foundation to encourage co-operation between students in conceptualising community. This is followed by a discussion of the research report '*Critical Minds*' from the DfES and a DCMS research project 'Inspiring Learning in Galleries' that was designed to develop 'a better understanding of the learning benefits to children and young people of engaging with contemporary art and artists' (Taylor 2006: 14). Finally, I look at a collaboration between PGCE artist/teachers and the artist Rasheed Araeen, '*Deconstruction Zero to Infinity*', to demonstrate how an understanding of the significance of 'communities of practice' (Wenger 1990; 1998; Lave & Wenger 1991; Watkins 2005a) can enable artist teachers to move beyond their 'passionate attachments' (Butler 1997) towards a more reflexive, collaborative practice.

Communities, collaboration, mutuality

The social organisation of pedagogy is of particular significance to the ways in which learning can be developed within schools. Schools are social institutions that, as Jean Lave and Etienne Wenger (1991) suggest, should be understood as 'communities of practice'. Their theory can be divided into two distinct aspects. First, a theory of learning and identity, 'an analytical viewpoint rather than a pedagogical strategy or learning technique ... a way of understanding learning' (p. 40). Second, as a sociological description of the forms of participation or 'communities of practice' that emerge from the reproduction and development of social practices. These communities are sites of shared experience that enable members to develop as critical thinkers through mutual engagement in common activities. For both pedagogic and social ends, the school community is often divided into distinct and overlapping units – year groups, departments, different sites – and, in this way, the school can be conceived as an organism, the different parts of which help it to function. Several commentators have used the metaphor of classrooms as ecosystems (e.g. Lambert and Balderstone 2000; Widdowson and Lambert 2006). They maintain that classrooms consist of diverse elements and transfers of energy, replete with complex interdependent processes and interactions. These systems-in-action, similar to the natural eco-system, can achieve harmony or become disrupted. Like the components of an ecosystem, the elements that make up a classroom exist within a particular environment. The environment is influenced by events and processes in local and regional contexts, as well as beyond in national and international arenas. From this position, insular, over-personalised and parochial practices are called into question. However, although schools are not islands, where a reality can be created separately from the cultural practices outside, they are able to put cultural practices at a distance. This process of distancing – the ability to look in on something – is a necessary stage in developing reflexivity. Reflexivity, the ability to reflect on practice and, if necessary, revise it in relation to alternatives found elsewhere, prevents communities from becoming stagnant. The pedagogic space of the art room can be used to organise learning experiences in such a way that the constraints of social positions and identities are discussed, and the restrictive nature of social identities is challenged.

As noted in Chapter 1, schools have traditionally been recognised as institutional spaces through which adults try to control children and through which differences between children are reinscribed; to an extent, this still remains true:

> A major purpose of school control is to socialize children with regards their roles in life and their place in society. It serves the larger stratified society by inculcating compliant citizens and productive workers who will be prepared to assume roles considered appropriate to the pretensions of their race, class and gender identities.
>
> (Aitkin 1994: 90)

Chapter 6 ('Critical Pedagogy') looks specifically at developing dialogue within the context of an art curriculum that is awkwardly positioned in relation to wider visual culture. What I want to focus on here is the construction of communities of learning through collaboration – whether within the school, local community or other agency – as a means of developing mutuality, a term that denotes a way of relating between people and organisations in which all participants can learn and benefit from the partnership and through which unhelpful hierarchies are exposed and challenged.

In a classroom where the aim is to promote dialogue (Mercer 2002) – in which personal, learning and thinking skills (PLTS) are a recognised ambition for art and design (QCA 2008) – you are likely to find yourself amid various conflicting voices (Moore 2004). What I want to suggest in this chapter is that the tensions arising from these conflicts, when orchestrated effectively, are not only necessary but constructive: what might be described as 'controlled contestation' rather that superficial consensus. Renee DePalma (2007), drawing on Nicholas Burbules (2000) and Peter Mayo (2002), suggests that what teachers need to foster is an 'incivility', a strategy that challenges civility as a silencing phenomenon and encourages a discomfort that leads to dialogue. As an art and design teacher, this can place you in a challenging position, one in which your pedagogic practice and position of authority as the teacher is not only called upon but called into question. A socially engaged approach to pedagogy can be recognised as appropriate in this context.

The notion of social engagement relates to bell hooks' theory of 'engaged pedagogy' that encourages a dialogic approach in which experiential and reflexive practice is fundamental to the development of a mutually supportive, if not consensual, learning community – one that 'recognises each classroom as different, that strategies must constantly be changed, invented, reconceptualised to address each new teaching experience' (hooks 1994: 10). Her approach to pedagogy avoids authoritarian teacher–student models, while recognising that the teacher still has a responsibility to 'orchestrate' the learning. This is an approach based on a commitment to continual shared investigation with a questioning of doxa, that is a questioning of society's taken-for-granted truths, truths that limit what can be thought and done.

You may find that these ideas of collaboration and mutuality do not correspond with what you have witnessed and experienced in schools where a culture of assessment and accountability militates against shared practices. Therefore, you may perceive the classroom as a demanding, densely populated, complex social environment and, although you are under constant scrutiny, feel psychologically 'alone'. Watkins (2005) points out: 'if you examine images, prints, paintings and photographs of classrooms over the centuries, you will readily list observable similarities – classroom walls, rows of pupils, status gender and power ... a social distance between pupils and teachers' (p. 8). Over recent years, these alienated relationships have been exacerbated by remote policy-makers who prescribe strategies for improvement in ways that do not always afford with teachers' professional vision, thereby reducing their agency as well as their morale (Ball 2002).

However, in the development of the new secondary curriculum (first implemented in September 2008), a shift in emphasis can be noted. Its declared aims recognise that 'education influences and reflects the values of society, and the kind of society we want to be' (QCA 2007a). It stipulates that all areas of the curriculum should enable young people to become 'successful learners', 'confident individuals' and 'responsible citizens'. It also acknowledges the importance of cross-curricular dimensions, including critical and creative thinking, cultural diversity and identity, global dimensions and sustainable development, community development, enterprise, technology and media. However, in the past, such laudable aims have all too often been elided by art and design teachers or translated into projects that fail to challenge the status quo sufficiently. Although the NSEAD, through their website (www.nsead.org.uk), workshops and publications, champion cross-curricular liaisons and show how art can take a lead in collaborative partnerships, at the time of writing there is little to suggest that many art and design teachers are inclined to follow this lead. The promise of additional time with the Workload Agreement (DfES 2003) and the introduction of additional teaching assistants, has had less impact on the arts than in areas of the curriculum previously described as the 'core' curriculum: English, Mathematics and Science. Established working practices, tried and trusted programmes of study validated by Ofsted and external examination boards are proving difficult to supplant.

As a teacher of art and design, although you are subject to the pressures of existing orthodoxies and subject boundaries, you will need to resist these pressures if you hope to change official rhetoric into classroom reality. To be an agent of change, teachers often find themselves in difficult, even contradictory, positions – promoting collaboration and mutuality through contestation. Even your attempts to promote partnership may be misinterpreted as trespassing. As Nirmal Puwar (2004) points out, 'social spaces are not blank and open for anyone to occupy. There is a connection between bodies and space, which is built, repeated and contested over time' (p. 8). It is easy to be 'of and in a space, while at the same time not quite belonging' (Rogoff 2000). Rather than see this peripheral position as one to be overcome, you need to recognise it as one of the moral and existential dilemmas that 'are so much part of the work of teachers and the rich complexities of social interaction, subjective experience, and dependency and struggle that characterize life in and outside the classroom' (Britzman in Moore 2004: 25). As QCA points out, it is your responsibility not only to take on board these issues yourself, but to provide opportunities to engage students in them too:

> The programme of study for art and design provides opportunities for pupils to work in groups, to take part in discussions and to present their observations. Such activities encourage pupils to collaborate with others, and to develop understanding of, and respect for, others. Exploring art, craft and design across both times and cultures deepens pupils' global understanding

and helps them to engage with local and national issues. Pupils recognize they can they can make a difference for the better.

(QCA 2007e)

Recognising learning as a dialogic, social process

As a way to regain a sense of agency, I recommend that you look to constructivist and co-constructivist learning theory, particularly as these theories have informed educational research in schools, galleries and museums for many years and are congruent with working in partnership (Goodman 1984; Gergen 1985; Hein 2001; Carnell and Lodge 2002; Falk and Dierking 2004; Watkins 2005). Links between co-constructivist and feminist pedagogy are also worthy of investigation (see Collar 2002).

In constructivist theory, the learner is recognised as a knowledgeable resource, a person who brings to every learning situation her or his understandings of the world. In this way, learning is conceived as a process of adaptation in which the learner's view of the world is constantly modified by new information and experience. Building on constructivist theory, co-constructivism emphasises that such learning is necessarily a social process in which language and dialogue are primary (Watkins 2005, Vygotsky 1978a). These dialogues take place between individuals who are socially situated within historically and culturally specific learning environments. In both formal and informal pedagogic situations, the values accruing to these environments enact particular power relations, and for co-constructivists they have to be acknowledged before any mutuality can be developed.

It is perhaps pertinent to refer to personalised learning in this context. According to the Gilbert Report '20 20 Vision' (DfES 2006), personalised learning '*is a matter of moral purpose and social justice*' and has the potential to '*transform education*'. But what is personalised learning? At face value, personalised learning can be seen to be at odds with any call for collaboration, but as David Miliband (2004) pointed out when he first introduced the idea at his now-famous North of England Conference, personalised learning promotes:

> High expectations of every child, given practical form by high quality teaching based on a sound knowledge and understanding of each child's needs. It is not individualised learning where pupils sit alone. Nor is it pupils left to their own devices – which too often reinforces low aspirations. It means shaping teaching around the way different youngsters learn; it means taking the care to nurture the unique talents of every pupil.

(Miliband 2004)

The personalised learning agenda recognises that students do not learn in isolation; it emphasises:

- responsive teaching strategies (including whole class and group work along-side individual teaching)
- flexibility and collaboration across the curriculum; and partnerships beyond the school
- reciprocity, that the ability to learn well in the company of others, and the development of learning relationships, are key to developing resilience and independent thinking. Staff and students are considered equally as learners
- support and collaboration between students, encouraged 'in a spirit of intellectual camaraderie', and through which group working is emphasised with attention to listening skills, body language and techniques of 'respectful disagreement'.

(ibid)

Personalised learning is not without its critics (Ledda 2007). It does not point to any particular ideology or activity and it is therefore easy to understand how it can be difficult to implement, and why teachers remain puzzled about delivery. Although it is true that, like many cross-phase cross-curricular directives, it can be perceived as a chimera, as a teacher intent on developing art and design in the secondary curriculum, it is important that you use such directives and initiatives strategically, gleaning from them aspects that support your advocacy for change within the subject and beyond.

Dialogue and collaborative work tend not to characterise teaching in art and design because traditional aims in the subject often valorise individual expression. Ironically, teachers realise these aims by directing students to reproduce stock signs of difference. As Addison argues (Chapter 1), within state-controlled schools, research has repeatedly shown that pedagogic power relations are predicated on the reproductive role of schooling (Bourdieu and Passerson 1977; Bernstein 1996; Reay 2007).

In the following section, I look at the ways in which art and design teachers have worked in partnership with the Prince's Foundation to encourage co-operation between students in conceptualising community, while at the same time embracing aspects of built environment and citizenship education.

Place Making: Linking the art of building to the making of community

'*Place Making*' was the title given to a built environment project that I co-directed with Catherine Williamson between 2002 and 2006. In this project, IoE partnership schools worked in collaboration with the Prince's Foundation to develop an understanding of the 'interdependence between the built and the live, between physical and social infrastructures' (muf 2001: 11) and, as noted above, to foster co-operation between students in conceptualising community.

A central aim therefore was to generate inquiry into the components that make up a place and to initiate a participatory learning process to develop an awareness of and consideration for individual and collective needs within a community. The project also provided a framework within which to explore the basic principles of citizenship as they relate to the processes through which communities evolve.

Underpinning the project was the belief that the built environment concerns everyone and that the quality of an environment has a direct influence on the quality of people's lives. How the built environment is made, looks and functions continually evolves. Its development is influenced by a diversity of people and agendas: historical, cultural, economic, political and environmental. As simple settlements evolve into large bustling cities, the tasks and decision-making processes of 'place making' have become assigned to planning bodies, architects and engineers. Design and construction processes have become more complex and are increasingly driven by commercial viability; consequently, there are fewer opportunities for public involvement, consultation and debate. As Ben Bolgar, Director of Architecture and Design for The Prince's Foundation, pointed out during the project: 'Too often people feel they have no contribution to make to their built environment, they feel no connection with it, as they have no part in building it'.

In addition, *Place Making* aimed to show how, despite limitations and temptations, art and design teachers (and their students) can become agents of change – making significant contributions not just to the developing art and design curriculum, but also to cross-curricular dimensions outlined in the new secondary curriculum. Cross-curricular dimensions provide important unifying areas of learning that help young people to make sense of the world and to give education relevance and authenticity. They help students to engage with the major ideas and challenges that face individuals and society – in this instance, Community Cohesion (DCFS 2007), citizenship and the built environment.

Art and Design contributes to citizenship through helping pupils to:

- recognise how artists, craftspeople and designers have responded to issues, problems and events in contemporary and past times
- express their own ideas, beliefs and values through creative work
- negotiate, make decisions and take responsibility in collaborative projects that explore the role and function of art and design in the school, locality and wider world.

(DfES 2007)

Clearly there are different ways in which teachers can involve young people in 'values' education and differing views on how this can be achieved (what it means to be an 'active citizen'). *Place Making* provides an example of how art and design can take the lead in making a 'meaningful contribution' to citizenship. It involves participants designing and making plans and models of spaces and places in response to given scenarios, while at the same time challenging them to reconsider taken-for-granted beliefs about identity, belonging and rights. It privileges the critical without denying the importance of praxis, where learning is simultaneously practical and dialogic.

David Buckingham (2000) suggests that 'young people today are postmodern citizens – cynical, distracted, no longer possessed of the civic virtues and responsibilities of older generations' (p. vii). He claims that this is a response to their own powerlessness, their exclusion from the discourses and the decision-making process. Similarly, other research (Wilkins 1999) reveals that young people's definition of the role of the 'good citizen' is restricted to minimal public duties and the defence of private property. Paulo Freire (1999) 'insists that the problem lies in the fact that students have not developed habits of critical dialogue sufficiently, that their discussions lack the rigour of reflection, reflection on how attitudes and values are formed and how they might be reformed' (Freire and Macedo 1999: 53). He suggests that this is the reason there is often an imbalance between chronological age and 'epistemological curiosity' and argues that, 'in many cases, epistemological curiosity remains truncated, giving rise to students who are intellectually immature' (ibid).

The *Place Making* 'experience' covers all aspects of creating a community: from understanding the need for basic shelter, exploring how structures are modified for functional and aesthetic reasons, to designing a settlement with consideration to the local environment and people's social and cultural needs. A participatory problem-solving approach, generated by a series of scenarios and challenges, looks at how the built environment evolves over time and investigates how it reflects and affects a community's quality of life. It brings to the fore not only how the built environment develops in response to physical and material resources, but also how its construction and habitation reflects people's attitudes and values, power and agency.

Outline: mapping the content

At the start of the project, each student was given an image of an uninhabited and undeveloped environment. As the project progressed, they discovered that they were not living in isolation but shared the same location with others and, still later, that these shared locations constituted an island. They had to consider the climate, physical features and available materials as they created (in the first instance) their personal shelter and (subsequently) a settlement. Simple frame structures made by each student were clad and decorated to create a personalised shelter. The scenarios and processes involved in creating these shelters were designed to nurture a sense of identity and establish a sense of ownership. Understanding was developed through reflection on how decoration can signify personal and cultural identity. Using examples of buildings from different historical, social and cultural contexts, participants were encouraged to investigate how buildings and public spaces can record and reflect the status and preoccupations of their owners and makers. Having determined the function of their shelter, each participant negotiated the role and position of it within the settlement. As the project developed, the focus shifted from individual to collective concerns and therefore students had to consider and discuss increasingly complex issues. The focus moved from a preoccupation with personal survival strategies towards consideration of how different cultural, economic, religious, social and political values influence the way that communities evolve. Throughout the project, key issues were introduced by the teacher to promote discussion, provoke enquiry and link the activities to students' lives. Speculative debate, a key feature of the project, encouraged high-order thinking skills and stimulated the need to know: this is exemplified in the following questions from a group of art and design students:

Does somebody have to be in charge?

Who makes the rules?

Why can't we share responsibility?

What happens if I don't want to be a part of this so-called community?

Their teacher noted:

[students] recognised that form and decoration could signify exclusivity as well as inclusivity ... It took them a while to realise why you couldn't put the public toilets upstream of the fish farm ... Where to position the church and the mosque provoked a lively debate.

Figure 4.1 Placemaking Project, IoE, photographer Nicholas Addison.

Figure 4.2 Placemaking Project, IoE, photographer Lesley Burgess.

Developing a discursive environment

> Dialogue as a process of learning and knowing must always involve a political project with the objective of dismantling oppressive structures and mechanisms prevalent in society ... Critical educators should avoid at all costs the blind embracing of approaches that pay lip service to democracy and should always be open to multiple and varied approaches that will enhance the possibility for epistemological curiosity with the object of knowledge.
> (Macedo in conversation with Freire, Freire and Macedo 1999: 53)

The role of the teacher in this process is significant. Since the introduction of the National Curriculum order for Art (DFE 1991), and the requirement for knowledge and understanding to inform making, art and design teachers have become progressively more skilful as critical educators, engaging students in the interpretation and analysis of visual and material culture through classroom dialogue. Drawing on the different methods used by art historians, cultural critics and gallery educators, they are able to move beyond formal analysis to a concern for wider discourses. Developing a discursive environment can be one of the hardest tasks for teachers, especially in subjects that, until recently, have concentrated on practice rather than theory. Clearly, there needs to be a unity between the two. Freire claims that, in order to achieve this unity, one must have 'epistemological curiosity', a curiosity that investigates the nature of knowledge, its foundations, scope and validity: one that is not always present in dialogue (Freire and Macedo 1999: 51). By staging scenarios and encouraging critical reflection and dialogue, the *Place Making* project goes some way towards achieving this unity and curiosity – it encourages a shift from cynical disengagement to critical citizenry using art and design as an interlocutor as well as an object of study.

Future action

> Knowledge territorialisation needs to be avoided in favour of some new object of knowledge in which a semblance of parity and reciprocity might take place between the constitutive components of study and through which a form of cultural politics could emerge from the work rather than be imposed on its materials.
>
> (Rogoff 2000: 8)

Having established an understanding of 'community' (alongside an understanding of architecture and critical aesthetics), the *Place Making* project went on to encourage students to think about how and why they could establish relationships with 'outsiders'. For example, how to design bridges to link with other islands, whether or not to develop advertising to promote trading and tourism and if, and why, it might be necessary to control and monitor access. Border-crossing, although one of the most overused metaphors in educational theory, is significant here – not just in the context of the project, but also more widely in Initial Teacher Education, where cross-curricular collaboration to address whole school issues remains limited.

David Lambert, Director of the Geographic Association, poses the question, 'Do geographers read landscapes differently to artists?' (2003: 17). Exploiting synergies between art and design and geography to develop citizenship through the built environment is one obvious way forward. Recent developments in the art and design curriculum to include a critical understanding of contemporary visual and material culture are mirrored in geography education, with its increased emphasis on cultural geography and enquiry-based learning. The responsibility of Initial Teacher Education providers is to identify common pedagogic links and to demonstrate how core skills and subject knowledge can be incorporated in new or unfamiliar ways. Teachers need to perceive themselves as agents of change and foster the political skills and advocacy required to make new things happen beyond a set of perceived boundaries or constraints. They also need to consider whether their aims can be best achieved independently or collaboratively, not only with outside agencies, but across subject boundaries too. This will enable educators to address global and local citizenship rather than resort to a traditional and historical data-bound perspective. *Place Making* sits within a pedagogic framework that promotes epistemological curiosity, creative enquiry, experiential learning and the notion of audience as community. Using scenarios to help young people reconstruct the past in order to deconstruct the present and envisage the future can encourage them to be agents of change too. It involves them in communities of learning and in a dialogue about what critical citizenry might mean.

With such initiatives, the move towards negotiated decision-making leads to increasing student collaboration and a realisation that the ideas of others are a valuable resource for learning. In *Place Making*, students recognised that their own learning is enriched and expanded by engaging with different points of view, a process that builds a learning environment built on mutuality.

Critical Minds

One effective way to establish this mutuality is through collaboration with external arts agencies – for example, in the context of the art curriculum with artists, galleries and museums. This makes it possible to develop a pedagogy situated somewhere between and across the school and external resources and institutions, an in-between space extending and enriching the role of all those involved.

The *Critical Minds* research project was a collaboration between artists, gallery educators, HE researchers and school students, through which they investigated how an engagement with contemporary art might inform learning and critical thinking in particular. There is evidence to suggest that many art and design teachers neglect or avoid contemporary art (SCAA 1997; Burgess 2003; Downing and Watson 2004). As a result, students' knowledge of contemporary practice tends to be mediated by the popular media, where it is often characterised in stereotypical ways – for example, as absurd, deficient or contentious. The contemporary art gallery is therefore a site where these assumptions can be questioned and a fruitful dialogue developed in which the concerns of artists, critics and curators can inform wider cultural debates and discourses. In this way, the project was informed by the drive to develop educational practices through partnerships. These partnerships enable young people to extend their education beyond the classroom and to engage with local and global discourses and practices, as they are represented not by the curriculum but within a professional field.

I want to focus my analysis of the research findings on the way that participants, but especially the students, received the partnership rather than explore the content of the project. I shall therefore concentrate on statements made by a representative sample of students from the four collaborating schools during semi-structured interviews, as well as adult voices. However, it is important to note that the way in which principles and working procedures were agreed between the different professional groups (some of whom had quite different perceptions about learning) was made possible by taking an action research model (McNiff and Whitehead 2002) in which the adult participants met frequently to negotiate aims, to plan, implement and evaluate as a collective. Partnerships rarely work if time is not built in for discussion and the negotiation of differences (for a discussion of dialogue, see Chapter 6). One of the collaborating artists pointed out that such professional dialogue is challenging but, nonetheless, worthwhile. Gradually, as participating adults learnt from this process, they encouraged students to work similarly to develop mutual relations:

> Artist: You have to be willing to not only collaborate but to compromise and to give up on every great idea being included. That's just not going to happen, but you subjugate to the greater good so you can create a seamless whole.

That definitely could not have happened with the groups if they were not working together, working on problem resolution, being willing to say 'alright I think this is a great idea but the group as a whole want to go in a different direction, then I'll deal with that.' It's very mature ... and it shows they did learn a number of the really salient lessons we were trying to get across.

(*Critical Minds* archive 2005)

Mutuality

Supportive structures are undoubtedly important in making learning possible (Bruner 1960), but support should not be mistaken for supervision and control. Students participating in *Critical Minds* showed a preference for pedagogic relationships in which there was mutual respect – in particular, they appreciated the chance to take decisions about the focus and direction of their work. As hooks (1994) claims: 'respect ... is essential if we are to provide the necessary conditions where learning can most deeply and intimately begin' (p. 13). Both the most positive and the most negative comments by pupils refer to these relationships.

GCSE student: *She [the artist] talked to us much more as if we were adults.*

(CM archive 2005)

GCSE student: *'x' was babying us and we found [it] really irritating ... then this person [the artist] that had supported all of our work before, suddenly turned around and agreed ... I know they probably had their reasons, we still felt hurt that we weren't trusted.*

(ibid)

Indeed, the evidence from *Critical Minds* suggests that most of the action researchers, at least initially, doubted students' capacity to work independently as they believed the process of schooling itself disables self-sufficiency.

Artist: *Going into schools rather than gallery education I've become aware that there isn't the chance for people to develop their own ideas. Projects are set, and what's nice about going in as an artist is that you don't necessarily have to follow that model.*

(ibid)

However, action researchers recognised that, in order to develop critical skills, it is vital that students ask questions and listen to others.

Artist: *... they are able to express their opinions too and be able to defend their position and ask questions. We, as a society, tend to try to dampen a lot of that down because if you ask too many questions then you're a troublemaker!*

(ibid)

Student ownership

By and large, participating students indicated that they accept the power relations within schooling, albeit reluctantly in some instances. This acceptance can be seen to be generational, simulating familial relations, where guidance, support and boundary setting characterise interactions. Nonetheless, it is evident that students wanted their voices to be taken seriously, appreciating a space for equitable if not equal relations. As a consequence, within schooling, students are unlikely to share their personal feelings unless adults recognise them as both subject to and agents of learning.

> GCSE student: *We were going there [the final exhibition of students' work in a public gallery] expecting like to be able to do our own thing and then we were given photos and told to arrange them and it was just like 'well this isn't what I was expecting'.*
>
> (ibid)

Here, expectations about what constitutes student production and what counts as art combine with a sense of disempowerment and alienation. This lack of ownership was felt by a number of students towards the end of the project.

> GCSE student: *I did like doing this project a lot and I liked the artists we were working with, but I don't think the final gallery is a fair representation of the work we've done.*
>
> (ibid)

Figure 4.3 Enquire exhibition, The Nunnery Gallery, Bow Arts 2005, photographer Nicholas Addison.

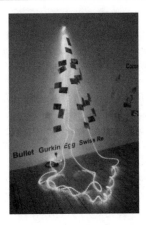

Figure 4.4 Enquire exhibition, The Nunnery Gallery, Bow Arts 2005, photographer Nicholas Addison.

The exhibition marked a stage when adults intervened in the student production both because of pressures of time and also a perceived need for a representative and coherent presentation that they assumed students were unlikely to realise by themselves.

> Gallery educator [choosing images for the exhibition PowerPoint]: *I thought this photograph kind of suggested conceptual, critical thinking more than some of the other images which were just workshop shots. And I guess it will come out more professionally than the other things, which I think is important to the girls.*

(ibid)

From this example, it is evident that public accountability can militate against mutuality. Although educators have a responsibility to 'orchestrate' student work, they need to ensure that students are acknowledged as agents throughout the whole process, from conception through production to dissemination.

Making sense of activities in relation to personal preferences

Despite the fact that the art and design curriculum is often critiqued as insular and removed from the everyday experiences and needs of young people, some pupils were able to identify with school practices. For example, it is notable that 50 per cent of the pupils (two of four) who were identified as 'resistant' by their teachers, contradict such labelling.

'resistant' GCSE student: ... *I actually do enjoy art a lot. It's like your own, you're expressing your own ... working through, not just writing, like through something else ... basically it's included to our environment as well, so it shows where we live and everything.*

Some students found it difficult to identify with the curriculum and they had to work at making sense of the project by relating it to practices beyond school. The student cited below identified himself as an imaginative person, despite the opinion of some of the adults involved in the project:

Artist: *He is confident playing football maybe; he is not-confident thinking about art. So I don't have any strong opinions about him except for he needed a lot of pushing, he needed a lot of direction. He needed a lot of attention.*

The student recognised that his project homework provided an outlet for therapeutic, expressive, almost cathartic responses. He suggested that he usually finds it difficult to work this way in a public forum, possibly because of the emphasis on emotional disclosure, a practice in which boys are often reluctant to participate (Moss 2005).

'resistant' GCSE student: ... *they gave us a sketchbook to take back home, we did pictures of how we felt. First I thought it was a bit strange. When I went home, I found it kind of easy ... cause I am a very imaginative person ... a kind of like release ... Eventually I got the idea. So I wanted to do like a cartoon book, where you kind of lift the pages and things that move. We did it with a video camera and play-dough.*

This student evidently prefers to work in haptic modes, engaging physically with plastic materials in combination with new technologies – preferences that correspond to the findings of Ofsted, who claims that 'the interests and achievements of boys, in particular, can be secured by starting with direct exploration of materials or the use of ICT' (Ofsted 2004). At a later stage in the interview, the student comments on the acoustic potential of the gallery space, 'Surroundings ... kind of, we just shout and echo'. In this different space, he revels in the materiality of 'noise', recognising that certain spaces afford a different acoustic, a place to foreground sound. This recognition reinforces his preferences for non-logocentric, physical experiences, preferences that in contemporary art are valued as multimodal resources (Jones 2006).

From personal and shared ownership to a recognition of audience

In traditional pedagogy, 'ownership' is the term often used to refer to the way in which students gradually take control of, rather than instigate, the learning process

– where they take possession of learning through a combination of teachers' guidance and their own efforts. This is in contradistinction to the transmission model, which produces a culture of dependency and blocks any possibility of autonomy, while ensuring 'good' results. In the former, ownership takes place at the moment at which the learner's interest appears to be self-generated, leading to initiative and resourcefulness, whether individual or collaborative.

> 'resistant' GCSE student: *They were kind of giving me ideas of their own as well to help me come up with ideas … So I made one idea, which I saw when I went further through the park, next to the palm tree thing, that says 'freezing' while it is supposed to be in the sun. I put a little sign that it says 'freezing' … like a postcard.*

In this project, students were taken out of the gallery and school context into the local environment, where they were invited to make textual interventions in an attempt to encourage audiences to see the familiar in unexpected ways. The artist suggested using the accessible procedure of inversion, whereby an expected characteristic is replaced by its opposite. Although the resistant pupil acknowledged that the artist and teacher initially gave him ideas, on reflection he claimed ownership of the inversion for himself. By encouraging ownership, educators enable students to find some sense of congruence between the curriculum and their interests; in effect, they generate an interest that might not occur without their intervention.

Ownership is something that can be understood entirely in relation to individual students. What *Critical Minds* attempted to do was to establish conditions for learning where ownership could be perceived as something shared. The individualistic, expressive paradigm of school art, complementing the perceptual/mimetic model, limits the extent to which students conceive collaboration as either feasible or ethical and also encourages them to neglect the idea of audience. This inward, solipsistic orientation negates any consideration of the ways in which art is viewed, interpreted and disseminated as a discourse, so that students' expressive work is presented as a closed declaration rather than a communicative statement or open question. Because most of the artists working on *Critical Minds* valued socially engaged practices, audience participation and collaboration figured prominently in their discussions. It is particularly notable how some students began to engage with these ideas and take into consideration the ways in which audiences might be encouraged to interact with their work. In this first statement, the interaction is not an afterthought but an integral part of the conception of the work. In this respect, students can be said to be refashioning the tradition of school art to accommodate the socially engaged practices of participation and 'undecidability' (here, troubling the public/private dichotomy).

> GCSE student: … *mine and Rosie's idea was to be, a thinking house … would be private … We could stick on the walls things we liked and no one else could see this. We knew it was our private little area. But we wanted people to think*

'what was inside there?' What could there be? What are their private thoughts? ... We were gonna get a little post box and people could put in the post box what they thought was in the house.

(ibid)

In the following statement, a student articulates an understanding of the work of Francis Alys (a contemporary artist whose video installations they had visited, see http://www.postmedia.net/alys/alys.htm) in terms of process rather than outcome, a way of working in interaction with a local environment that s/he recognises as a resource to be adapted and used for meaning-making.

Figure 4.5 Enquire project 2005: still from video, GCSE students.

'resistant' GCSE student: *He (Francis Alys) does like lots of walks and videos them, but he uses like rules and things that tell him how to go and where to walk ... He maps out like walks that he takes and he uses either string, or a map ... he has a certain pattern to his walk ... he'll stay on the left side of the road, or when he reaches a bridge he'll cross the bridge and keep walking, things like that ... That's what we did. We all like had our own routes and ways to walk and then it was videoed, but we linked up as well, like when we met other people walking, so they changed our walk.*

(ibid)

In this description, the student recognises that, although the film s/he made with her peers in collaboration with the *Critical Minds* artist is somewhat imitative of Alys, it is, nonetheless, an appropriation of a way of thinking and mode of practice (establishing rules, etc.) that affords them the opportunity to express something about their subject positions within the school environment. The work they saw by Alys suggested how everyday street paraphernalia can be utilised to construct an alternative soundscape, a sign of resistance to regulated behaviours (he taps objects as he passes them). In response, the students developed rules to condition the trajectory of their walk, which took them to peripheral parts of the school grounds, territory about which they feel some ownership. At this significant moment, they signal a sense of ownership by setting up a barrier between themselves and viewers who are positioned on the other side of the school railings. This marks a hiatus in an otherwise regimented performance, before they eventually return to the predictable constraints of the school corridors.

Reconstructions

Reconstructions was a research project in which artist/teachers were invited by Rasheed Araeen to mediate as interlocutors between the general public and a collaborative art installation first conceived in 1968, *Deconstructions: Zero to Infinity* (1968–2007) (see Figs 4.5, 4.6 and 4.7). In this final section, I discuss these events – first, to reveal the ease with which, as a teacher, you can unwittingly reinvest in a limited and limiting curriculum; and second, to help you recognise the significance of 'communities of practice' (Lave and Wenger 1991) as a way of promoting collaboration, discussion and reflexivity as an antidote to such limitations.

The project involved artist/teachers (PGCE students who continue their studio, curatorial and/or commercial practice alongside teaching part-time in 14–19 education). As 'friendly interventionists', artist/teachers are in a unique position to contribute to curriculum development – bridging the gap between classroom pragmatism and the 'not yet possible' (Addison and Burgess 2005). However, my recent research has shown that, although a number of artist/teachers successfully maintain this position as agents of change, others rely too exclusively on their own art practice as the basis for their teaching. This position may become counterproductive in those instances where alternative practices are ignored so

Figure 4.6 Rasheed Araeen *Deconstructions: Zero to Infinity* 2005, 291 Gallery, photographer Lesley Burgess.

Figure 4.7 Rasheed Araeen and public *Deconstructions: Zero to Infinity* 2005, 291 Gallery, photographer Lesley Burgess.

that teaching becomes inflexible, due to a reluctance to shift out of their 'comfort zones'. In other words, artist/teachers become trapped in a self-referential loop, reinforcing a niche practice that 'speaks' to a limited audience or restricted field. Artist/teachers' own practice becomes their primary passion, a 'passionate attachment' on which they depend (Butler 1997:8). Dennis Atkinson (2005) describes the way in which experienced teachers form 'passionate attachments' to particular practices and develop policing mechanisms to help maintain them.

Figure 4.8 Rasheed Araeen and public *Deconstructions: Zero to Infinity* 2005, Spitalfields Market, photographer artist/teacher.

He points out that any push to embrace new discourses and practices is likely to create uncertainty and anxiety. He reminds you that 'as subjects we are only able to understand our existence through the parameters of those discourses, practices, ideas and so-on, to which we are subjected and simultaneously, through which we achieve subjectivity' (p. 25).

Through the *Reconstructions* project, the extent to which artist/teachers can be isolated within a restricted field was highlighted. Nonetheless, it also proved a locus for disruption, an event that incited them to engage reflexively with their own practice in relation to another's – namely, Araeen's. This took place on three consecutive days in three different venues in east London as part of a contemporary art festival. In order to prepare them for this role, Araeen introduced them to the issues and ideas informing his work, as well as the discourses and debates involved in its reception.

Araeen is known as a tireless campaigner for the visibility of artists who have been marginalised by the institutional system, especially black and Third World practitioners. He is the author of many articles on the implications of Britain's emergence as a multi-racial society. Internationally, he is widely known as the first editor of *Third Text*, a journal he founded in 1987 to promote Third World perspectives on contemporary art and culture. His work is informed by a critique of 'ethnic pigeon holing' as played out within art discourses – for example, in minimalism, multiculturalism and globalisation. In particular, he interrogates Eurocentric institutional structures and promotes a form of socially engaged practice. He is also critical of the superficiality of much contemporary art practice, which he sees as colluding with commercialism and the media, and which, like society at large, is 'fuelled by an obsession with narcissism and ego and only wants to entertain' (Araeen 2005: in discussion with artist/teachers).

Deconstructions: Zero to Infinity was originally conceived in 1968 but was never realised, although a smaller version comprising four cubes was produced at that time.

The reconstruction in 2005 was displayed over three days, each day at a different site. Araeen was present during the three-day event, and he and the artist/teacher interlocutors were onhand to encourage audiences to discuss and interact with the work. At the start of the first day, Araeen constructed the 100 cubes in a 10 × 10 symmetrical configuration. The audience was invited to dismantle this Minimalist structure and reconstruct it without specific instructions from the artist but with prompts from the interlocutors. These new structures were recorded before being removed from the site at the end of each day. The operation was repeated the next morning at a new site.

On the surface, this event appears to correspond to an intervention within a formalist aesthetic, whereby the participation of an audience questions notions of authorship; it does not appear to challenge ethnocentrism in any obvious way. In his rationale for the installation, Araeen explains how his conception of *Deconstruction: Zero to Infinity* draws on the tenets of Minimalism, while at the same time critiquing and extending them:

> What I am trying to do is engage with ideas, structurally and formally, which are inherent within our culture, and in art. The art which is often described as 'art for art's sake', may appear to be innocent of political affiliations, but when its Form is analysed structurally it reveals an ideological underpinning representing a particular and specific position or worldview. In this work I want to show that it's possible to confront and challenge the established view of things or the status quo within the formal framework and without resorting to iconographic references or representations of reality realistically. This challenge doesn't have to occur at personal or individual level but the mass of people can be involved in the artistic process. This re-defines not only the nature of art but the role of the artist in it, as well as of the audience.
>
> (Araeen 2004: 3)

By arranging 100 open cubes in a symmetrical configuration (ostensibly as a Minimalist sculpture), Araeen establishes a simple metaphor for mutual relations. However, the way in which he invites the audience to intervene within the work questions the seeming fixity of this metaphor by potentially altering the relations through asymmetrical reconfigurations. Araeen argues that symmetrical systems can be recognised as an equalising force both socially and economically, whereas asymmetrical systems indicate hierarchies. However, despite the seeming benevolence of symmetry within this equation, it can also oblige individuals to forfeit individuality: 'everyone becomes the same with the same appearance, same haircuts, same housing, etc and is expected to express the same thing' (Araeen 2005: in discussion with artist/teachers). This results in an unnecessary gap (or false binary opposition) between symmetry and asymmetry that ignores the dialectical relationships between the two. *Deconstructions: Zero to Infinity* attempts to bridge this gap: the basic symmetrical structure (equality) is maintained, it is the starting point for each day of its presentation, but it is allowed to manifest itself asymmetrically when transformed by groups and individuals in different social contexts.

After the event, artist/teachers were asked to consider how their experience as interlocutors had informed their work in education and how they might integrate the issues informing Araeen's work into 14–19 teaching. Initially, they claimed that the issues informing Araeen's work were out of line with their own practice. In their estimation, he was 'of an earlier generation' and, although they recognised how his work could usefully form part of an art history lesson or be integrated into a project on modernist building structures, most thought his political stance made it difficult to see how it could be included in their teaching.

> *It's of another generation, not our concerns and there is a this a gap in under-standing, I can't see what it's is trying to communicate that's relevant today.*
>
> *It still remains for me an historical re-enactment, I can't see links with con-temporary practice ... there are lots of artists/curators working in this way in London at the moment ... there's a lot of interest in public collaboration so it makes comparison possible ... but Rasheed doesn't fit in with any of these really.*
>
> *I don't know ... we certainly positioned it within an art history perhaps that's the easy solution.*

Artist/teachers were also very defensive about his critique of younger British artists. Clearly, the discussions did not stop here. They were asked to justify their position through a process of critical reflection, which entailed additional research and posing new questions, a process drawing on the tradition of the 'reflective practitioner' (Schon 1987). Over a number of sessions, their positions did indeed shift. However, their initial responses had revealed how reluctant many of them were to engage with issues that fell outside the safety zone provided by their 'passionate attachments'.

Reflexivity not reflection

Reflection, in this instance, did enable artist/teachers to reconsider their position, but what they did needs to be differentiated from the introspective reflection that so often characterises practice in Initial Teacher Education. As Taylor Webb (2001) points out:

> when reflection is conceived as a process of looking back alone it may not improve pedagogy/practice. Definitions that describe reflection as an individual cognitive process do not explain how personal biases generate the framing of situations ... The assumption that reflection is an objective and rational act is misleading and maintains teachers in isolated positions.
>
> (p. 15)

Bourdieu describes such introspection as the 'epistemology of the individual', a type of reflection that fails to take into account the social and cultural attitudes and values through which subjectivities are constructed (Bourdieu and Wacquant 2002). In a similar vein, Atkinson (2003) cautions against the wholesale adoption of introspective reflection because it all too often results in PGCE students pathologising their own or their students' behaviours.

With hindsight, one of the most significant aspects of the *Reconstruction* project was the way it eventually promoted an understanding of reflexivity, as defined by Bourdieu (1997). The primary focus of reflexivity is not individual analysis (introspection) or self-reflection, but a recognition of the social and intellectual unconscious embedded in practice. This can be reached most effectively through collective enterprise rather than through the struggles of the 'lone academic' or creative practitioner constrained by doxa or passionate attachments. Being explicit about the social, historical and cultural contexts within which Araeen's work is embedded undoubtedly helped artist/teachers to evaluate knowledge claims and understand how their own attitudes and values are constructed. This was not a comfortable practice.

> We thought that perhaps Rasheed was rooted in the 1960/70s and wasn't engaging sufficiently with the contemporary issues ... we approached the project with a degree of scepticism but found that people's, children and adults' responses to Deconstruction was surprisingly easy. They readily engaged with the work, they made sense of it in relation to their own experiences. This made us reflect on our response and be more open to different interpretations.
>
> Socially engaged, collaborative art is very topical at the moment. Rasheed's project repositioned this and made us think [about] rejecting simple definitions and extend[ing] its history and context. The idea of different histories, different cultural and financial agendas, different interpretations from different perspectives, isn't part of the curriculum. When I introduce artists or art institutions in my teaching it will be more considered as a result of this experience ... more critical and complex at least that is what I hope ... But perhaps the institution is more powerful and negating than we realise, that's why it continues to be reproduced.

Loic Wacquant (2004) suggests that the most fruitful form of critical thought effectively weds epistemological and social critique by continuously questioning 'both established forms of thought and established forms of collective life – "common sense" or *doxa* along with the social and political relations that obtain to a particular moment in history' (p. 97). The rationale behind this synergy is that it enables us to question the given world in order to invent futures other than the one inscribed in the given order of things, 'to *think the world* as it is and as *it could be*' (ibid.). Wacquant warns against the narcissistic preoccupations of the moment, preoccupations perpetuated through '*weak critical thought*', which is so insular that it 'runs uselessly in circles and ends up biting its own tail, like a dog that has been

driven mad after being locked up in a closet'. In addition, there
thought, which is under cover of apparently progressive tropes,
'subject', 'identity', 'diversity' and 'globalisation', and invites us to
prevailing forces of the world – in particular, market forces, thus pe
inequalities produced by the new global capitalism (ibid: 98–100).

Conclusion

The fragmented nature of the school curriculum is often cited as the reason why
teachers are unable to establish continuity and build constructive relationships with
students (see Burgess 2007). However, through their research into practices within
informal education, Lave and Wenger (1991: 98) have developed an understanding of how communities of practice are developed and sustained. They explain
that, for a community of practice to function, it needs to generate and engender
a shared repertoire of ideas, commitments and memories, and that it takes time
for a shared sense of joint enterprise and identity to take place.

There is always a danger that projects such as *Place Making, Critical Minds*
and *Reconstructions* serve to reinforce normative relations because they act as
'one-offs', merely limited outsider interventions. Alan Kaprow warns of this effect
when he claims:

> Almost anyone will seem to flower if unusual attention is paid to them. It's
> what happens over the long term that matters. Rephrasing the question to
> 'What happened to the kids after they left us?' must probably be answered:
> 'They returned to the way they were'. And so, if sustained instruction and
> growth are necessary for lasting value, as I believe they are, the whole thing
> was an educational diversion. At best, they were entertained.
>
> (in Lacy 1995: 156)

As a way to ensure that projects like these can be sustained, it is vital that you build
lasting relationships with local galleries and other art agencies.

To ensure changes in practice are more than 'educational diversions', it is not
just the regularity of partnership that needs to be considered. As noted above, the
Gilbert Report (2006) points to flexibility, reciprocity, resilience and independent thinking as important skills for teachers to foster in young people. It also
recommends that students are encouraged to develop techniques of 'respectful
disagreement'. Sustaining partnerships that do not encourage these skills can result
in the reproduction of restrictive practices rather than reflexive practices in both
students and teachers.

The artist and critic David Beech (2008) echoes this sentiment when he
describes, as dubious, any claim that participatory practice can create cohesion
without confrontation. He points out that participatory practice too often neu-
tralises both the individual and cultural conflict more generally; it does so by
presenting itself as a viable route to consensual relations. Like Bishop (2006), he

too believes that antagonism is fundamental to, and sustains, democratic society. The projects outlined above set out to show how controlled contestation is an important element of effective and sustained collaboration, one that art and design teachers need to promote if art and design education is to be understood as a social practice that can have an impact on the lives of young people beyond, as well as within, the art classroom.

Lave and Wenger (1991) claim that teachers new to the profession can be seen to be engaged in 'legitimate peripheral participation', one that gradually becomes increasingly centralised and embedded. What I am suggesting here is that you sustain your relationship at the edges, rather than engage too readily with the certainties at the centre. What I have been trying to demonstrate here with the example of PGCE artist/teachers is an understanding of epistemic reflexivity, as defined by Bourdieu (1997) – a reflexivity whose primary target is not individual analysis or self reflection, but a recognition of the social and intellectual unconscious embedded in practice. This can be reached most effectively through collective enterprise rather than through the struggles of the 'lone academic' or creative practitioner constrained by passionate attachments.

Chapter 5

Assessment and learning

Nicholas Addison

Introduction

What is assessment for? Is it a way to mediate young people's learning by helping them to understand, develop and apply different forms of knowledge in ways that are meaningful to them and their communities? Or (and) should it be a means to secure a benchmark for excellence, measuring outcomes, and establishing norms of practice to account for national standards? From the position of a classroom teacher, you might well suppose that its primary purpose is to ensure the former, for education, so the rhetoric has it, is all about learning and developing knowledge by applying it to real-life situations. Indeed, some educators claim that when starting to teach, it is essential to understand the ways in which young people learn, to appreciate their motivations and interests, and only then to consider exactly what and how to teach and what and how to assess it.

In 2004, the UK government began to promote an approach called 'Assessment for Learning' in which the apparent dichotomies between the two strands above are reconciled through a process of continuous assessment aimed to 'raise pupils' achievement' by enabling them to understand how they learn (QCA 2004). In thinking about reconciliation, it is therefore important to revisit definitions and wonder whether these two positions are as polarised within art and design as current debate would have you think. From the very start, it is important to understand the relationship between assessment and learning as a continuous, dynamic process rather than merely a post-event appraisal of products or outcomes. As such, I intend to look at concrete examples of ways in which learning can be aided through assessment. This is of particular significance for art, craft and design, where learning is often creative rather than reproductive and is thus not easily measured. At the same time, the knowledge that results from art, craft and design activities is often of a practical and embodied kind – not factual or accurate, but developed through material, expressive, symbolic and exploratory means. Because of this richness and uncertainty, assessors require domain-specific interpretative skills in order to reach understandings of quality, aesthetic integrity, use, persuasiveness, resolution and so on (Eisner 1985). But, as you have seen in Chapter 2, such creative work does not spring from nowhere; it is generated within or in relation to specific traditions and, in this way, students, teachers and assessors also need to understand the various contexts in which production takes place.

There is increasing literature on assessment in general (Gardner 2006; Swafield 2008) and in art and design specifically (Eisner 1998; Atkinson 2002; 2008; Hulks 2003; Cowan 2006; Mason and Steers 2006; Ash *et al.* 2007; Rayment 2007) and there is much advice online (Assessment Reform Group; National Curriculum Online; QCA 2004; Wiliam 2007). It is therefore not difficult to find useful information on ways to go about assessing, what works in different pedagogic contexts and with different age groups, how research findings relate to theory, but also why assessment remains such a contentious issue in art and design (Atkinson; Cunliffe; Hardy in Rayment 2007). Because of this welcome proliferation, I want to concentrate here on assessing learning and its development for creative activity (with reference to the working definitions argued in Chapter 2), particularly as creativity is perceived as central to the needs of a post-industrial, service economy such as that of Britain, and increasingly the USA (Blair in NACCCE 1999: 6; NCEE 2006). I am going to ask: Can creative work be nurtured through collaborative work while enabling students to develop understandings of their own learning? What types of criteria acknowledge the various contexts of production and assist in finding out what students have intended and achieved rather than what they have not? What types of assessment limit students' practice or indeed might harm them? And, in respect to the positions outlined at the opening of this chapter, might such approaches serve both the interests of learners and government accountability?

But, first, it would be useful to look at the nature of learning and to do so I want to take the theories of the influential Soviet psychologist Vygotsky as a point of departure. In recent years, his work has been particularly significant for the development of constructivist theory in the west (Daniels 2005). For example, when the US educationalist Bruner (1960) first contributed to the so-called 'cognitive revolution' in the 1950s, he adapted Piaget's theory of the progression of cognitive development to form a taxonomy of skills necessary for effective learning: enactive (manipulation of objects, spatial co-ordination, adaptation to environments), iconic (visual recognition, the ability to compare and contrast) and symbolic (abstract reasoning, using words and numbers). Since then, in response to Vygotsky, Bruner (1996) argues that learning is less a matter of personal maturation and more one of social interaction within cultural settings. A teacher's role is to support this interactive process by means of 'scaffolding', thereby enabling young people to 'construct meanings'. This process of meaning-making is always embedded in the 'ways of one's culture' and it is through cultural practices such as the arts, as William's suggests (1983), that students are introduced to a culture's 'structure of feeling' (p. 21). Despite this interest in learning as an interpersonal, historical and cultural process rather than only an intrapersonal one, there has been little discussion of the significance of Vygotsky's theories for art education, partly because he valorised the role of language in higher-order thinking (however, see Matuga c1994; Cunliffe 2008). Nonetheless, I hope to demonstrate that his ideas can help you to consider what sort of learning takes place and how it can be facilitated within a domain that prizes practical knowledge. Throughout, I discuss the implications of his theories for assessment.

Learning

Learning is the process through which people make meaning from experience. The situated events that make up experience are characterised by social and dialogical relations and, as such, people come to know things that can be applied in specific situations to affect the way in which they interact with other people and their environment. In the formal context of schooling, both the content of learning and the designated means for learning it correspond to the values of those members of society who determine educational policy – the dominant class at any particular moment. But how individual students make sense of the experience of schooling – that is, construct knowledge from the curriculum and the social contexts in which it is embedded – will depend on a complex range of variables that have genetic, social and cultural bases. In this sense, knowledge is not something separate, out there, to be acquired and assimilated, rather it is something made anew with each social and pedagogic interaction (mediation), an event in which the individual relates new sensory and conceptual data to existing patterns of knowledge, and this may not necessarily accord with the dominant values.

Now certain types of knowledge can be arrived at through instruction: a young student can be informed that, when mixed, yellow and blue pigments produce green – this type of procedural knowledge can be adduced as factual, and can be tested as such. Indeed, because such value is placed on individual 'ability' within contemporary societies, students are often tested on what they know through the reiteration of information or by solving domain-specific problems. As such tests isolate individuals, the results conclude what they can do on their own. Yet as Vygotsky (1978a) has demonstrated, what young people can do with the help of others is more indicative of their 'mental development' than what they can achieve on their own, and it is certainly more indicative of the way in which people learn and work in society at large, as collectives of domain-specific workers – what Lave and Wenger (1991) call 'situated learning' within 'communities of practice'. In this sense, what is important for the development of thinking and making in art and design is not the reiteration of facts in linguistic terms – a type of declarative knowledge (Cunliffe 2005) – but the way in which students in action, by them-selves or in partnership with others, develop and use such knowledge. For example, in the instance cited above: by mixing a vibrant veridian because the green paint provided in the school series is dull; approximating an earth green (terre-verte) to use as an under-painting for the shadows in light-skinned, flesh tones (drawing on early Renaissance practice); calculating a series of leaf greens as camouflage for a hide that students are constructing in order to observe and record local fauna; colouring a recycling bin to symbolise its function; or establishing a point of con-trast in an over-pink composition. In these cases, factual knowledge is remembered and used in both habituated and improvisatory ways to realise particular intentions and solve problems arising from specific cultural situations.

Given this theory, teachers can be seen to provide a type of factual, technical knowledge, which is often taught through demonstration supported by language (Franks 2003). Such procedural knowledge provides students with resources for development and use, resources that are additional to their prior knowledge. It is by mastering and coordinating these resources that students can do things that matter, can realise a whole range of needs around representation, the formation of histories and identities, building the domestic and civic environment, questioning and possibly contesting dominant values, even imagining alternative futures. Now, whether the form these uses take is stipulated as a part of the curriculum, invented by you as the teacher, arrived at through negotiation (either among students or you and students), generated by students as individuals or provided by an external agency as a live brief will depend on the degree of interest from students or whether you aim to encourage collaboration and so on. All of these options have their benefits and you should deploy them at different moments, where appropriate, within a programme of study (e.g. KS3). What is significant for you to consider in all instances is how you might assist students in doing things that they would not be able to do on their own. Vygotsky called this space, 'the zone of proximal development' (ZPD) which he defined as: '*the distance between the actual development level as determined by independent problem solving and the level of development as determined through problem solving under adult guidance or in collaboration with more capable peers*' (1978b: 86). Just so, it should be remembered that students may know things that you do not, perhaps a craft that they have learned at home (see Mason 2005), and you may wish to invite them to share this knowledge; the ZPD does not only exist between teacher and students, although, given your role and subject specialism, it is here that its significance is pivotal. The sort of advice you proffer and construct within this zone – maybe as a series of options or a sequence of questions with which you elicit a solution to a problem through students' own powers of reasoning – can be seen as a type of formative assessment: What options have you got here? What if ... ? Do you remember the way so-and-so did this? This can be achieved one-to-one, in discussion with small groups or in more formalised, whole class reviews or 'crits'.

The central tenet here is the idea of a discursive environment, one in which talk not only supports action through instruction, but where a dialogical process of reflection and speculation leads to a shared, subject-specific vocabulary and critical knowledge of practice. For many years, this has been sidelined in art and design (despite the advice from QCA to provide plenaries in every lesson at KS3) because many teachers thought that there was not enough time or that serious talk was alien to the character of the subject and would get in the way of, or even ruin, those treasured intuitive responses. When reflective practice is introduced as a duty, as an add-on, without clear structure or direction, perhaps as a written assessment exercise where a uniform proforma is filled in, it is no wonder that students receive it as a chore. However, the type of metacognitive skills that can be developed through immersion in a discursive environment can help to negotiate shared understandings and, gradually, student independence and autonomy (for a strong critique of intuitive practice and assessment, as well as an argument for metacognition in art and design, see Cunliffe 2005). Metacognition is a term used to denote the process of thinking about thinking and/or action through which individuals come to self-understanding – here, of the ways in which they best learn (Watkins 2005b). From the moment they enter the art and design classroom, if students are encouraged to contribute to an environment in which dialogue is an expectation, it will become an habituated practice, as if second nature.

Perhaps the reticence to talk art in the artroom stems from the Romantic myth of the isolated, mute practitioner for whom creation is supposedly a force of nature rather than a cognised, social and cultural process. This myth mutated into an extreme form of individualism in the mid-twentieth century, but the history of modernism as a collective enterprise belies these myths (consider the café/bar as a site for symposia, the written manifesto, theoretical polemic and pedagogical treatise; Harrison and Wood 1992), as does the trajectory of craft with its communities of practice as well as design, which has always had to acknowledge the dialogical role between clients and practitioners.

As you have seen in Chapter 2, reflection is always a part of creative action, even if for some such reflection is mute, carried out within a sort of contemplative state, where one action leads to another as if by intuition. There are a number of theories that attempt to account for this: Ehrenzweig (1967) calls it 'unconscious scanning' and Schon (1987) 'reflection-in-action', but I wish to consider Bourdieu's theory of 'the logic of practice' (1990) at a later point in this chapter as a way to account for this phenomenon. In the context of school, learning is undoubtedly a public, shared process. It is true there may be exceptional circumstances – for example, individual students who require different conditions to work productively – but theories that stipulate the impossibility of education in art or the need for splendid isolation are not helpful to the fundamental givens; exceptional or atypical needs should not form the basis for either a general method of teaching, nor a curriculum, although ways should be sought to accommodate those needs within larger structures through systems of personalised learning (see DES 2004). Dialogue is then a central tenet for art education, but it is not a panacea, an issue that is discussed in Chapter 7 on critical pedagogy.

Vygotsky (1978b) was keen to question a number of educational theories that he realised were counter-productive for learning and it would be useful to look briefly at his thoughts before trying to take on what he said does work. First, he argued that the naturally occurring maturation of children – their biological *development*, if you like – is not the premise for learning (as encapsulated in Piaget's idea of 'readiness to learn', which often limits possibilities), neither is learning and development one and the same thing (where development is understood as the elaboration of 'conditioned reflexes', p. 80), nor can these two positions be combined to form a coextensive and interdependent process, the one symbiotically pushing forward the other to develop transferable skills. Rather, Vygotsky suggests:

Learning does not alter our overall ability to focus attention but rather develops various abilities to focus attention on a variety of things. According to this view, special training affects overall development only when its elements, material, and processes are similar across specific domains: habit governs us. This leads to the conclusion that because each activity depends on the material with which it operates, the development of consciousness is the development of a set of particular, independent qualities or a set of particular habits.

(1978b: 83)

If you look at the instance of the use of 'terre-verte' mentioned above, suppose in one of your lessons that a GCSE student is attempting to paint a portrait from life of a person with exceptionally pale skin. All the painter's attempts to achieve a modelled surface have led to strong tonal contrasts as s/he adds strong greys to the ivory colours used elsewhere. But s/he realises that this is uncharacteristic of the person seen in this specific light and s/he finds this quality significant and wants to represent it. Given this wish, and with your knowledge of colour theory, you ask the student to observe the face closely and note the way that, in shaded areas, shadows take on a complementary hue to the light source, so that if the light is warm, shadows will appear a cool blue/green, colours that combine with the local colour of the skin to produce a sort of pale, duck egg colour. The student, however, can't see it; theory doesn't appear to be carried through to perception. You take a different tack by investigating how historical painters have applied this theory, showing reproductions from a book that includes portraits by the Impressionists; but the student says they look like distortions. Undeterred, through your knowledge of western painting, you have recourse to the Internet, searching for and finding a website on which there is an illustrated discussion of the technique of under-painting used for representing the figure in the early Renaissance, with close details of surfaces, particularly those where the top layer of paint has flaked off to reveal the green beneath. From the image of the whole painting, the student is convinced by the subtlety and vibrancy of the face, and has to admit, when looking at the detail, that it has been achieved by the contrast of colour rather than tone.

The ZPD is clear here – your mixture of theoretical and historical knowledge has enabled you to mediate between the student and a variety of others' work to find a strategy to convince, a demonstration that a particular combination works; without your support, the student couldn't see this effect. Admittedly, for this student, seeing is believing and s/he takes on a rule because it is seen to work, rather like the Renaissance painters who would have been instructed to use this technique in the workshop.

Despite such habituation, Vygotsky claims that when adults set new practical problems for children they begin to search for a solution by manipulating the objects that are specific to the task. However, the moment that they are hindered or frustrated, they speak to an adult for guidance (Vygotsky and Luria 1994: 117). Children use language in this way to mediate their actions, asking for tools,

→ backed up

constructing a narrative to explain what they are doing, just as language tends to be the basis for posing the problem in the first place and for providing instruction (although this may be augmented by demonstration). In this way, young learners realise that adapting to their environment is most successfully achieved as a social activity in which *action and language are structured as one*, a process in which they plan their actions through dialogue at the very moment they are enacted; this is the process that enables development. *Attention* is an essential function in all this, one that ensures children can commit to an action. But it is also a *'transferable property'* – something to shift depending on interest, goal and instruction – thereby freeing children from their immediate *'field of perception'* (Vygotsky and Luria 1994: 132–133). Language, insists Vygotsky, allows children to think other than what is before them. With this skill, children begin to understand the significance of time, working towards a desired outcome by using *memory* to recall what has happened before in order to construct a *'field of possibility'*: past *'sensory fields'* in relation to present ones suggest possible futures. Vygotsky is discussing quite young children here, but the significance of all this for the example above is to suggest how it can be productive to contribute knowledge outside the students' experience to increase the 'field of possibility', not to determine and limit it. This contribution is mediated through language, but also through exemplification and, potentially, demonstration, a type of mediation that Vygogtsky somewhat neglects.

If, in the future, the student becomes interested in the theory itself and realises how it can be redistributed to represent instances of general perception, s/he may begin to 'see it'. Then again, the theory could become a sort of rule or strategy for vibrancy as with the Fauves, where you encourage the student to intensify the colour dynamic and thus move away from an initial reticence. Or it may be that you decide to encourage the student to use digital photography to seek out the colour of things, moving close in on the pixels to observe 'empirically' the oscillation between warm and cool colours. Whatever strategy you choose, the student becomes aware of the particular qualities of the material (colour) due to your mediating role and is able to deploy them in similar (habitual) circumstances (as Vygotsky notes above).

Learning and assessment

As this same student moves from GCSE to a higher qualification, you might suggest that s/he begins the course by developing a previous interest, perhaps building on earlier colour work by exploring how painters in the 1950s and 1960s isolated colour and made it central to their concerns. Suppose s/he examines the way in which Bridget Riley and others explored optical effects by juxtaposing colour bands to construct patterned fields, paintings that produce powerful bodily sensations in viewers. Building on her past experience, s/he begins a series of studies exploring how a whole subtle dynamic can be achieved by using the same tonal range but with different contrasts of hue. Although technically competent, they do little beyond replicating the possibilities already explored by the Op artists;

any possible future seems already to be mapped out. However, by happenstance, the student sees an opportunity to extend the studies outside of painting when a group of music and dance students advertise for a visual collaborator in a performance. The musical work is the given starting point, a piece that is composed around a cluster of close notes in which the dynamic is produced through rhythm (rather than melody or harmony) as well as contrast, where the grouping and regrouping of similar instruments set up different combinatory possibilities of timbre or 'colour'. These quite severe limitations lay down a framework or series of options, which the dancers wish to replicate. The art student realises that the colour exercises s/he has been involved with, isolated as they are from any representational or symbolic function, might provide an equivalent set of limitations.

At a first collective meeting, the collaborating students talk through and agree the constraints: the only ingredients besides the musical composition should be the dancers' draped bodies and a colour projection. Initially, the art student experiments with coloured acetate and a projector, improvising different combinations and time sequences, working alone in the art and design lessons and outside the official timetable with the dancers and musicians. After the experimentation and during a further meeting to discuss putting on a performance before the year group, students predict that the formal basis of the work might seem alien to many of their peers. After much discussion, they decide to interrupt the formal sequences with moments in which dancers, musicians and the artist introduce elements selected from the immediate cultural landscape of students' lives as points of identification. The art student produces a digital colour projection as a moving colour field occasionally interrupting the beam of light with a succession of small everyday objects so that they are silhouetted against the dancers' bodies. Likewise, the musicians produce a taped version on a loop over which they improvise, occasionally sampling from a favoured radio station. Meantime, the dancers organise a strict sequence of group movements and gestures out of which individuals are allowed to move, depending on the throw of a dice, in order to improvise to the radio, deploying dance steps from appropriate genres.

Where learning is collaborative like this, how can it be assessed? Well, in this instance, contributing students keep personal records of their work in progress (variously using audio and visual recordings, notes and drawings, as appropriate); in this way, they accumulate evidence of their thinking/practice as it progresses, monitoring and evaluating the development of their ideas and identifying their specific contribution. Schon (1987) describes the process of reflection-in-action, which many creative practitioners use – a process that is not necessarily articulated through language (reflection-on-action), but through which decisions are taken through modifications and revisions in the making (see Prentice 2007a for a further consideration of how this impacts on art and design). Teachers should thus acknowledge this possibility when it comes to assessment, looking for development in the visual evidence. Nonetheless, in the performance project, the collective decision-making is written down, each student taking turns to scribe a meeting, a copy being provided for all; these documents join each individual students' portfolio of evidence. Any shared decisions are attributed to all (that is, unless an individual wishes to record their opposition, subsequently overruled). It should be noted that a small group like this, rather than a whole class, is more likely to reach consensus. Although there is evidence of polarisation in group work (Torronen in Balchin 2006: 177), 'so too is the evidence that groups can become, as it were, depolarised, and that small groups make better decisions and come up with better answers than most of its members, and, surprisingly often, the group outperforms even its best member' (Sunstein in Balchin: ibid). The events themselves – both the work in progress and a public performance – are recorded digitally using video and still photography and stored on a central computer available to all collaborators. It is no doubt possible to single out individuals and roles within this evidence but, as a collective, each contributor owns something of the whole and should therefore be assessed both for their particular contribution and in relation to the totality.

Within this collaboration, the art student's application of knowledge requires the imaginative transformation of a phenomenon of human perception into an aesthetic principle (the dynamism of colour contrast), something which begins with empirical study, moves into the cultural field (a history of optical painting), but which is then used dialogically to complement other forms of expression (relations and equivalences across modes). As with most creative practice, the student has had to work within certain constraints, the musical composition is already formed, and, along with the dancers, responds to its specific qualities. Initially, rather than work in contrast to the music's forms, or independently of them (which could both be strategies), the student decides to configure a visual equivalent for the music's formal procedures. Later, with a consideration of audience, the strict formalism of the work is interrupted, a decision that could be seen as an aesthetic contamination that serves the purposes of accessibility or that might be understood as a deliberate choice to use bricollage, perhaps as an index of diversity. Whether decisions are articulated in this way will depend on the knowledge base of the collaborating students, their awareness of why decisions are made, and perhaps the degree of support provided by teachers in the collective enterprise. If this collective can be formed into a mutually informing, mutually supportive community, then the likelihood of understanding is greatly increased, as Balchin (2006) notes: 'Teachers and students should form an appropriate community of learners within which understandings and meanings of creativity can be socially constructed and evaluated in the precise situations and contexts for learning' (p. 176).

In this example, learning is a process in which resources are used dialogically to make something new, both for domain-specific and cross-domain purposes and with the intention of creating a valued experience. This value is multifaceted, with cognitive, aesthetic and social elements held together by material, developmental and performative procedures; all should be acknowledged within the assessment process, including the social abilities to cooperate, collaborate and empathise with and address the needs of audiences. (Take the opportunity to look at current post-16 assessment criteria within a number of art and design courses, and map how they relate to these values; if there is no easy fit, can they be interpreted to accommodate them?)

Creativity and context

However novel a creative act may appear in the precise situation in which it is enacted, such instances of making anew are always constrained by the historical and social circumstances in which participants live, the cultural resources that people use to find things out or produce useful and/or interesting artefacts/ events. For example, Turner's interest in Goethe's colour theory and its application to the representation of light required both the poet's work, its international dissemination through translation and printing, and the manufacture of new types of metal-based, chrome pigments (Townsend 1993), whereby the painter could, for the first time, approximate to a full colour spectrum. In this way, it can be seen that knowledge is always embedded in specific cultural circumstances so that what interests the individual is part of a larger network of interests, values and knowledge.

These interests usually inform, if not determine, the criteria by which a cultural product is assessed. For example, the New-York-based, Iranian-born artist Shirin Neshat explores the way that women in twentieth and twenty-first century Iran work within the conventions of a revolutionary, patriarchal Islamic culture to assert their gendered identities. In an interview with the critic Arthur Danto (2000), Neshat, despite her exilic status, identifies with the Iranian film movement (using the phrase 'our culture'), discussing its positive role within a revolution in which 'Western influences' have been eliminated. Before arriving at this statement, Danto provides a short introduction that frames the conversation with a series of oppositions: modern and traditional, Western and Middle Eastern, gender and culture, which he insists 'touch our essential humanity'. In this way, he tends to simplify the complex experience of diaspora, neglecting the specific historical conditions under which Neshat has been working, as if all revolutions were the same. In this way, he provides a series of 'universal' criteria that give the viewer permission to neglect language and context (something that Taylor has attempted to formalise for school art and design, in Hickman 2005).

Neshat continues by considering the ways in which the creativity of Iranian cinema is partly produced through the government's regime of censorship, a constraint that forces film-makers to rethink their work by inventing 'stronger', more 'humanistic' approaches to representation; she contrasts this quest with the ubiquitous exploitation of western cinema (sex, violence, etc.). In relation to the reception of her work by western audiences, she acknowledges the way that her use of Arabic and Farsi script could lead to misunderstanding, and how this possibility was one motivation for her to change her work from a 'didactic' to a 'lyrical, philosophical and poetic' mode. With this, Danto is able to assert the universality of her work once again and the way in which he and others are able to respond to it through 'feeling' rather than understanding.

The central and longest part of the interview centres on the relationship between men and women. Neshat claims that because women are more oppressed in Iran, they are impelled to find forms of resistance and ultimately free themselves. For example, women cannot sing in public, yet one of the main female characters in her film *Turbulent* (1998) out-sings her male counterpart and, in the process, breaks all the rules of Islamic music. In this way, her song is a form of resistance, which non-Iranian viewers would not understand without Neshat's explanation. Similarly, her claim that women in Iran are powerful might confuse non-Islamic viewers who are used to stereotypical representations. Her films could be assessed on purely technical and formal procedures, examining the use of mis-en-scène, lighting, acting, editing, perhaps culminating in a general sense of the affective impact of the work, its emotional punch; but this would surely be to miss the point? Without knowledge of the conventions that are being questioned, audiences may well misrecognise Neshat's ethical concerns, the risk-taking and inventiveness of the action. So, school students should be encouraged to think about the contexts of their making, and the way in which their work can be presented to specific audiences in order to produce or perhaps challenge understandings. To enable this, students need to be provided with an opportunity to frame, explain and/or complicate their work through discussion or writing, although this should not be a prerequisite for success (see the last section on practical knowledge).

In the school setting, it is therefore important to consider what it is that is of interest at a given time: locally, nationally and internationally. History is significant because it traces how a community has reached a particular point of development and why it holds specific values. One function of education is undoubtedly to induct students into the values of the community/culture and, in a time of diversity and democratic principles, this is a complex and rich process in itself (see Addison and Dash 2007). But, perhaps more significantly, education should invite students to consider possible futures: given this past and these presents, how might art, craft and design contribute by creating a more beautiful world, or a more just world, or, perhaps, a more sustainable world?

Creativity and assessment

As an example of the latter, I want to look at the built environment project that Lesley Burgess discusses in Chapter 4 (see also Burgess and Williamson 2005). The sequence of problems and activities held within it invite a range of creative responses to an imaginary situation that utilises practical knowledge of materials, associating ideas, using scale to model intentions, discussing, reflecting, evaluating and revising ideas, processes that invite formative assessment strategies, accommodating individual, peer- and teacher-led instances. Imagine that this project is being followed by a KS3 group, a large class of 30 students. The project is introduced using a narrative, as Burgess explains. The initial problem after the shipwreck requires individual work in which students build a shelter to protect themselves using the units of rolled paper as a building form, joined by tying thread unwoven from old clothes (all materials can be recycled). Aware of prevailing conditions – weather, ground base, fauna, etc. – the next task is to build in relation to these conditions. At this point, students explain their build to one another in pairs, and the teacher invites explanations to the whole class from one representative from each of the four basic conditions in which they imagine they are building – wet/ swamp; dry/sand/windy; high/sloping/cold; grassland/temperate. The criteria for assessment revolve around: Stability, does the structure stand, is it well crafted? And fitness for context/purpose: Would the structure provide shelter from prevailing conditions? The teacher might discuss one or two examples with the whole class, exploring what works and what needs developing. Students are then given time to modify their piece to meet these criteria.

Stability and protection guaranteed, students then concern themselves with refining their structure, constructing extensions, taking into consideration both utility and aesthetics: Do I want the woven skin of my building to act as camouflage? Do I want to signal to others something of my identity? This time, the criteria move into the more subjective territory of taste. Balchin (2006) examines a similar set of assessment possibilities in the research that he conducted for school design and technology teachers to help them form 'consensual' groups to judge students' work, dividing criteria under two main categories: 'concept' and 'quality of build' (p. 178). Concept has four factors: 'uniqueness, associations of ideas, risk-taking, potential', and the quality of build has three factors: 'operability, well-craftedness and attractiveness' (ibid). It may well be that you wish to encourage students to use a more formalised set of criteria such as these at this stage, or perhaps, to look at them as a framework to be interpreted, modified, negotiated. For example, if a local community decide that they wish to present a unified front through a uniform building process and design, and thus deny the individuality of its members, is the ability to compromise, to agree, more significant than uniqueness? Or should it be that uniqueness is assessed in relation to the group aesthetic rather than individuals?

The students are then invited to meet their immediate neighbours – for example, those in the swamp. Suppose the classroom is divided into two islands – 15 students a piece, with four basic groups on each – then each group consists of three or four students. These groups explain their work to one another and begin to discuss how to build a local community. They have to ask: What are our needs? What resources do we have? Which values do we share and how can this be manifested through the built environment? For example, do we want boundaries or open networks? All these points are written down and the immediate environment is modelled so that the four groups join to make each island. Next, each group meets with their immediate neighbour, thus the need for an even number of basic conditions. They discuss their needs and consider the possibilities of exchange, communication, sharing, or indeed lack of trust, protectionist strategies and so on. Again, the teacher asks for representatives from the four new groupings in the class to present their discussions, asking the whole class to mediate unresolved questions or points of tension.

As Burgess recounts, the project may move into a consideration of wider structures as the islanders move towards constructing a larger society, looking at civic organisation and responsibilities, communications, education, health, trade, transport (drawing on knowledge and working methods transferred from citizenship, geography and science) and on to belief systems and identities (drawing on English, history and religious education). The project could be developed though processes of mapping and modelling, possibly developing the existing scale model or perhaps using ICT, but always within a discursive and reflective framework.

Dos and don'ts

This art and design project is just one example of the way in which you can enable students to learn through interdisciplinary activities by developing a social environment and sequence of experiences in which students actively produce knowledge and within which you help them to understand how they have done so. In this way, your students will gradually become both collaborative and autonomous learners. In contradistinction, the system in which the teacher, as subject expert, provides knowledge through its transmission – the 'banking system' that is criticised by Freire (see Chapter 6) – denies the student any agency (that is, any participation in the construction of knowledge itself). Interestingly, there is also a largely unspoken tactic in art and design where the teacher abnegates their responsibility to teach, ignoring the ZPD (perhaps because of a belief in 'natural' talent) and, instead, encourages students to imitate, for example, a school art prototype (the past work of 'A' grade students) by relying on technical abilities they may well have developed elsewhere (what they are capable of doing on their own). However, more usually, teachers have recourse to the formal elements – line, tone, colour, etc. – that are used as the building blocks to help students understand, analytically, how two-dimensional work (sometimes three) is constructed. But the elements are often used in the service of 'truthful' representations, the look of things – what Bryson (1991) calls 'Perceptualism, the notion that artistic process can be described exclusively in terms of cognition, perception, and optical truth' (p. 66), and this is relatively easily assessed in terms of a spurious accuracy (for an extended analysis of how such terms as 'accuracy' and 'correct' are misapplied to the semiotic practices of art and design students, see Atkinson 2002). The example of the use of under-painting that I made above could be accused of falling into this paradigm. However, it should be remembered that neither the formal elements nor accurate representations are in themselves insignificant, but they have rarely been, nor are they in the present, the principle objectives of artists, craftspeople and designers. Their prominence in schools today is a legacy of the technical training and pictorial imperative of the Victorian era, as discussed in Chapter 1. This criticism is therefore not given to encourage you to neglect the formal elements in the production of art, craft and design, nor the importance of privileged or dominant forms of representation in circulation today (e.g. photography, painting and other forms of naturalistic picture-making). It is merely to point out that the formal elements are a means, not an end, and that privileged and dominant forms become naturalised over time and should therefore be subject to investigation and analysis, especially in the context of inclusive education and the intercultural classroom (see Addison 2007; Hickman 2005).

Atkinson (2002; 2008) and Moore (1996) have looked at assessment practices in which the '*natural attitude* to representation' (Bryson 1983: 10–11) determines grades by holding up faithfulness to appearances, or 'accuracy', as the main criteria. Students who cannot work within the conventions of this tradition are assessed as being deficient in some way: of low ability, immature, naïve or even 'educationally subnormal'. Often, the students will say themselves, 'I can't draw', and may resist your attempts to help them 'conform'. I don't wish to rehearse Atkinson's and Moore's arguments here, but recommend that you read them as they both convincingly argue the detrimental effect that such practices have on the identities of students (in the instance of Moore's case study, it is particularly pernicious as judgements revolve around issues of race). What I want to emphasise here in response to their critique is twofold: first, naturalistic and photographic-dependent representations are conventions with multiple traditions (consider the differences between seventeenth-century Dutch still-life and twentieth-century US photorealism – they do not mirror a world out there but interpret it in relation to the values and interests pertaining to the society in which they are embedded, see Bryson 1990; Leppert 1996). Second, art, craft and design are not limited to representational functions alone, as you might suppose when you look at school art, but can be investigative, constructive of the environment, exploratory of materials and their physical properties. However, in relation to the first point, when you do embark on a project involving a representational goal, students should be introduced to a diversity of conventions, not only within supposedly like approaches, but across traditions. For example, if you are working with still-life, in addition to the above, show students foodstuffs within Roman mosaic, domestic paraphernalia painted on Japanese screens, materials deployed within cubist constructions, objects of desire in contemporary advertising and so on. In this way, you can demonstrate that there is no one way, an accurate way, to make representations. You will also provide a repertoire of conventional resources, and if students choose to work in relation to a particular convention, you need to work with them to understand analytically what that convention involves. If they are concerned with spatial systems (Willats 1997) – for example, as used by Japanese ukiyo-e artists – then they will need to understand and deploy a form of axonometric perspective and may choose to ban shadows and shading in favour of a type of line drawing based on calligraphy in which the varied weight of each line signifies the volume of objects. If they are intent on illustrating a cookery book, they might look at the way in which commercial photographers use multiple light sources, glycerine and water vapour to conjure luminous solids and velvety surfaces, while collaging multiple shots in Photoshop to produce an illusion of a unified image.

Negotiated assessment

Each of these approaches and the conventions within them imply specific types of criteria that are peculiar to the function of the outcome, and the procedures and processes that help makers get there: these may be about persuasiveness (propaganda/awareness campaign), fitness for purpose (the built environment project above), identity construction (rewriting history by representing the visual presence of a minority and/or marginal group). These examples are clearly not comprehensive or exhaustive and you need to work with students to negotiate which criteria are appropriate. These types of negotiation recognise the particularity of domain-specific knowledge that Vygotsky argued for, rather than the generic criteria used within most forms of summative assessment, or even the cognitive skills that Vygotsky valorises elsewhere and that Cunliffe (2005) promotes as the basis for art and design assessment. Relying on cognitive criteria alone can over-determine learning objectives and neglect the functional and affective dimension of aesthetic practices.

The idea that you might negotiate assessment criteria with students may seem strange to you, given that you will undoubtedly have, at some stage, to accommodate assessment to the requirements of external examination systems. You may therefore find that you are advised to plan for assessment by considering learning as identified in pre-set learning outcomes rather than as something situated and negotiated. It is, no doubt, important to predict what may be learned – perhaps very broadly in terms of general concepts, critical approaches, technical competencies, valued traditions and social skills – but these can be identified as a series of aims rather than specific sets of knowledge. Strongly delimited learning objectives, such as 'students will draw such-and-such an object accurately', can blinker you so that you only look for evidence of the objective while missing what has actually been learned because it doesn't conform to your expectations. It is important to remember that, in each pedagogic situation, what is learned is qualitatively different from individual to individual. Learning is not a process of transmission in which a body of knowledge is passed from expert to novice in the way that those who want a purely reproductive education might wish.

As has been explored in the previous sections, assessment criteria need to respond to specific situations and intentions, so that even externally imposed criteria should be subject to translation and interpretation. Discussion of criteria therefore involves the negotiation of shared meanings – this is a limited type of negotiation, but it is a first step. The more you engage students in understanding the criteria by which they are to be judged, the more transparent the process and the more likely it is that they can meet them. The more they discuss them, the more likely it is that they will begin to understand how they can serve as a driver for revision and development. The more they use them, the more they will understand how some might open up possibilities where others limit and contain practice and should therefore be subject to critique. But students may also see the benefits of forming them for themselves, either individually or collectively, because they have witnessed how they can provide a productive framework. All judgements are criteria-based, whether they involve personal preferences (I like this brand, not that one), group identifications (this music is so out-of-date) or ethical principles (I couldn't use that because it is produced through exploitative means). In helping young people to acknowledge, use and articulate such criteria, you can build on this everyday process before encouraging them to devise criteria formed to meet immediate and emerging concerns – this is especially so once students are expected to initiate individual research.

Practical knowledge

In this chapter, I have tended to look at the role of discussion for learning, a means to help students develop ideas and assess work within the social matrix of the classroom. In the context of schooling, despite the emphasis on information and its regurgitation through testing, propositional knowledge is often the type that is most highly valued, taking the form of an evidenced argument around what has, is or might be within a specific domain, and it often takes the form of discussion. Nonetheless, under examination conditions, it is usually assessed by judging written argument. But valued knowledge can also be of a practical kind (riding a bicycle is the example cited by the philosopher Polanyi, 1966) and much of what is done in art and design has its basis in this second type, where material and technical resources are deployed for specific purposes. But, in art and design, purposes are not only utilitarian, competitive or recreational, as with bike riding, but affective, communicative, symbolic and transformational. Thus, it is practical knowledge that constitutes the main concern at the close of this chapter, for it is not only central to art and design but it is also vital to the way in which people live their lives. This is especially so in the context of a rapidly changing world within which the mobility of populations, communications and capital ensures new forms of social practice (e.g. transcultural, inter-generational interactions) and movement between and across different value systems (e.g. market novelty and sustainability). Creative ways of responding to emergent and unforeseen situations are therefore acutely required in practice, particularly if the mutating and redeveloping configurations of values and systems are not necessarily compatible.

In these circumstances, people often need to adapt to changing circumstances very rapidly – they need to do things, practical things, at the same time as talking about them. In his analysis of the logic of practice, Bourdieu calls on Plato himself – possibly the thinker most responsible for the theoretical turn in western philosophy – to recognise this 'race for life' (Plato in Bourdieu 1990: 287). Not much of what happens in school art and design is a matter of life and death, but the ways in which students may engage with the domain, working within, across or against traditions, deploying materials in habituated and improvisatory ways, both individually and collaboratively, develops habits of action in which risk-taking (in the sense of acting without knowing the future for certain), along with sensitivity to the multiplicities of the situation (aesthetic, ethical, social, utilitarian), are paramount. At its best, the experience of making in the subject has something of the intensity and complexity of wider aspects of social practice in that learning is not abstracted from real events. Mediated by language, practice is not determined by it; drawing on the conceptual habits of ideation, generalisation and abstraction, the processes and outcomes of practice are nonetheless embodied in the sensuous and particular.

In his far-reaching and taxing examination of practice, Bourdieu (1990) characterises its qualities by stressing its temporal and risk-laden nature and provides the example of a player (e.g. of soccer) to exemplify the experience of being in the moment for the future:

> A player who is involved and caught up in the game adjusts not to what he [sic] sees but to what he fore-sees, sees in advance in the directly perceived present; he passes the ball not to the spot where his team mate is but to the spot he will reach – before his opponent – a moment later, anticipating the anticipations of others and, as with 'selling a dummy', seeking to confound them. He decides in terms of *objective probabilities*, that is, in response to an overall, instantaneous assessment of the whole set of his opponents and the whole set of this team mates, seen not as they are but in impending positions. And he does so 'on the spot', 'in the twinkling of an eye', 'in the heat of the moment', that is, in conditions which exclude distance, perspective, detachment and reflexion ... Urgency, which is rightly seen as one of the essential properties of practice, is the product of playing the game and the presence in the future that it implies.
>
> (1990: 81–82; my italics)

Art, craft and design practices are not quite like this, although as with dance, music, sport and theatre, when practitioners work within a performative arena, they can be exactly like this. But the necessary immersion, rehearsal, knowledge of materials, conventions, rules and social relations required for art practices have much in common with Bourdieu's example and they can be risky: certain paints or resins afford slow and deliberate handling, others have to be worked quickly; when carving a solid, too much taken away cannot be reversed; two hours left before the exhibition and one installation presents materials that some of the audience may find offensive, the student is intransigent insisting they are essential, you are not quite so sure. Despite the urgency of these situations, as you have witnessed throughout this chapter, one difference is that art, craft and design practices often do allow for reflective attention. This can happen not only at the end of the sequence of actions – after the event, as it were like a synoptic analyst from a distance – but during them; reflexivity is integral to many art practices. In this sense, learners in art and design can be seen to have the best of both worlds – moments of spontaneity and improvisation occurring from time to time within sustained and intentional activity. The important matter for you to consider here is how to ensure that assessment is formative of what Bourdieu terms 'objective probabilities' and Vygotsky 'a field of possibility', options for approaching things to be done. Bourdieu explains and complicates: 'Reflexive attention to action itself, when it occurs … remains subordinate to the pursuit of the result and to the search … for maximum effectiveness of the effort expended. So it has nothing in common with the aim of explaining how the result has been achieved, still less of seeking to understand (for understanding's sake) the logic of practice, which flouts logical logic' (1990: 91).

So assessment needs to be of this kind, a type of formative assessment, assessment for, not of, learning. It should serve the process of the 'pursuit', however uncertain the end; assessment as a thing in itself, a thing that has no impact on driving the process to its resolution, is little more than a fetish, a means to applaud the ascendancy of bureaucracy and the death of creativity. You, as a teacher, with the help of your students, need to monitor this process, keeping records both of its procedures and of its efficacy. Only with this evidence can you advocate its benefits to others and seek to alter policy so that assessment becomes meaningful and necessary.

Part III

Relocating Practice

Chapter 6

Critical pedagogy

Nicholas Addison

No tradition should ever be seen as received, because when it is received it becomes sacred, its terms suggest reverence, silence, and passivity. Democratic societies are noisy. They're about traditions that need to be critically reevaluated by each generation.

(Giroux 1992: 156)

Introduction

This book has been promoting the idea that art education can be both creative and critical, an education of possibility through which individual students learn within a community of practice. Such communities are not necessarily harbours of contentment, continuity and consensus, but energetic places in which purposeful action is fuelled by enquiry and debate. There is a danger that creative aims can be subsumed within liberal, apolitical models where education becomes a competitive process of self-actualisation or indeed where they are paraded as rhetorical devices disguising a programme primarily designed to secure a viable workforce. As Cochrane *et al.* (2008) analyse:

The discourse at the core of the NACCCE report (1999) suggesting creativity is an essential capacity for preparation for the complexities and challenges of twenty-first century living, the pace of change and a range of employment beyond the creative industries per se does not appear in the Children's Plan (2007). Instead it is replaced by a functional view of creativity largely as preparation for employment in the creative industries'.

(p. 35)

Therefore, it would be useful to consider how a creative and critical education is different to such individualistic or instrumental models, one that contributes to the participatory aims of democracy. To facilitate this, I wish to propose two questions: What does critical pedagogy offer an education for democracy? How can art teachers develop practices to oppose discriminatory systems and thereby undo privilege?

As an approach and set of practices, critical pedagogy grew out of the recognition that education is always a form of social and political practice, the effects of which condition students' subsequent engagement with, and agency within, wider cultural formations. In the context of a developing democratic, postcolonial society, I shall argue that (as teachers of art and design) you can learn from the ethical integrity of critical pedagogy and adapt some of the pedagogic methods of cultural studies – a dual tactic of strategic borrowings and interventions that can challenge the insularity of school art (Hughes 1998; Steers 2003). (As such, I focus here on the reception of art, craft and design rather than with its production, although I look at two instances of critical practice.)

It is also important to examine the claims made for critical pedagogy as a means to empower people who suffer oppression of some kind. During the late 1980s/early 1990s, critical pedagogy was severely criticised for its totalising agenda, its abstractions, its focus on schooling and its indifference to any differences that fell outside its specific vision (Ellsworth 1997). Critics pointed out that its aim to empower young people hadn't worked; all it provided was an emancipatory rhetoric that went nowhere (Ellsworth 1989).

I close the chapter by looking at the potential of dialogue to help reshape the curriculum. I do so because dialogue is often promoted as the panacea to the recalcitrant and emerging cultural differences that can play themselves out uncomfortably in the diasporic communities of major cities in the USA and Europe (Shohat and Stam 1995; Cahan and Kocur 1996; unesco.org/dialogue 2001). I therefore suggest some of the questions you might ask yourself and your students in order to break the insularity that has dogged development in the subject for the past 40 years or so. Gradually, but incrementally (a continuation of Raymond William's *The Long Revolution*, 1965), it is possible to regain a significant place for art and design in the school curriculum.

But first I want to introduce the various elements that have informed these questions: the development of a radical alliance known as critical pedagogy, the emancipatory claims made for art, and the possibilities of a dialogical pedagogy that goes beyond the liberal need for consensus.

Education for democracy

Critical pedagogy is a recent, emancipatory project developing from within the practice of mass education but rooted in democratic philosophy and theories of progressive education (Dewey 1916; Freire 1990). Mass education, intimately connected with industrialisation and empire, is often assumed to be democratic in its aims – education for the social advancement of all. But this is not necessarily so, for it has been cogently argued that mass education can constrain just as easily as advance the individual (Dewey 1916; Swift 1995). Bourdieu and Passerson (1970) coined the term 'symbolic violence' to indicate the way in which schooling, as a set of values designed to unify a national population, produces normative rules and behaviours and thus violates students' sense of themselves as unique or different. Likewise, Foucault (1977) looked at the way in which disciplinary institutions such as schools produce 'docile bodies' – that is, a dutiful and deferential population that accepts authority without question. Such obedience is ensured through behaviourist strategies in which repetition and replication underpin learning and assessment (Skinner 1953), a process that has affinities with the industrial production line (see Kanpol 1994: 6–8 for a critique).

One of the philosophers who first opposed such instrumental models was Dewey (1852–1952) who made a democratic, community-based education central to his philosophy:

> [we must] make each one of our schools an embryonic community life, active with types of occupations that reflect the life of the larger society, and throughout permeated with the spirit of art, history, and science. When the school introduces and trains each child of society into membership within such a little community, saturating him [sic] in the spirit of service, and providing him with the instruments of effective self-direction, we shall have the deepest and best guarantor of a larger society which is worthy, lovely, and harmonious.
>
> (1899: 39–40)

For Dewey (1934), it was creativity that produced the generative and positive forces for growth and cultural renewal and, unlike his English contemporaries Fry and Bell (see Chapter 1), he envisaged creativity in education as a pre-eminently social entity.

It is important, however, to differentiate the critical, democratic wing of progressive education from other progressive developments due to the emphasis in critical pedagogy on social emancipation rather than, for example, the natural harmony of Johann Heinrich Pestalozzi (1801), the 'cosmic unity' of Rudolf Steiner (1904) or the familial community of Maria Montessori (1909).

By the close of the last century, the revolutionary Brazilian educationalist Paulo Freire had become the most influential thinker and practitioner of critical pedagogy, and his philosophy underscores the distinction between critical and progressive tendencies (1990). Although his theories were articulated in a social, political and economic climate quite unlike that of the UK today, it is evident from his writing that he believed teachers should always acknowledge context before elaborating and implementing programmes of educational reform (1990); his instance of practice is no blueprint for universal application.

Freire wished to replace what he termed the 'banking method' of education in which 'the teacher is the subject of the learning process, while the students are the mere objects' (1990: 59), with 'problem-posing education' in which:

men [sic] develop their power to perceive critically *the way they exist* in the world with which and in which they find themselves; they come to see the world not as a static reality but as a reality in the process of transformation ... Problem-posing education is revolutionary futurity ... Hence it identifies with the movement which engages men as beings aware of their incompletion – an historical movement which has its point of departure, its subjects and its objective.

(ibid: 71–2)

Rather than being given answers, as opposed to there being set problems, Freire asks that students pose their own questions and seek answers that will affect their own lives and futures. To enable this in the context of art education, it is therefore necessary to construct a social environment in which students engage discursively with visual cultures (local, national and global) both to understand how people are constructed as subjects within systems of representation (Hall 1997), but also how they can come to inform, contribute to and potentially change such systems. The rhetoric here may seem grand, yet such understandings can be gradual and incremental, and they can develop from an accumulation of insights provided by the continual habit of relating practices to social and cultural contexts and functions – for example, by enabling students to set their own briefs or to consider such issues as: audience, who is representing whom and why, and the sustainability of their practice. These last considerations raise questions of power and the way in which systems of representation, such as advertising or portraiture, are produced in relation to the interests of a particular social group who aim to persuade others that their interests are somehow mutual.

In the 1960s, Freire, along with many critical thinkers before and since, diagnosed such mutuality as a fiction. He argued, echoing Althusser (1971), that the modern nation state has to deploy a system and apparatus of oppression to maintain its power. Within the process of emancipation, the most pressing problem is the way that oppressed people (subalterns) are paradoxically complicit with their oppression, a complicity that for Freire is born of fear. Aronowitz (1994) examines the psychological premise on which Freire posits this problem:

Oppression is not only externally imposed but ... the oppressed introject, at the psychological level, domination. This introjection takes the form of the fear by members of the oppressed classes that learning and the praxis to which it is ineluctably linked will alter their life's situation. The implication is that the oppressed have an investment in their oppression because it represents the already-known, however grim are the conditions of everyday existence. In fact, Freire's pedagogy seems crucially directed to breaking the cycle of psychological oppression by engaging students in confronting their own lives, that is, to engage in a dialogue with their own fear as the representation within themselves of the power of the oppressor. Freire's pedagogy is directed, then, to the project of assisting the oppressed not only to overcome material oppression but also to attain freedom from the sado-masochism that these relationships embody.

(p. 226)

For Freire (1985), the only way to 'eject' the dominator and their 'style of life' is 'by a type of cultural action in which culture negates culture. That is, culture, as an interiorized product that in turn conditions men's [sic] subsequent acts, must become the object of men's knowledge so that they can perceive its conditioning power' (pp. 52–53).

Abdul JanMohamed (1994) argues that perceiving this conditioning power is an impossible task without first going through a process of 'disidentification', 'a process of forming affiliations with other positions, of defining equivalences and constructing alliances' (p. 246). The first part of this process is what I would wish to call 'thinking other' (see Chapter 5: 'on emotions'). If art is one form of embodied evidence of others' ways of thinking and being, then the process of interpretation across cultural and historical artefacts is one way to achieve thinking other, to achieve the 'naïve transitive consciousness' of Freire. This imaginative practice opens up a space in which a new subjectivity can begin to be articulated (ibid: 245; Burgess 2003; Addison 2006).

Art, class and distinction

If then the purpose of critical pedagogy is to help students to understand how they exist in the world and how they can come to inform and change that world, in what ways can the practice and interpretation of art help them to question the goals of a system of social rewards that the majority realise is beyond their reach? If Bourdieu's analysis is to be credited (1984; 1993), the majority of school students (from working and lower middle-class backgrounds) know they cannot aspire to the cultural or academic aristocracies who view art, especially in its canonic form, as a necessary expression of what it is to be truly human. Instead, they satisfy consumerist desire and appetite by accumulating those products that the elites disdain but which provides them with credibility and satisfaction in their habitu-ated social situation. As Bourdieu asserts, taste is statistically shown to be almost entirely conditioned by class, 'the choice of the necessary' (1984: 379) (although such taste will be infused with gendered and cultural differences).

In a series of critiques, Bourdieu (1984; 1993) concludes that modernist claims for the resistance of art and its transformational potential are largely illusory. For him, the field of art is a set of cultural practices through which the dominant classes distinguish themselves from others by their love for and ownership of art; the modern artist is nothing but the 'fool', '*the idiot of the bourgeois family*' (Bourdieu 1993c: 165). For artists, the goal of originality is merely a posture, a sign of radicalism with which to situate themselves at the forefront of a self-serving, insular network that has historically worked hard to render itself independent of wider social structures and thus establish an autonomous and restricted intellectual field; but this is an illusion that masks its ideological function. It is the 'aesthetic disposition' that claims to be the ultimate sign of distinction which, internalised by the middle classes, marks their entitlement to know and understand the canon, supposedly the highest form of cultural expression.

Bourdieu's theories are still highly respected in sociological circles, although his critics point out that the data for his research was made in the 1960s/1970s in France, a cultural situation somewhat different from today's in the UK. It is true that, in his later work, he collaborated with critically engaged artists such as Hans Haacke and modified his views (Bourdieu and Haacke 1995), but outside the field it is often his central thesis that stands. His method has thus been taken up by many sociologists as a means to further question the place of agency in cultural practices. Skeggs (2004), for example, shows on the one hand how the middle classes take ownership of culture by using it as a resource for self-advancement, producing a regime of 'compulsory individuality' (art and design and its stated quest for self-expression is thus viewed positively). On the other hand, the entitle-ment to culture is denied to working-class students because they lack both access to knowledge and the competencies necessary for its appropriation and/or con-sumption. Although Skeggs highlights the various forms of resistance taken up by working-class dissidents, these tend to bypass those cultural institutions, such as galleries and museums, where the competencies they lack, and often consciously reject, are foregrounded.

There is undoubtedly a tendency for art teachers in schools to work with a mod-ernist canon (SCAA 1997; Downing and Watson 2004), ignoring the pre-modern (except in the context of multiculturalism) and neglecting the contemporary (especially in the context of multiculturalism). In some respects, this focus is neither surprising, nor necessarily a problem, after all, as Clark (1999) suggests, 'Modernism is our antiquity' (p. 3). However, modernism was and is an intercul-tural phenomenon so that the popular history promoted in schools is only a partial, western and phallocentric view (Burgess 2007). Equally, the banning of popular visual culture from the art room does not reflect the way in which modernism drew on popular means of expression to counter the moribund practices of aca-demic art. At the same time, modernism emerged alongside an increasingly visual commercial culture with which many artists worked in dialogue, from Toulouse Lautrec through Dali to Warhol and the market-led phenomenon of the Young British Artists, a process that both the social history of art and cultural studies has revealed as widespread. Just as with artists, research has shown that young people, in particular, are able to appropriate popular products and use them as a vehicle for expression (Hebdidge 1988; Fiske 1989; Willis 1990; McRobbie 1994). It is not therefore the products of consumerist culture that are the problem, rather it is people's passivity and acritical acceptance, for perpetual acquisition can be a symptom both of privilege and under-privilege, a process through which people signal commonalities and differences.

In the USA, in recognition of the dialogue between popular and restricted forms of cultural production, critical pedagogy is affiliated to a form of cultural studies that has permeated the art curriculum in high schools (albeit to a limited and localised extent) (Giroux 1992; Giroux and Mclaren 1994; hooks 1994; Efland *et al.* 1996; Freedman 2003). In the hands of some dedicatees, it has transformed traditional art teaching into a socially engaged pedagogy (Paley 1994). In many ways, Giroux (1992) has been the most vocal and astute advocate of what he terms 'border pedagogy', a way of approaching learning that is at once interdisciplinary and grounded in the lived experiences of young people. Giroux and Mclaren (1994) and hooks (1994) have been particularly attentive to the emergence of popular visual culture as a site for resistance, but also as a tool for the consolidating forces of Neo-conservatism (Giroux 1997a). Art therefore entered their deliberations in the context of visual culture studies, a concern that had already informed the work of the Birmingham school and their contribution to FE and HE teaching (Hall 1988; 1997).

Critical approaches in practice

I wish to explore two of many possible practice-based approaches to critical practice: first, a dialogue between popular and restricted forms; and second, an examination of the ways in which language frames and conditions viewers' responses to works of art, craft and design. The first is an investigation designed for student teachers but which is eminently adaptable for use with different age groups, whereas the second is a critical intervention by a design historian into the 'A'-level textiles curriculum, a part of the research project Art Critics and Art Historians in Schools (Addison *et al.* 2003).

Within the history of human culture, but particularly in western education, values have often been secured by deploying binary oppositions to structure the world: right/wrong, conformist/rebellious, male/female, white/black. Similarly, the high/low binary that determines specific forms of taste in the visual arts conditions what is acceptable or appropriate within formal education. Binary oppositions are thus ripe for investigation through art and design and can potentially destabilise naturalised meanings to transform consciousness (Addison 2007: 263–265). However, in the context of schooling, teachers themselves need to engage reflexively and dialogically with their situation before attempting to transform that of students – that is, they need to work to understand the historical conditions and relations of power that position them in their specific role, one that potentially limits their ability to make active choices (Atkinson 2008). In this way, critical pedagogy aims to incite people to take control of their lives by questioning naturalised values and practices (ideology) and thereby begin to unsettle the social norms that determine unjust relations. This process recognises that the knowledge/power relations of any existing or potential state are unlikely ever to attain the condition of perfect equity that would make critique redundant; such a teleological project is, in fact, antithetical to democracy.

For the first approach, I ask student teachers to visit a gallery or museum to establish ways in which binary oppositions structure not only the building and its exhibits but the behaviours of staff and visitors, and select one binary for study. This has yielded a range of investigations from entrance/exit, original/replica through sacred/profane, science/magic and on to able/disabled, rich/poor. The aim is to identify an opposition and investigate how it is manifested in terms of the material fabric of the building or exhibits and the ways that people are allowed to engage with them, whether it is constructed, for example, through physical juxtapositions or absences, rules and regulations, or the structuring of space (for example, what is central or peripheral). The idea is to analyse the opposition to find out whether its either/or construction can be sustained. Following deconstructive methods, students inevitably find exceptions to the rule: looking at male/female, they may come across a Roman sculpture of a hermaphrodite or they notice that a signi-fier of masculinity/femininity that is understood in the UK today as biologically determined is inverted in another culture/historical period, thereby questioning its 'natural' status. Students are then asked to consider whether the opposition is specific to their ways of thinking or whether it has historical/transcultural validity, a question that requires further investigation with reference to museum archives, the internet, books, etc. They keep visual records of the opposition (some photo-graphic, having gained permission) and present their investigations to the other students (as a PowerPoint presentation) for discussion.

Students are then invited to propose an intervention (a now ubiquitous way for artists to engage dialogically with museums, see Putman 2001 and the Statuephilia exhibition at the British Museum 2008–2009). The intervention is realised by making an artefact/text that is digitally recorded and inserted virtually (through Photoshop or similar) into the gallery/museum site using the photographs taken previously. I complicate this task by imposing a further constraint: if the opposi-tion they identify is manifest through high or legitimated cultural forms, their intervention must be drawn from popular or illegitimate ones and vice versa (an opposition that is itself often subsequently collapsed). The intervention I wish to focus on revolves around a legitimate/illegitimate opposition.

After visiting one of the Great Courts at the Victoria and Albert Museum housing casts of significant, canonic works from Renaissance Europe, the stu-dent teacher concerned, let me call him Jack, selected a cast of Michelangelo's giant 'David' (http://www.vam.ac.uk/images/image/17246-popup.html). Michelangelo's original, completed in 1504, marked both a revival and a transi-tion to something new (already complicating the binary old/new). In reviving the nude sculpture of antiquity, the David sculpture re-legitimises the heroic, naked male, altering his potential significance within Christian iconography where it had tended to symbolise innocence before the fall, the incarnation, martyrdom or abjection of some kind. The David is also very familiar through reproductions and its appropriation within commercial culture, whether as a tourist souvenir, garden ornament or jeans advert. Its pre-eminent status was secured early on by Vasari, Michelangelo's younger contemporary, who claimed:

It certainly bears the palm among all modern and ancient works, whether

Greek or Roman ... The legs are finely turned, the slender flanks divine, and the graceful pose unequalled, while such feet, hands and head have never been excelled. After seeing this no one need wish to look at any other sculpture or the work of any other artist.

(Vasari 1568)

The reception of its cast in England in 1857 was initially less rapturous. The sculpture was a diplomatic gift to Queen Victoria from the Grand Duke of Tuscany. The Queen, apparently shocked by its nudity, was unwilling to house the gift and offered it to the newly formed South Kensington museum. On subsequent visits by the monarch and other female dignitaries, the David's genitals were masked by a detachable fig leaf lest their modesty be compromised. During his visit (in the last year of the twentieth century), Jack observed a group of school students observing the cast with their teacher. Some of them at the edges of the group, were, like Queen Victoria, notably 'embarrassed', although they behaved 'disrespectfully' rather than censorially, sniggering and gesticulating. From their gestures, Jack understood that it was not only the breaking of the taboo outlawing the public exposure of adult genitalia that disconcerted them (a taboo that can be broken within the 'sacred' confines of art), but the diminutive size of David's penis. Solomon-Godeau (1997) locates the historical explanation of this proportion for male statuary within antiquity:

Athenian conventions governing the representations of male sex organs were themselves structured by the beliefs, preferences and sexual practices specific to Attic culture and society. Athenian men considered genitalia beautiful when small and taut, possibly because the socially sanctioned object of desire was an adolescent, not a mature man ... this aesthetic/erotic preference was even provided with a biological rationale, by no less an authority than Aristotle himself, who theorized that the small penis was more fertile than the large one because the distance for the seed to travel was shorter, and therefore had less time to cool.

(pp. 181–182)

In the twenty-first century, both fashion-based and pornographic representations of male genitalia tend to favour large, even excessive proportions, so that the cast's penis, as a masculine signifier, did not correspond to contemporaneous expectations. The combination of the 'sublime' David with the students' profanities produced the legitimate/illegitimate opposition for investigation.

Earlier in the PGCE year, Jack had collected a series of drawings discarded by year 9 students after a 'recreational' cover lesson. As a basis for the activity, he had introduced them to the drawing process entitled 'exquisite corpse' (something like the party game 'Consequences'), a Surrealist strategy used to construct chance juxtapositions through multiple authorship (see Addison and Burgess 2007). Jack, joined by three students, demonstrated the process by collectively drawing a figure, each author folding the paper to conceal her/his drawing from the others to ensure chance configurations. Before students began, Jack invited them to work in exploratory and playful ways, telling them that the drawings would not be assessed and could therefore remain unsigned. Given the freedom of anonymity and a certain license, it appears that students took the opportunity to work transgressively, not so much as a form of recreation but more as a type of release. They did so by visualising the illicit discourses of their unsupervised conversations and fantasies around the body to render the figure an excessive site of bodily pleasure and disorder (see Fiske 1989). The resulting drawings were full of insults, obscenities, and sexual and scatological references. In his examination of taboo and transgression, Bataille (1957) notes the profound animosity between legitimate, or sanctified, discourses and illegitimate, or degraded ones:

> The sexual organs and the sexual act in particular are referred to by degrading names from the jargon of the dregs of society ... The dirty words for love are closely and irrevocably associated with that secret life we lead concurrently with our profession of the loftiest sentiments. These unnamable names formulate the general horror for us, in fact, if we do not belong to the degraded class. They express it with violence, and are themselves violently rejected from the world of decency. No communication is conceivable between the two worlds.

(p. 138)

Figure 6.1   Installation 1999, IoE PGCE student, photographer Nicholas Addison.

Despite, or perhaps because of, the frisson of illegitimacy, the students' violent expressions were simultaneously inventive and humorous, moving with some ease between image and text, the genres of life drawing, biological diagram and comic strip. I am not suggesting that this was an ideal lesson, something you should plan for. Nonetheless, as an event, it became a useful resource for Jack, evidence of transgressive actions that he could use critically in his intervention. Alternatively, for the critical pedagogue, such evidence might form the basis for critical reflection, a tool with which a teacher might discuss normative values with students and how, within humour, difference and/or conformity can be the locus for victimisation and abuse, as well as a site of resistance to authority.

Jack decided to graft elements of the students' drawings onto two souvenir-like replicas of the David, modelling them in clay (see Figure 6.1). The figurines support a range of prostheses and accessories, from a giant phallus to a daisy tutu, while around them, subsidiary, less 'ideal' figures circle and mock the twin Davids' indifference to their presence by mouthing expletives and farting (sounds indicated by text written on balloon speech bubbles and plasticine puff-balls). The students' actions here mirror the way in which the Soviet cultural theorist, Bhaktin (1984), characterised the carnival, a procession in which the people invert moral authority so as to parody the hierarchical structures of normative social relations. Jack appropriated students' excesses to produce an intervention in which the one-off inversion of carnival is more sustained as a provocation; art has the potential to embody, and thus make permanent, acts of resistance that have only symbolic rather than structural force – after all, the official carnival can be used by the authorities to ensure the cathartic release of the masses only to return to normative relations more forcibly after the event (Bataille 1957: 66).

There are different degrees of ambivalence, however. While making visible the 'knowingness' of childhood, a phenomenon often denied by adults (Burgess 2003), the legitimised object of Jack's assault – nominally youthful courage and beauty embodied in a work of art – is itself already degraded. In being transposed photographically to the Victoria and Albert Museum, Jack merely despoils a replica, and by working on a table-top scale it could be the souvenir that is the target of ridicule rather than the original and its surrogates. The way in which Jack presented the outcomes, both as subversive photographic intervention and actual, small-scale installation, demonstrate how contexts for, and methods of, display can be used critically to produce different possibilities and potential meanings.

In the second example, the design historian and researcher Georgaki worked with first year 'A'-level textile students in a girls' comprehensive school to unravel such discourses of display. Specifically, she was concerned with examining the ways in which language is used to reinforce hierarchical distinctions, particularly between art, craft and design.

It appears that both the textiles teachers and students understood their practice to be a form of 'craft', a designation that signalled an approach to ensuring skills acquisition within prescribed traditions (a way of working that Bourdieu characterises as 'middle-brow art' [1993a: 125–131]). It was generally agreed that there could be little creative or self-generated practice until these skills were mastered. Although this perception was not radically altered in students' definitions of art in schools, they differentiated between the two by noting that, in craft, the tactile is privileged. When it came to discussing and evaluating practice, this produced difficulties, for, as Georgaki notes: 'the theme of tactility is resistant to established analysis which assigns to language the function of the key to the process of encoding and decoding artefacts' (2000: 6). In order to explore this further, Georgaki conceived a project in which students acted as curators and critics of one another's work.

Every student selected a textile by one of their peers, presenting it through reproductions in three, independent formats: as a work of art, of craft and of design, presentations which included written descriptions and evaluations. This entailed research into the modes of display (market- and museum-based) and genres of criticism deployed in their respective discourses, and particularly the way that discourses on class, gender and race intersect with and inform them (Livingstone and Ploof 2007). Georgaki intended that students would come to understand Bourdieu's claim about language as a tool of mediation: 'Discourse about a work is not a mere accompaniment, intended to assist its perception and appreciation, but a stage in the production of the work, of its meaning and value' (1993b: 110). But students also became keenly aware of the way that monetary value has become a parameter of cultural value, retailing their 'designed' object in tens of pounds, the fine art textile at several thousand, while the craft piece approximated the latter, a price influenced by a visit to the Crafts Council. Georgaki concludes:

> Perhaps the most challenging task for the group was to try and identify their own status within the cultural models presented to them. Interestingly they were keen to consider themselves craftspeople, yet their understanding of the term relied on equating craft production with fine art production. I view this as an implicit strategy to circumnavigate problems of value creation and overcome the low status associated with handicraft.
>
> (2000: 9)

The exercise opened up a debate in which students were encouraged to articulate how craft is valued within society and how these values circulate within discourses that determine its status and thus the people who engage with it. Although the group (15 female and 1 male imported from the neighbouring boy's school, which did not offer textiles) were unwilling at this point to consider the gendered implications of their practice, and despite a certain denial in their disidentification with handicraft and an alliance with fine art, they had at least recognised Bourdieu's contention that:

> The opposition between art for art's sake and middle brow art which on the ideological plane, becomes transformed into an opposition between the idealism of devotion to art and the cynicism of submission to the market, should

not hide the fact that the desire to oppose a specifically cultural legitimacy to the prerogatives of power and money constitutes one more way of recognizing that business is business.

(1993a: 128)

Galleries and museums: resistance and complicity

Both of the papers by Bourdieu cited above were first published in the 1980s and it could be argued that the principles of, and conditions for, state patronage (as opposed to market forces) have altered significantly since then. Although governments still foreground national heritage and cultural excellence, these imperatives are accompanied by a rhetoric of inclusion that accommodates resistance to privilege. The recommended way in which this undoing of privilege is to be facilitated is through partnerships between cultural institutions, schools and communities (nationally: Anderson 1997; MLA 2001; DCMS 2005; internationally: ICOM). Because artists today are so concerned with dialogical practices, the ever-present conversation between restricted and popular cultural forms, for example, and the border crossing between art, craft, design and wider disciplines is particularly evident in galleries of contemporary art. As Bourriard observes:

> This is the precise nature of the contemporary art exhibition in the arena of representational commerce: it creates free areas, and time spans whose rhythm contrasts with those structuring everyday life, and it encourages an inter-human commerce that differs from the 'communication zones' that are imposed upon us.

(Bourriard 2002: 16)

Therefore, in notable ways, and unlike school art, the contemporary field of art appears to stand somewhat apart from the institutions of government and its instrumental 'communication zones'. These zones are administered by a bureaucracy in which the agency of individuals is severely curtailed by regimes of surveillance and accountability. As you may have witnessed, schools can be experienced as one such site, a place where young people are socialised into becoming productive citizens by undergoing a process of monitoring and assessment through which they are positioned in relation to prevailing norms. The contemporary art gallery can therefore prove an interesting partner to engage young people in considering social norms and their position within them – after all, such galleries pride themselves on their ability to establish a symbolic space of difference and divergence.

Within this space, the artist (as artist and/or educator, and unlike the role of the school art teacher) is intentionally positioned as an agent of change, a potential catalyst for social and cultural transformation. In turn, this places the spectator in a position where they are asked to question the tastes, habits and impositions of the 'privileged' or dominant class by engaging in dialogue with symbolic forms of difference or, more traditionally, by suspending the instrumental reasoning that surrounds everyday interactions in favour of aesthetic contemplation. In this sense, and unlike the national museums that Bennett (1995) argues have supported the oppressive grand narratives of a Eurocentric modernity, the gallery of contemporary art seems to proffer an alternative space. If one views the gallery within the history of early modernism (the avant-garde) and postmodernism (accommodating feminist, postcolonial and queer positions), it has evidently been a space where agents have worked collectively to reveal and oppose dominant and normative discourses, and even participated in anti-discriminatory practices (Allen 2008). Hence, as a critical space, the gallery of contemporary art has actively contributed to democratic debate.

The larger galleries and museums are, however, often experienced by school children as forbidding (Duncan 1995). How then might participation avoid the ritualised nature of traditional gallery-going so that young people feel more familiar with such cultural resources? There is much current advice for teachers to work in partnerships with external agencies (Creative Partnerships 2002 ongoing) and, since the advent of the National Curriculum in the late 1980s, art galleries have proved proactive in supporting learning in art and design. Hooper-Greenhill (2007) examines one such generic initiative, 'The Learning Impact Research Project', which investigated the potential of galleries and museums to motivate learning. She reports that the school students and teachers who participated found the experience enjoyable, inspiring and conducive to creativity, arguing that galleries and museums can contribute to inclusive education by providing a space and pedagogic approach to complement state school provision, particularly for those students who find logocentric pedagogies difficult and/or alienating. She draws on Claxton (1999), among others, to develop a theory of learning that foregrounds the embodied nature of the individual, and the importance of experiential, immersive and playful strategies providing evidence of the way in which participation in educational events opens up possibilities for the learner to widen their cultural knowledge, develop self-esteem and arrive at an empathetic view of the world. Rooted in psychological perspectives and recognising the significance of cultural constructivism (Vygotsky 1978a), she nonetheless tends to universalise the learning subject as someone who recognises and respects others even though s/he is primarily bent on the liberal, humanist quest for self-actualisation. As such, Hooper-Greenhill's argument is somewhat apolitical in orientation and, in this sense, despite the reference to radical thinkers, she prefers to use such 'neutral' terms as 'pupils' voice', 'active self-image', to the uncomfortable and more politically inflected terms 'self-knowledge' or 'agency' that are more typical of critical pedagogues.

Alternatively, the possibilities of rupturing the decorum of gallery-going have been and are being explored, particularly through forms of play (Engage 2003; Harding 2005). But there is a danger here that these practices form a parallel, imaginary realm, where art promises an escape from, rather than a transformation of, everyday reality. As such, participation in these events can promise possibility but ultimately prove isolated – a moment lost once participants re-enter everyday realities.

Burgess, in Chapter 4, examines how, through partnerships, artists, art teachers and gallery educators might work together to develop more sustained pedagogies. Trowell, in Chapter 7, also examines this; her focus is on active engagement in community. The key to the possibility of transformation does not only revolve around issues of ownership and purpose, but around agency – the ability of students to participate actively in meaning-making.

Agency, alliances and the possibility of transformation

'Agency' is a term borrowed from philosophy that has entered educational discourse as a central aim. In anthropological terms, it means 'the power of people to act purposively and reflectively, in more or less complex interrelationships with one another, to reiterate and remake the world in which they live, in circumstances where they may consider different courses of action possible and desirable, though not necessarily from the same point of view' (Inden in Holland *et al.* 1998: 42). In the context of critical pedagogy, the 'point of view' of participants is supposedly in common so that, here, agency refers to the actions of a person who makes conscious choices to act in the world so as to transform the unjust cultural, social and political constraints that limit both their own and others' lives. Only within a culture of questioning can young people become agents in the transformation of society through a pedagogy of hope (Giroux 1997b).

Giroux (1992) suggests that the first stage is for educators to recognise how they are inscribed within institutions of power so that they come to represent particular forms of conventional authority rather than 'themselves'. He offers a series of actions:

> This means we [progressive educators?] must make an attempt to develop a *shared language* around the issue of pedagogy and struggle, develop a *set of relevancies* that can be recognized in each other's work, and articulate a *common political project* that addresses the relationship between pedagogical work and the reconstruction of *oppositional spheres*. Second, we need to form alliances around the issue of *censorship* both in and out of the schools. The question of *representation* is central to issues of pedagogy as a form of cultural politics and cultural politics as practice *related to the struggles of everyday life*. Third we need to articulate these issues in a *public* manner, in which … we're really addressing a *variety of cultural workers* and not simply a narrowly defined audience. This points to the need to broaden the definition of culture and political struggle and in doing so *invite others to participate* in both the purpose and practice central to such tasks.
>
> (p. 159)

Giroux's politics are evident: he belongs to a Left alliance that denounces all forms of oppressive organisation – in particular, the capitalist system that is so valorised within the USA. This system is manifest today in its most ambitious and absolute form as corporate capitalism (Fukuyama 1989) – a type of faceless authority that determines the international circulation of goods, capital and people, a system that (in relation to banking) was severely undermined in 2008. Taking this dominant system into account, it could be argued that one way in which school students are oppressed within contemporary culture is by being entrapped within the class-inflected culture of consumption that Lukács (1971) points to. One of the reasons for the power of capitalist economies is their ability to coerce the subject/consumer to introject the 'laws' of fetishism and commodification. Consumers regulate themselves: work enables leisure, leisure becomes a space in which to purchase the products of work, consumption satisfies those internalised desires that people know are contrived by the capitalist system but misrecognise because they are addicted to, and 'guided by, the fetishistic illusion' (Zizeck 1989). Education itself, despite its rhetorics of empowerment and inclusivity, is far from immune to consumerist metaphors and frequently deploys them to indicate its potential to deliver competitive advantage (Ball 2007): public examinations, the specialist voice, the aura of high culture, all can be viewed as commodities for social advancement – the 'academic capital' that is described by Bourdieu (1984). How then do art, craft and design figure within this system?

Well, despite many instances of modernist art practice (from both Left and Right) as a form of resistance to dominant, particularly capitalist, systems, during the same historical period art has also functioned as a site for fetishistic illusion, a part of the apparatus of oppression, whether engineered by the totalitarian state (Ades *et al.* 1995) or encouraged by the 'free' market (Stallabrass 2006). By engaging with works of art in the gallery, how then can educators hope to help students disentangle themselves from their enmeshed position within a matrix of class, gendered, raced determinants?

The work of art, craft or design is both a thing in itself and embodied evidence of the agency of others' values, a concretisation of their values. It is a site not only for appreciation but investigation and interpretation, a means for young people to work through differences and particularities, but also the possibility of shared values. If you accept Bourdieu's thesis that the dispositions required to enable appreciation are class inflected (Bourdieu *et al.* 1991), the other two are less so. Various approaches to investigation and interpretation exist: descriptive and narrativising, analytical, conversational (see Charman *et al.* 2006; Addison 2007: 256–266). These approaches can be used in combination – in particular, sequences, allied to practical work or as independent enquiries. In the context of critical pedagogy, one of the strategies I would recommend is that advocated by Rogoff (2000), who discusses the work of art as an 'interlocuter'; she explains: 'Art is my interlocutor rather than my object of study, it is the entity that chases me around and forces me to think things differently, at a different register or through the permissions provided by another angle' (p. 10). Because of the power of art to disrupt everyday thinking, she engages with it in a sort of conversation, a means to revisit assumptions and values, almost as an irritant to upset everyday commerce. Within this conversation, the work of art has things to say. Nonetheless, as the conventions of art are historically and culturally conditioned, intended meanings need to be worked at analytically. In order to ensure that you are less likely to misinterpret intentions, it is advisable to work in dialogue with others, perhaps as small groups of students, with a teacher, gallery educator or artist, to extend the discursive environment that you have constructed in the artroom.

It might be useful therefore to look at dialogue as a process through which investigation can be facilitated and through which the alliances that Giroux calls for might be formed. Although dialogue can be defined as a transparent and fair exchange of views, it is, however, also conditioned by power relations. As such, Nicholas Burbules (2000), among other commentators (Ellsworth 1997; Smith 1999; Cameron 2000), is suspicious of the 'hegemony of reasonableness' that sustains its benevolent status. The discursive environment that Lesley Burgess and I have been proposing for art and design follows the dialogical imperative and is potentially the strongest support for securing a critical subject. I must therefore spend some time recounting Burbules' argument before defending the potential of dialogue as a critical, creative and democratic tool.

Dialogue

The critical pedagogic process par excellence is dialogue, a process that enables participants to acknowledge their possible differences and to voice their positions, a process that holds the potential if not of resolution, then at least of understanding. Burbules (2000) usefully categorises six conceptions of dialogue: 1) liberal, debate; 2) feminist, reciprocity; 3) Socratic, argument; 4) hermeneutic, intersubjective understanding; 5) Freirian, emancipation; 6) post-liberal (Habermasian) negotiation (pp. 252–255) (the terms identified are, in some instances, my own interpretations). Whatever the differences of these positions, Burbules contends:

> They all place primary emphasis on dialogue as the adjudicative basis for social and political discussion and disagreement. They all privilege dialogue as the basis for arriving at valid intersubjective understanding or knowledge. And they all, in the educational domain, recommend dialogue as the mode of pedagogical engagement best able to promote learning, autonomy, and an understanding of one's self in relation to others. The prominence of these six views, particularly among educational theorists and practitioners of what might be called broadly the 'progressivist' stripe, has meant that dialogue is the topic of the day and that promoting dialogue and the conditions that can support it is taken as a central educational task.
>
> (p. 257)

Burbules' objections to the dialogic panacea revolve around the problem of power relations and the way in which proponents of dialogue suppose that, because in principle anyone can contribute, it follows that as an inclusive process dialogue is thereby democratic. What this elides is threefold: who instigates and thus frames dialogue? (a group who will inevitably hold the moral high ground for initiating a 'benevolent' process); on whose and what terms are contributors invited? (the selection of venue, time, representatives, ground rules and procedural structures, topics for discussion, the language for discussion); who is most at risk from contributing? (in the event of a lack of consensus, some groups, by exposing their beliefs, may have laid themselves open to sanctions by people who, outside the dialogue, are in a position of power over them and who are now forewarned with knowledge that could be used against the very group most in need of empowerment).

Burbules characterises three dialogic models that have been devised and deployed in the name of social justice in an attempt to address the issue of diversity in education: pluralism, multiculturalism, cosmopolitanism. Although he admits that the intentions of those promoting each strain have many virtues, he also discloses what he believes to be the weaknesses of each in practice.

The first, pluralism, is a 'melting pot' in which *exchange* is the main vehicle for reaching a *reconciliation* of differences. Such dialogue involves agreements and compromises and, perhaps, *new understandings* with which all contributors can identify because they are produced together. However, it 'comes to the end of *assimilating* diverse groups into predominantly mainstream beliefs and values ... this asymmetry of change threatens ... to erase significant cultural difference or to relegate it entirely to the private, not public sphere' (Burbules 2000: 258) [my italics]. In this way, pluralist approaches can unwittingly reinforce dominant perspectives because they represent the norm from which difference is identified and with which any negotiation must be informed. Often 'common sense', pragmatic solutions result because the ideal outcome is *social harmony.*

The second, multiculturalism (see Mason 1995), takes as its founding principle *respect* for difference. Given this maxim, multiculturalists attempt to *preserve* differences through *celebration* (enjoying difference for the sake of difference). However, multicultural visibility 'can have the effect of *exoticizing* differences, rendering them quaint or interesting as artifacts and not as critical points of reference against which to view oneself' (Burbules 2000: 258). This approach was once sanctified in the National Curriculum order for Art and design (DfEE 1999) and has therefore been subject to most criticism in England. For example, John Holt (1996) cautions against what he calls a 'cultural kaleidoscope' (p. 131) because the spectacular, indiscriminate exposure of difference can distort cultures by misrepresenting them through stereotypes – for example, by allowing historical artefacts/practices to stand in for today's (see Addison and Dash 2007). The multiculturalist is therefore in danger of essentialising difference, of limiting its manifestations to fixed historical, ethnic signs that can be played out in harmless distractions while the main business of life goes on as usual. Here, the ideal outcome is *cultural tolerance.*

The third, cosmopolitanism, is a recognition of the '*unreconciled coexistence* of diverse cultures and groups' (Burbules 2000: 259). This approach acknowledges the past history of colonisation and the contemporary conditions of globalisation so that divisions may, at times, throw into relief the 'limits of assimilation, agreement, or even understanding' (ibid). It follows that, in some instances, 'there must simply be an end to talk that seeks to bridge or minimize differences ... it *abrogates* – and sometimes prejudices and rejects out of hand – the *value of agreement*, excluding both the possibility of mutual accommodation and the possibility of a critical questioning of one view from a radically different other' (ibid). This approach has no ideal because it professes *realism*.

In response to the domestications of the first two approaches and the pessimism of the third, Burbules goes on to state: 'differences are enacted. They change over time. They take shape differently in varied contexts. They surpass our attempts to classify or define them' (p. 261). The implication of this statement is that, for a variety of reasons, different groups and individuals may choose to change the strategies through which identification is made possible depending on the conditions, particularly the power relations, in which the choice is made. Therefore, in the educational context, all approaches are worth considering as long as they are stripped of their *neutral* clothing by denaturalising the norms around which they are structured and as long as the *power relations* that frame the specific pedagogic situation are acknowledged. Additionally, participants should critique the categorial distinctions that mislead through the fixed identities of hostile binary oppositions in three ways: by accepting the possibility of internal difference – 'the unexplored and unrecognized dimension of one's self', 'differences within'; by subjecting naturalised concepts to redefinition – 'differences beyond'; by refusing to capitulate to normative discourses and employing strategies of resistance to dominant conventions – 'differences against' (p. 261). Furthermore, in order for there to be equity, all participants should participate in the deployment of the approaches so that their supposed neutrality is exposed and so that dialogue is recognised as a socio/historical, interactive and situated practice.

In the approaches taken by cultural studies (Hall 1997) and visual culture (Mirzoeff 2002), art becomes just one facet of the multiplicity of social relations and its critical and historical study becomes a way of analysing that constitution. However, this emphasis on social structures and practices enables some critics to wag an accusatory finger: 'Cultural studies may sometimes be primarily thematic, paraphristic and diagnostic in their way of reading ... The orientation is more toward the culture and less toward the work itself, even though the heterogeneity of each culture is in principle recognised' (Miller 1992: 17). According to Miller, cultural studies is a politically motivated discipline in which, on the one hand, a dominant culture is dismantled through theoretical critique, while on the other, peripheral, minority cultures are celebrated and empowered to assure their ascendancy, a transformative process of enfranchisement and reparation (ibid: 18–19). It follows that, for the cultural critic, the art of a dominant culture is interesting only in so far as it reflects that culture and only in so far as it represents its ideological structures (thus the critique of canon formation). When choosing to analyse such art, the cultural critic does so to expose and/or demonstrate its coercive properties and its injustices; it is used merely as an *illustration* of power relations that are external to the works themselves and not as something *productive* of power relations.

Alternatively, according to Miller, when championing the art of a minority culture, the cultural critic finds it necessary to take a different approach, promoting campaigns of visibility with their recontextualisations and preservations and their necessary redefinitions of art and identity (Parker and Pollock 1981) – often by means of 'strategic essentialism' (Spivak 1988: 13). The intention here is that such campaigns of revision will lift minorities out from their position of subjugation towards self-determination, a position of subjecthood and agency. However, there is the danger that a dominant culture, in learning from its critics and adopting a rhetoric of inclusivity, is able to make difference visible in the belief that assimilation will inevitably follow. There is also a danger – if a minority culture is able to establish a form of dominance, as in the case of African/American traditions in popular music and athletics – that it will have recourse to the aesthetic categories that were once perceived as antithetical to it, thus jazz has been called the authentic classical music of the USA (Miller 1992) (this instance is not so much an example of assimilation so much as appropriation by a dominant culture). As Mercer (1999) argues:

> Visibility has been won, in the African American world, through complicity with the compromise formation of cultural substitutionism. 'Hyperblackness' in the media and entertainment industries serves not to critique social injustice, but to cover over and conceal increasingly sharp inequalities that are most polarised *within* black society itself, namely between a so-called urban underclass and an expanded middle class that benefited from affirmative action.
>
> (p. 56)

For Miller, therefore, a focus on marginalised or sub-cultures through forms of multiculturalism dilutes what is good and valuable, whereas for Mercer it has the effect of valorising and thus accommodating difference within existing patterns of injustice.

Within existing educational structures, teachers, drawn from the community, are, however, evidently not fully representative of its diversity. Therefore it may be strategically vital to support and/or represent the views of others but in such a way that the histories of their lives are made credible. Shohat and Stam (1995) emphasise that:

> Any substantive multiculturalism has to recognise the existential realities of pain, anger and resentment, since the multiple cultures invoked by the term 'multiculturalism' have not historically co-existed in relations of equality and mutual respect. It is therefore not merely a question of communicating across borders but of discerning the forces which generate the borders in the

first place. Multiculturalism has to recognise not only difference but even bitter, irreconcilable difference ... But these historical gaps in perception do not preclude alliances, dialogical coalitions, intercommunal identifications and affinities. Multiculturalism and the critique of Eurocentrism, we have tried to show, are inseparable concepts; each becomes impoverished without the other.

(p. 15)

While progressive educators argue that the diasporic realities of contemporary culture are a productive resource, from a traditionalist perspective it is incumbent on the teacher to introduce young people to the western canon (those works agreed by experts within the disciplinary field to represent cultural excellence). For conservatives such as the philosopher/critic Scruton, the canon is a means to ensure that students are acculturated to the transcendent values it embodies – what he terms 'an historical community of sentiment ... celebrating universal human values' (1999). Yet there are also calls from the Left suggesting that the canon, far from being transcendent, is a useful material resource for the empowerment of oppressed groups. Gretton (2003) argues that within existing pedagogic power relations, young people have little agency and those whose social backgrounds marginalise them further from the centres of power have even less. The canons of art do represent power, and it is therefore important to allow young people access to them as an intellectual and social resource. As Gretton articulates:

> Instead of wishing the canon to oblivion teachers should identify for and with our students the sources of its power and the logic of cultural reproduction and distinction of which it gives such clear evidence, and then use the loose canon because it is an adequate resource for their cognitive training, because it is an indispensable resource for cultural entryism, and because it can form the focus of a critical debate with and among students on the realities of cultural power.
>
> (2003: 186)

With this type of 'critical pragmatism', in combination with intercultural dialogue, the borders that Giroux is so keen to dismantle are more successfully eroded from within by slow, cumulative action.

It is my contention that, however difficult to promote, such a process is crucial to the practice of a critical pedagogy, one where differences are not categorial but contingent and strategic and one in which the possibility of failure is recognised due to the incommensurability of some differences. Strategically, galleries are a rich educational resource in which the past, the canon, and the present, doubt and new formulations, quite often meet. They are therefore uniquely positioned as a site where you can engage students in making meaning through discussion and negotiation, not feel-good self-advancement, but dogged work in making dialogue.

Chapter 7

Collaborative liberatory practices for global citizenship

Jane Trowell

'Trespassing ... is a prerequisite for ... advance'
(Bourdieu and Wacquant 1989: 46)

Young people and the world

As an artist/teacher, you are educating young people at a time when it is less possible than ever to insulate them from complex issues of national and global significance. Digital technologies such as the internet, e-networking groups and mobile phones means that serious issues constantly permeate young people's worlds – issues such as the recent increase in the UK of brutal murders of teenagers by teenagers, struggles over race and immigration, chronic eating disorders, or wars, climate change and credit crunches. Indeed, if you hope to equip young people to take care of each other and the future, you will be actively and optimistically fostering a rolling discussion on many such issues. After all, aren't you educating young 'citizens'?

Art educationalist Jonathan Barnes states in his book *Cross-Curricular Learning 3–14*:

> Almost undoubtedly our children will have to face the realities of global warming, rising sea levels, pandemics, human cloning, increasing terrorism ... water, oil and food shortages, frequent job changes and economic meltdown ... Today's children are already living in a century of unparalleled rapid and global transformation which will quite literally *change our minds*.
>
> (2007: 17 my italics)

Beyond the school gates, culture, politics, joys and conflicts flow messily and seamlessly through the lives of young people, from the music they listen to and the clothes they wear, to the language they speak. Inside the gates, young people grapple daily with huge intimate realities and excitements around power: who's in and who's out; coercive uses of race; class, sexualities and gender; comparisons of material wealth; hierarchies of beauty, intelligences, language and physicality and, on top of all that, what school is trying to do to them or for them.

Children aren't born seeing the world as chopped up into 'subjects'. For them, everything is related and connected, and primary school children in the UK have benefited from the state's recognition of this since the 1960s (Barnes 2007: 11). Young people at secondary school, however, are suddenly confronted with this segregated specialist mode by an ideological curriculum model that requires the mind to split one thing from another, to develop boundaries and hierarchies between knowledge (Apple 2004; Moore 2006). It is proposed as a norm, as being part of becoming an adult, just as the focus on individual work is seen as superior (and easier to assess) than collaborative work. Yet, more than ever, young people need regular spaces where they can consider, debate and make critical meaning of their own daily experiences and freely connect them to the politics, justices and injustices of the wider world. When subjects under discussion matter to young people and are framed in genuine open enquiry, this kind of unboundaried learning is not only powerful and exciting, but also deeply meaningful to them (Burke & Grosvenor 2003: 68; Field & Stow 2002: 271). Provision of such spaces urgently needs to be facilitated and, ironically, given its compulsory and state-controlled nature, school is one of the few regular environments where it could be.

Despite Ivan Illich's weighty argument that compulsory education should be abolished due to its unavoidable 'institutionalisation of values ..., social polarisation, and psychological impotence' (1971: 9), I believe that, with vision and courage, it is possible for schools to enable young people to become critical deconstructors of their present and critical actors in a constructive, liberatory and hopeful future (Hutchinson 1996; Giroux 2005). Indeed, if liberatory educators don't engage with schools, the mass of young people will be abandoned to conformism. 'Liberatory' teaching and learning should foster critical ownership over the very questions being asked, rather than teaching and learning to fit someone else's pre-existent answers (Freire and Faundez 1989; hooks 1994). This process, crucially, includes deconstructing with young people the meaning of 'school' itself.

Art and design's liberatory potential

Within this, I argue that the subject art and design can be a potent, critical force in the lives of young people, and in some schools this is indeed the case. There is, after all, a lingering tradition of the art department as a haven for free speech, welcoming the non-conformist and misfit from the logocentric curriculum. The downside is that art and design can be the apogee of isolation from the rest of the school, an outmoded romantic cocktail of feeling misunderstood and relishing exile.

However, the subject, especially when interpreted in its widest scope as 'visual culture', has an enormous capacity to connect intimately and powerfully with the lives of young people. Given visual culture's ubiquity, it can profoundly assist them in meaning-making, in addressing complex and big ideas, in honing critical skills, in collaborating and in producing work (alone and together) that shows understanding of the power of the visual, tactile, spatial, digital, commercial and social world (Duncum 2005). All too often, however, this is precisely not what is happening in our art and design departments. All too often art and design is a bastion of conservatism in every conceivable way. There is frequently a fear by art and design teachers of 'the difficulty' of contemporary art and contemporary visual culture, which Lesley Burgess has vividly characterised as 'the monsters in the playground' (Burgess 2003; Downing & Watson 2004).

For the global context of today, what is urgently needed is a rethink in terms of how the subject operates within the broader liberatory education of young people. This can only be done, I suggest, by looking again at what the field outside school is offering. My question is, therefore, what can the area of contemporary practice concerned with social and environmental justice and global issues uniquely offer to young people's present and future lives? How can you, in collaboration with artist educators, learn from these liberatory practices to help address the pressing global issues that they are inheriting? How can you, together, equip and embolden each other to think beyond borders and to encourage young people to work alongside you?

The field we're in: art and activism

> Contemporary practice in art, craft and design blurs the boundaries ... Just as the sites of practice can be anywhere, from the natural environment to cyberspace, its methods can be interdisciplinary, from the anthropological to the psychoanalytical.
>
> (Addison and Burgess 2007: 2)

Contemporary artists, designers and craftspeople are increasingly choosing to work in contexts and on projects that address major social, cultural, economic and environmental issues. These may or may not have overt liberatory intent in the terms I have outlined. Internationally, the phenomenon is a result of invigoration of 'activist' art practice, which has been growing fast since the emergence of the broader anti-corporate, social justice, anti-imperialist and environmental movements of the late 1980s and beyond (well-documented by Gupta 1993; Lacy 1995; Felshin 1995; Gablik 1995; McKay 1996 and, later, Notes from Nowhere 2003).

For these dedicated practitioners, political, ethical and artistic concerns are expressed holistically. Such practitioners believe in crossing borders and many simply do not acknowledge them. This range can be seen where artists are committed to social contexts, such as prisons, hospitals, rehab units, schools, particular communities, or are campaigning against a proposed airport, road or power station. Such work can also be found in science through the pioneering work of Arts Catalyst, on environmental projects through collaborations with a local City Farm or the Eden Project.

Many practitioners run their own organisations, such as littoral working on rural issues, or Virtual Migrants on issues of asylum and immigration, or the UHC Collective who combine graphic design with an activist practice. The case study outlined later in this chapter focuses on the work of interdisciplinary group PLATFORM, who work on issues of oil, justice and climate change.

In the UK, a controversial change in UK state arts funding policy in 1999 has driven a further boom in artists working in social and environmental contexts. As a result of the 'Policy Action Team 10 Report to the Social Exclusion Unit' (PAT 10), all branches of government are required to demonstrate how they will fulfill the current Labour government's social inclusion and regeneration agenda, and this includes the Arts Council England (DCMS 1999). There is a controversial flood of new funding in this area, which has been criticised from the left and the right as a misuse of the arts in the name of social engineering.

The Government's major initiative 'Creative Partnerships' (2002 ongoing) is part of the PAT 10 agenda. It focuses on localities where multiple deprivation is in evidence, and, whatever critics say, has given a great deal of opportunity for artists, scientists and other creative people to work in a range of collaborations across schooling and other settings, as long as they address the central agenda. However problematic, there is a belief at the highest level in the current government that the arts can change things in ways that other means cannot (Smith 1999). Ironically, his view matches that of many artist-activists whose politics may be opposed to the government in many other respects. The mainstreaming of 'liberatory' practices can also be seen in the groundbreaking Dokumenta 11 in Kassel (2002) curated by Okwui Enwezor, which was the first international art fair that actively promoted collaborative work on social and global issues, and many other smaller recent exhibitions and projects. Thus, curatorship and government have both followed and then driven, even co-opted, agendas for arts practices that address social and political issues.

Whoever is the initiator and for whatever motives, all such practices are intrinsically interdisciplinary, collaborative and multimodal. They are inescapably accompanied by serious ethical implications that are often naively underestimated. If they come with a political commitment to liberatory pedagogies, what is required is an ongoing engagement with debates on ethics, aesthetics, collectivity, environmental sustainability and other-centred, non-Eurocentric thinking (Trapese Collective 2007). Projects can all too easily involve abuses of power, be unsustainable, or leave very damaging legacies of tokenism (Cooke and Kothari 2001). For artists with a long-term commitment to working in these areas, a primary skill is understanding the politics of how social relations are constructed and perpetuated. Because of the primacy of social relations and ethics in this emerging field, Bourriaud (1998) has called it 'relational aesthetics' and Kester (2004) 'dialogic aesthetics'. It also goes without saying that social justice practices, in art or otherwise, are always inherently zones of fierce contention and disruption. Practitioners have to be willing to be humble. They have to understand their own power, their own privilege, as well as their own potential self-delusion about the 'good' they are attempting to do in the world (see Ellsworth 1989; Burbules 2000; Cooke and Kothari 2001). This, suggests Giroux, is also the central work of the teacher (1992).

Disjuncture with formal education

As with many other aspects of contemporary practice, the subject art and design struggles to reflect this new movement. Nonetheless, increasing numbers of those entering into a PGCE in art and design are arriving with just such global concerns and social practices, keen to explore their potential in secondary school. Yet, within the art and design department these practices are almost never presented, let alone taught and learnt. As a contemporary artist, craftsperson or designer who has entered formal education in a teaching role, you may have found that these practices are rendered invisible, impossible or, worse, taboo. There is a bewildering disjuncture between what you consider to be a relevant engaged art practice and that which is taught in the institution of school or college. You may conclude that it is not in the interest of school or college to promulgate such a practice, or you may have hoped that it is just the zone where it is most needed and most possible. Either way, how can you make your way? How might your artistic experience and commitment to liberatory education be brought into a formal learning context?

In the next section, I look at a case study of a liberatory primary school project initiated in 1995 by PLATFORM, an interdisciplinary group of artists, activists, researchers and campaigners of which I am a member. I examine *Tides and Tributes* to reflect on the ways that it shaped my understanding of the potential to intervene in mainstream education, and to consider how such experience bears on teacher education in secondary school art and design.

Tides and Tributes: 'It's very insighting, Miss!'

A group of fifteen 8-year-olds are trying not to run along a street next to the urban river Wandle in south-west London, near where it flows into the Thames at Wandsworth. A few stretch a banner between them proclaiming the word 'Citizens'. They are all armed with clipboards and pens and are accompanied by their class teacher, a classroom assistant and two interdisciplinary artists from PLATFORM. They are on the lookout for six fellow citizens, of the adult variety, whom they will recognise by the large gold-ribboned rosette on their coats. The citizens are local campaigners who work on different aspects of the Wandle, including The Wandsworth Society and Wandsworth Action Volunteers for the Environment. The children are champing at the bit, having prepared for this moment very carefully. They've been on a number of exploratory walks around different parts of their local river's delta and they're pretty outraged by its polluted and neglected state. They weren't to begin with. Most of them didn't even think of it as a river, more as a dirty ditch (if they had even noticed it at all).

On the way back to their old Victorian building with its outdoor toilets, we walk past the building site that is the beginnings of their brand new school – an eco-school that will have many environmental features, including a large intercultural garden. It will also have a music room powered by renewable electricity generated by a micro-hydro turbine that PLATFORM and a hydro-engineer have installed in a sluice gate in the nearby river Wandle. The school will go on to win awards for its ecological values and ethos.

Back in the classrooms, the group discusses their findings with their Wandle animal affinity group: Salmon, Swan, Heron, Eel. They discuss their own perspectives and that of their animals. They then recombine for their elected project strand, taking their new-found insights with them – insights from real people and real animals, grappling with real problems, in the world out there that the children walk through every day.

The Delta TV group are making a news programme about the river's present condition, as it should be, not as it is, along the lines of the BBC's children's programme 'Newsround'. The writing group are creating poetry and prose around the river's rich history and future and creating ideas towards a grand performance. The music group are exploring, through sound and rhythm, how the past, present and future of the Wandle might be evoked, and will later join the writing group. The art and design group are hard at work on drawings and designs for the project's multifunctional poster, studying issues about the wildlife that depend on the river, as well as those that are likely to return should it be cleaned up. The pupils are from two different year groups, which breaks the age-banding and enlivens the learning and teaching further. Periodically, the whole group comes together for performances/presentations by the artists and each other, sharing new ideas about how the work is going and other aspects of project business.

Tides and Tributes was a strategic part of PLATFORM's long-term project *Delta* (1993–2001), which aimed to raise the profile of the neglected river as well as connect it to issues of resource justice and energy efficiency by contributing hydro-electricity from the river Wandle to the music room of the new school. The collaborative team of a sculptor and a green economist worked with a hydro-engineer, a stonecarver and Whitechapel Bell Foundry to install the micro-hydro, and to mark this by enabling tidal movement to ring an engraved ex-church bell. To PLATFORM's knowledge, it was the first micro-hydro turbine in a global north context, as micro-hydro technology is more usually used in remote mountain or rural areas for small-scale generation. Its presence in an energy-saturated city was a deliberate provocation and, as such, the project received a lot of press attention.

Funded by the Arts Council of England, *Tides and Tributes* involved a writer, musician, artist and video-maker working with the children for one day a week over 10 weeks. Or perhaps, revealing a more truthful inner interdisciplinarity, I should say a writer/campaigner, a musician/art teacher, an artist/naturalist and a performance artist/activist. We returned to the school for a shorter period of work later in 1995 to create the performance for the grand opening of the eco-school and its turbine connection. We returned yearly for visits, and again in 2001 for a second residency *The River Detectives*. We took a long-term view of the relation-ship and formed bonds (and fundraised) accordingly.

So far, so good. But what of the tensions and difficulties inherent in such social and relational practices? In this project, the tensions lay chiefly in three areas. First, the new headteacher had heralded a revolution that caused her to be seen as controversial among some influential school governors and also some staff. This revolution included embracing a politicising artists' residency, which had some very uncomfortable knock-on effects that proved tricky to handle. Second, PLATFORM shielded the school and pupils from political and jurisdictional struggles that we were to encounter a few years later in the wider *Delta* project regarding the working of the turbine. This was inconsistent with our approach. With hindsight, both we and the headteacher considered that this was a mistake, a missed opportunity for pupils to engage in the very issues with which I began this chapter. Finally, but tellingly, some of the teachers who did not work with us were very troubled at hearing of the children walking and holding the 'citizens' banner. It seems they worried that we were propagandising the pupils, although this was never said explicitly. What is telling is that the word 'citizens', held up proudly by children, caused some teachers discomfort.

These tensions notwithstanding, during one cliffhanger moment during the project, a wide-eyed girl said to me, 'It's very insighting, Miss!' It was clear at the time that she had meant 'exciting', but somehow the mis-said word took on a meaning for us which, over a dozen years later, and for the purposes of this chap-ter, has resonance. The carefully planned yet also responsive project was achieving more than we had hoped: each week, the children simply could not wait to get on with it, and their teachers made use of this excitement for connecting to the work undertaken in between.

Exciting, insighting *or inciting*? With regards to the aims of PLATFORM as an interdisciplinary practice dedicated to advancing social and ecological justice, all three adjectives combine to create a working and creatively problematic defini-tion of an active, liberatory pedagogy. If incitement literally means 'to move to action', then, if it is coupled with reflective practice grounded in debates on social justice, there is the potential for an exciting, meaning-making education that emerges from critical, engaged and progressive pedagogies (Freire 1972; hooks 1994; Giroux 1995; Trapese Collective 2007; Addison and Burgess, this volume). 'Educate, Agitate and Organise' goes the old propagandising socialist slogan, made famous again in the 1980s in the conclusion to the soul classic 'How we gonna make the Black Nation rise?' In terms of the aims of a vivid, informed and activat-ing learning experience for young people, I surmise that it was the interdisciplinary nature of the *Tides and Tributes* project (between art, environment, technology and politics), combined with engagement with the reality of a contested future for a local place, plus the contact with a range of real and active people (including the risk-taking Headteacher), that gave this education project its electricity, not the pioneering micro-hydro turbine.

Using this primary school project as a jumping-off point, I next suggest what you can learn about how art and design in secondary contexts can contribute to exciting, insightful and liberatory education from the perspective of both teacher and student. Below, I explore eight provisional areas that could crossover from PLATFORM's experience with primary schools to the secondary art and design context.

1. *Holistic approach: blurring subject boundaries, multiple perspectives*
   In *Tides and Tributes*, it was clear to PLATFORM that the two collaborating primary teachers immediately understood how the proposed project could work for their children. We did not come across any epistemological blocks – that is, blocks based on teachers feeling uncomfortable with the range of knowledge, meanings and skills that the project could encompass (Bernstein 1996: 20). The fact that it was artist-led but would involve renewable energy, nature, industrial history, study of rivers and discussion about active citizenship, sat well with the teachers' understanding of their job. Furthermore, they accepted that PLATFORM could facilitate an interdisciplinary collaboration with appropriate expertise. Many primary schools understand issue-based teaching and learning very well and can flex their already integrated curriculum structures (one class teacher, teaching across all subjects) to enable the children to benefit from the experience (Barnes 1993: 68). Yet the secondary school art and design department with its norms of discrete subject specialisms may have difficulty embracing it for a host of reasons. The challenge lies in two crucial gaps. First, there is the gap between the more integrated primary model and secondary's subject-specific model; and second, the gap between contemporary liberatory art practices and school art. In collaboration with other like-minded secondary teachers, you will need to equip yourself to challenge these norms in terms that the department and institution can understand. Using the practices of interdisciplinary collaborative artists will be invaluable in helping you achieve this.

2. *The local and the real: uses of the unknown past, present and future*
   During the project, pupils and their teachers were particularly excited by engaging with the very local, very immediate contested environment in unexpected ways while simultaneously working to relate it to wider issues (Lippard 1997). The everyday and neglected environs of the Wandsworth Town one-way system became extraordinary, through making the life of the river the focus of attention and not the road traffic. By researching its history and nature, pupils became aware of the fact that everything can change, not only for the worse, but also for the better. Giroux's injunction to 'make the familiar strange and the given problematic' was a central plank of the project's future-orientated thinking (1993: 25). The children began to imagine an alternative future for the area. It didn't end there, however. The possibility for change was reinforced by meeting very real, local and active 'citizens'.
   The local and the real are more practically available to teachers and young

people than a trek to an important gallery, and are arguably more productive in terms of liberatory education, although critically juxtaposing the two can produce extremely fertile discussion about cultural hierarchies and snobberies. Young people may be more cyber-networked than ever, but the point at which both everyday and global issues touch the ground is on their doorstep, at the bus stop, or hanging out on street corners. There is no doubt, however, that the crucial tool in stimulating participation was having new people (both local and from elsewhere) who could refresh tired eyes and share fascination for the places on the doorstep (Barnes 2007: 167).

3. *Embodiment: feeling and sharing the issue through the senses*
    Pupils regularly went out to investigate different aspects of the nearby river and its delta. Each visit had a clear focus while encouraging diverse investigative methods and procedures. In this way, pupils not only put themselves (literally) in the picture but they also deployed multimodal means to record their observations and understandings using written word, storytelling, factual researching, enacting, photography, drawing, videoing, collecting, listening, comparing and, importantly (given the muddy river), smelling! By later electing a specific project strand, pupils could extend their knowledge by building on their collective investigations to date, a search that had become urgent because of its embodied, experiential nature. This use of what Gardner (1999) terms 'multiple intelligences' gave a depth and ownership to the experience, while the regular discussions helped pupils to contextualise their findings critically. Gardner notes: 'The brain works best and retains most when ... actively involved in exploring physical sites and materials and is asking questions to which it craves the answers' (Gardner in Barnes 2007: 164). In *Tides and Tributes*, this sense of active, experiential learning connected with Freire's 'learning to question' outlined earlier to produce an embodied engagement with the local that proved invaluable. Walking from school to a nearby place with a series of new questions in mind created a connectedness that counteracted the mental splitting mentioned earlier. In this way, pupils lived the questions and extended them. Additionally, in this situation, pupils' local knowledge brought about a reversal of power as they frequently knew a lot more about aspects of the locality than the teacher/artist. This was a dynamic that gave the shared work enormous veracity and energy.

4. *Metaphor and thinking 'other': extension through the self to the world*
    There are many inner-city issues that you could choose from to stimulate an investigative project. By peeling the city off the land and revealing the river's healthier past and its current neglected state, *Tides and Tributes* opened up not only a wealth of urban environmental issues but also a rich seam of metaphor. As pupils learnt about springs and sources and how, in the past, people used to drink from the river, their conversations moved from historical considerations to their own lives. These were conversations that enabled them to make

connections between past, present and potential futures. Innocence, misuse, neglect and care are all powerful themes for inner-city children. Pupils learnt that, should the campaign lead to the river being restored, certain animals would thrive. This symbiotic relationship with the environment encouraged a kind of identification that became apparent when the pupils chose animal affinity groups. Alternatively, by considering how one micro-hydro can power a whole village in Nepal, but only the music room in their London school, the children found themselves immediately inside the question of social and resource justice. This layering of empathies and identifications allowed a deepening of ownership and a way of demonstrating views, tensions and experience that moved from the literal descriptions of their earlier investigations to metaphorical understandings.

5. *Inner and outer interdisciplinarity: uncovering our many selves*
Why do so many secondary teachers keep their inner interdisciplinarity from their students? For example, do you imagine that you yourself are perceived by students as just an 'art teacher'? By keeping private your other passions and interests you can certainly maintain a certain wall of standardised safety between 'us' and 'them', giving 'them' less personal information, but at the same time you lose the potential to reverse the potential to surprise students, to challenge their stereotype of the 'art and design teacher'. Adult life is complex and interdisciplinary. Teachers, too, are learners, enthusiasts, experts in a number of areas, yet secondary teachers are officially forced to identify with one subject. Everyone can remember a moment when they realised that an indifferent teacher of X was actually interested in something you were interested in. In my case, it was Mr G, a dull maths teacher, who astounded everyone in an assembly with his performance as a bass guitarist in a staff rock band. Or music teacher Mr E, who sometimes loved lateral thinking exercises more than teaching us music. I did not look at them the same way again, and have remembered them vividly 30 years on.

In a primary school setting, it is absolutely accepted that teachers cross boundaries and have stakes (although unequal) in many subjects. Yet, in secondary schools, this fact is institutionally undermined by the segregated subject-specialist curriculum. As Bernstein asks, '... in whose interest is the apartness of things and in whose interest is the new togetherness and the new integration' (1996: 25). I would argue that if you reveal your inner interdisciplinarity to students and, additionally, acknowledge that you are still a learner, a profound and exciting shift in power relations will result and in such a way to aid the project of liberatory education (Lackey 2005: 207). This 'revelation' is the beginning of being able to collaborate with others beyond your specialism (Wentworth & Davis 2002: 21–2). For members of PLATFORM it was easy to be ourselves in *Tides and Tributes*, yet in secondary school it can take courage to interrupt the stern hegemony of 'subject specialism' and 'subject knowledge'. In the past two years, however, there has been a significant and positive change that can help here. You should now take full advantage of the fact that the new National Curriculum (QCA 2007a) actively encourages cross-curricularity at Key Stage 3, a potential that I will return to later.

6. *Responsiveness: planning for spontaneity and risk*
    In *Tides and Tributes*, four members of PLATFORM had to plan rigorously for the 10-day project with two mixed age-groups and two teachers. Yet, the adult team (PLATFORM and teachers) agreed that things would change once we had met the children and would continue to do so as the project unfolded. In this sense, it is possible to be exact about overall liberatory aims while encompassing the possibility of major rethinks on process and outcome (Seabury 2002: 87). If the liberatory aims are clear and negotiated, then the detail can evolve. Life outside is not laid down with a ruler and young people need to learn skills for managing disruption, for making decisions about sudden change within a wider critical and ethical framework.

    Certain ingredients must be safeguarded, however: there must be room for 'the prophetic imagination' to gestate (hooks 2003: 185). There must be periods of inactivity and silence where the 'unthinkable' and the 'yet to be thought' can emerge (Bernstein 1996: 44–45). Teachers and young people should have space to 'make leaps … try out the unexpected' and 'let knowledge out of the boxes' (Seabury 2002: 56; 69). This aerated kind of teaching takes confidence and forethought in an era where, despite the loosening of the National Curriculum, there is still a culture of targets, surveillance and audit that pervades schools (Barnes 2007: 245). But it is precisely this environment of possibility that generates excitement in learning.

7. *Sense-making: critically sharing reflection and action*
    Sense-making in the context of liberatory education involves both teachers and students reflecting regularly on social and artistic process as much as product, and failures or complete changes of directions, as much as fulfilling a clearly envisioned path (hooks 1994: 21). Sense-making encourages the making of meaning in relation to an endeavour or encounter. It validates whatever is learnt. It is done individually by teachers and students, and is shared in groups. The latter encourages a culture of listening, reciprocal critique between student and student, students and teacher, and also assistance in untangling complex processes and reactions. It is not without conflict, especially if the teacher is honest in wanting feedback, but it is undertaken in the context of co-constructing the future of the learning (see Chapter 5, 'Negotiated assessment'). Asking a young person to make sense of their learning is a separate thing to asking them to assess or evaluate it. Sense-making is very personal and is about having time to sift and connect ideas. This is invaluable in interdisciplinary multilayered issue-based projects. Modes such as journal-writing and audio/video diaries, which are honest and reflective, aid the student here (Seabury 2002). Such a culture goes completely against

the 'trial-by-fire', which is the common divisive mode of the art school 'crit', a version of which can all too often be found in the secondary school art and design department (Mitchell 1996).

8. *Citizenship by example: negotiating rights, wrongs and responsibilities*
Throughout this chapter there have been references to the notion of the 'citizen' in the context of liberatory education. 'Citizen' is a deeply complex, contested and entirely ideological term, but Audrey Osler's 'cosmopolitan citizenship' (2008) is rooted in the premise of the co-existence of difference. This is far wider than any nation-state's definition. She states that cosmopolitan citizenship:

acknowledges our global interconnectedness, recognises our multiple and shifting identities and equips young people to contribute and to engage constructively with difference at local, national and international level, while at the same time acknowledging our humanity and human rights.

(p. 22)

The issue and the school subject Citizenship has quite rightly been a continuous site for political struggle in the UK and must be approached with care. It comes heavily loaded with a provocative government agenda. What is important here is to draw your attention to the ways in which liberatory education in art and design can draw on and engage with the school subject 'Citizenship'. However, as always, the devil is in the detail. While at first glance there may be much of use in the NC for Citizenship, and certainly much to debate with young people, the interpretation of this subject (as with any) will be crucially determined by the politics and values of the teachers involved.

For PLATFORM, the notion of the child as citizen is not related in any way to the needs of the state. It was enacted through working with young people as co-actors in a shared future. Co-actors work together, they envision together, but also pay attention to individual needs, difference and tensions. Perhaps art and design has a unique role to play here in that there is a fertile contradiction that can be put to use. The artist in the European Romantic tradition has been enduringly constructed as competitive, alone and misunderstood (Wolff 1981: 11), an identity which Black artist-collaborators Rodney and Piper ably deconstruct in the context of Higher Education:

In Britain's art schools, where the mythology of the individual is held at a premium, collaborative activity is discouraged. Apart from throwing a spanner into bureaucratic machinery geared to assess the virtuoso, collaborative activities begin to counter many of the negative effects of individualism which leaves the art student isolated and vulnerable.

(Piper & Rodney 1988: 113)

Although capitalist individualism is indeed the antithesis of a liberatory ethos, the contradiction is that it breeds a certain expectation (both positive and negative) of being responsible for your own fate. Therefore, to choose to learn to listen to others when everything in culture has celebrated ego and individual achievement is a major rebuttal. To choose to collaborate on liberatory projects becomes a doubly powerful message. It denies the exclusivity of yourself and your field – in this case, art and design (which has been predicated on exclusivity) – and upholds the power of what can be achieved by working collectively, negotiating in collaboration, dealing with difference and contending with each others' value systems.

In *Tides and Tributes* the children experienced themselves and adults (teachers, 'citizens', teaching assistants and artists) negotiating, organising and renegotiating with each other on issues that were immediate and important. This notion of 'citizenship' is inherently relational, levelling and interdisciplinary. It is all about borders, behaviours and negotiating notions of transgression. In the context of relational aesthetics (Bourriaud 2002), liberatory practices in contemporary art have a lot to offer to young people around the contested area of 'citizenship', as I hope I have demonstrated, not least in giving exemplars of how to work together on difficult issues.

Conclusion

To conclude, I return to the key issue outlined at the beginning of this chapter. As Moore puts it, 'What sort of people are being constructed via the curriculum, and what kind of society is envisioned in that construction?' (2006: 74). Curriculum, and especially a national curriculum, is a reflection of the kinds of citizens that the teacher, department, school or government of the day wishes to create. Strong curricular classification and belief in a subject's 'singularity' keeps subjects and issues insulated from each other (Bernstein 1996: 23). While keeping out the suspected chaos, conflict and risk, it also excludes connectivity, creativity, leaps in understanding and intellectual fertility. However, as mentioned previously, the National Curriculum for England (QCA 2007a) explicitly encourages looser and weaker subject classification and greater integration between subjects and issues. This is a major opportunity for teachers who wish to work on a holistic liberatory education with young people.

Although it may take time for aspects of teachers' self-censorship on content or method to wear off, the new opportunity endorses the riskiness of the liberatory practices that I have been arguing for in this chapter. Cross-curricular practices or themes either within art and design, or between it and other areas, can begin to be fostered anew, while making unthought-of connections and alliances.

It is my contention that the new National Curriculum for art and design can make a very particular contribution to the future capacity of young people as global citizens who are able to cross intellectual and actual borders, debate ethics, rights and responsibilities, and collaborate to make their world. By engaging with the growing movement of collaborative, liberatory art practices, the fierce debate around 'citizenship' and the new possibilities in art and design, you, alongside other teachers, can begin to recast yourself as a public intellectual, a teacher who doesn't 'deliver' but actively fosters liberatory learning (Giroux 1993). Art and design teachers themselves can begin to see themselves as co-actors, co-constructing knowledge with young people. These critical self-positionings are the prerequisite for working with young people as activated, creative cosmopolitan citizens. In the report '*The School I'd Like: Children and young people's reflections on education for the 21st century*', Burke and Grosvenor compile and analyse many fascinating submissions made by young people as a result of an open call distributed to primary and secondary schools (2003). I leave the last word with Lorna, 14: 'Psychology, Sociology, Politics and Philosophy, [art and design?] ... all have something in common that may be responsible for their neglect. They may all be perceived as 'dangerous' as they can incite people to think freely and originally, and possibly to challenge school's authority. A good system need not fear analysis and scrutiny' (Burke & Grosvenor 2003: 65, my insertion).

Bibliography

Abbs, P. (ed.) (1987) *Living Powers: the arts and education*, London: Falmer Press.

Abbs, P. (1989) 'The Pattern of Art Making', in P. Abbs (ed.) *The Symbolic Order*, London: Falmer Press.

Abbs, P. (1994) *The Educational Imperative: a defence of Socratic and Aesthetic Learning*, London: Falmer Press.

Addison, N. (2006) 'Acknowledging the gap between sex education and the lived experiences of young people: a discussion of Paula Rego's *The Pillowman* (2004) and other cautionary tales', *Sex Education*, 6(4): 351–365.

Addison, N. (2007) 'Critical Studies', in N. Addison and L. Burgess (eds) (2007) (second edition) *Learning to Teach Art and Design in the Secondary School: A companion to school experience*, London: Routledge.

Addison, N. and Burgess, L. (eds) (2003) *Issues in Art and Design Education*, London: RoutledgeFalmer.

Addison, N. and Burgess, L. (2005) 'The friendly interventionist: reflections on the relationship between critical practice and artist teachers in secondary schools', in D. Atkinson and P. Dash (eds) *Social and Critical Practices in Art Education*, Stoke on Trent: Trentham Books.

Addison, N. and Burgess, L. (2006) '"Critical Minds", the London Cluster Research Report', in *Inspiring Learning in Galleries*, London: Arts Council of England and Engage, 44–87.

Addison, N. and Burgess, L. (2007) (second edition) 'Learning' in N. Addison and L. Burgess (eds) *Learning to Teach Art and Design in the Secondary School: A companion to school experience*, London: Routledge.

Addison, N., Asbury, M., Chittenden, T., De Souza, P., Georgaki, M., Hulks, D., Papazafiriou, G., Perret, C. and Trowell, J. (2003) *ACHiS Synoptic Report*, London: Institute of Education, University of London.

Addison, N. and Dash, P. (2007) 'Towards a Plural Curriculum in Art and Design' in N. Addison and L. Burgess (eds) (second edition) *Learning to Teach Art and Design in the Secondary School: A companion to school experience*, London: Routledge.

Ades, D., Benton, T., Elliott, D. and Whyte, I. B. (1995) *Art and Power*, London: Thames and Hudson.

Adorno, T. (1997 [1970]) *Aesthetic Theory*, Minneapolis: University of Minnesota Press.

Aitkin, S. (1994) *Putting Children in their Place*, Washington DC: American Association of Geographers.

Allen, F. (2008) 'Situating Gallery Education', Online. Available at: <http://www.tate.org.uk/research/tateresearch/majorprojects/tate-encounters/edition-2/tateencounters2_felicity_allen.pdf> (accessed 26 November 2008).

Allison, B. (1972) *Art Education and Teaching about Arts of Africa, Asia and Latin America*, London: The Voluntary Committee for Overseas Aid and Development.

Althusser, L. (1971) 'Ideology and Ideological State Apparatuses', in *Lenin and Philosophy and other Essays*, London: New Left Books.

Anderson, D. (1997) *A Common Wealth: Museums & Learning in the UK*, London: Department of National Heritage.

Apple, M. W. (2004) (third edition) *Ideology and Curriculum*, London: Routledge.

Araeen, R. (2004) *Proposal for Deconstructions: Zero to Infinity*, London: Unpublished.

Araeen, R. (2005) Discussion with Artist teachers at 291 Gallery, Hackney, London.

Arieti, S. (1976) *Creativity: the magic synthesis*, New York: Basic Books.

Arnheim, R. (1962) 'Notes on Creativity' in *Picasso's Guernica: The Genesis of a Painting*, London: Faber and Faber.

Aronowitz, S. (1994) *Dead Artists Live Theories and other Cultural Problems*. New York: Routledge.

Arts Council England (2004) *Keys to Imagination: ICT in art education*, London: ACE.

Ash, A., Schofield, K. and Steers, J. (2007) 'Assessment and Examinations in Art and Design' in N. Addison and L. Burgess (eds) (second edition) *Learning to Teach Art and Design in the Secondary School: A companion to school experience*, London: Routledge.

Assessment Reform Group (ARG). Online. Available at: <http://www.assessment-reform-group.org/> (accessed 26 November 2008).

Atkinson, D. (2002) *Art in Education: Identity and Practice*. Dordrecht, Boston, London: Kluwer Academic Publishers.

Atkinson, D. (2005) 'Approaching the Future in School Art Education: Learning How to Swim' in D. Atkinson and P. Dash (eds) *Social and Critical Practices in Art Education*, Stoke on Trent: Trentham Books.

Atkinson, D. (2006) 'School Art Education: Mourning the Past and Opening a Future', *International Journal of Art and Design Education*, (25)1: 16–27.

Atkinson, D. (2008) 'Pedagogy Against the State', *International Journal of Art and Design Education*, 27(3): 226–240.

Averill, J. R. (2005) 'Emotions as Mediators and Products of Creative Activity', in J. Kaufman and J. Baer (eds) *Creativity Across Domains: Faces of the muse*, Mahwah, NJ: Erlbaum.

Bakhtin, M. M. (1984 [1941]) *Rabelais and His World*, Bloomington: Indiana University Press.

Balchin, T. (2006) 'Evaluating Creativity Through Creative-Thinking Techniques', in N. Jackson, M. Oliver, M. Shaw and J. Wisdom (eds) *Developing Creativity in Higher Education*, London: Routledge.

Ball, S. (2002) 'Better Read: Theorising the teacher', in J. Dillon and M. Maguire (eds) *Becoming a Teacher: Issues in secondary teaching*, Buckingham: Open University Press.

Ball, S. (2007) *Education PLC: Understanding private sector participation in public sector education*, London: Taylor and Francis.

Banaji, S., Burn, A. and Buckingham, D. (2006) *The Rhetorics of Creativity: A review of the literature*, London: The Arts Council of England.

Barkan, M. and Chapman, L. H. (1967) *Guidelines for Art Instruction through Television for the Elementary Schools*. Bloomington, IN: National Center for School and College Television.

Barnes, R. (1993) 'Getting the Act Together: It may be Cross-Curricular, but is it Really Art?' *International Journal of Art and Design Education*, 12(1): 61–72.

Barnes, J. (2007) *Cross-Curricular Learning 3–14*, London: Paul Chapman.

Bataille, G. (2006 [1957]) *Eroticism*, tr. M. Dalwood, London: Marion Boyars.

Baudrillard, J. (2005) *The Conspiracy of Art: Manifestos, texts, interviews*, S. Lotringer (ed.) London, Cambridge, MA: Semiotext.

Baynes, K. (1985) 'Defining a Design Dimension of the Curriculum', *Journal of Art and Design Education*, 4(3): 237–243.

Baynes, K. (2006) 'A design dimension of the curriculum', unpublished paper. Available at: <http://www.nsead.org/downloads/Design_Ed_Report_2006.doc> (accessed 16 June 2008).

Beech, D. (2008) 'Include me out! Dave Beech on participation in art', *Art Monthly*, April 2008, London: Britannia Art Publications Ltd.

Benjamin, W. (2003 [1934]) 'The Author as Producer', in *Understanding Brecht*, tr. A. Bostock, London: Verso.

Bennett, T. (1995) *The Birth Of the Museum*, London: Routledge.

Berger, J (1972) *Ways of Seeing*, London: Pelican.

Bernstein, B. (1996) *Pedagogy, Symbolic Control, and Identity: Theory, research, critique*, London: Taylor & Francis.

Best, D. (1985) *Feeling and Reason in the Arts*, London: George Allen and Unwin.

Beuys, J. (2006 [1973]) 'I am Searching for Field Character', in C. Bishop (ed.) *Participation: documents of contemporary art*, London and Cambridge, MA: Whitechapel and MIT Press.

Bishop, C. (ed.) (2006) *Participation: Documents of contemporary art*, London and Cambridge, MA: Whitechapel and MIT Press.

Boden, M. A. (2004) (second edition, revised and expanded) *The Creative Mind: Myths and mechanisms*, London: Routledge.

Bourriaud, N. (2002 [1998]) *Relational Aesthetics*, Dijon-Quetigny: Les Presses du Reel.

Bourdieu, P. (1984) *Distinction: A social critique of the judgement of taste*. London: Routledge and Kegan Paul Ltd.

Bourdieu, P. (1993) *The Field of Cultural Reproduction*, Cambridge: Polity.

Bourdieu, P. (1993a) 'The Market of Symbolic Goods' in *The Field of Cultural Reproduction*, Cambridge: Polity.

Bourdieu, P. (1993b) 'The Production of Belief' in *The Field of Cultural Reproduction*, Cambridge: Polity.

Bourdieu, P. (1993c) 'The Field of Power, Literary Field and Habitus', In *The Field of Cultural Reproduction*, Cambridge: Polity.

Bourdieu, P. (1990) *The Logic of Practice*, Cambridge: Polity Press.

Bourdieu, P. (1997 [1982]) *Pascalian Meditations*, Cambridge: Polity Press.

Bourdieu, P., Darbel, A. and Schnapper, D. (1991) *The Love of Art: European art museums and their public*, Cambridge: Polity.

Bourdieu, P. and Haacke, H. (1995) *Free Exchange*, Cambridge: Polity.

Bourdieu, P. and Wacquant, L. (1989) 'Towards a Reflexive Sociology: A Workshop with Pierre Bourdieu' *Sociological Review*, 7(1): 26–63.

Bourdieu, P. and Passeron, J. (1977) *Reproduction in Education, Society and Culture*, tr. R. Nice, London: Sage.

Bourdieu, P. and Wacquant, L. (2002) *An Invitation to Reflexive Sociology*, Cambridge: Polity Press.

Bruner, J. (1960) *The Process of Education*, New York: Vintage Books.

Bruner, J. (1996) *The Culture of Education*, Cambridge, MA: Harvard University Press.

Bryson, N. (1983) *Vision and Painting: The logic of the gaze*. New Haven, CT: Yale University Press.

Bryson, N. (1991) 'Semiology and Visual Interpretation', in N. Bryson, M. A. Holly and K. Moxey (eds) *Visual Theory*, Oxford: Polity Press.

Bryson, N. (1990) *Looking at the Overlooked: Four essays on still life painting*, London: Reaktion.

Buckingham, D. (2000) *The Making of Citizens*, London: Routledge.

Burbules, N. C. (2000) 'The Limits of Dialogue as a Critical Pedagogy', in P. Trifonas (ed.) *Revolutionary Pedagogies*, New York, London: Routledge.

Burgess, L (2003) 'Monsters in the Playground', in N. Addison and L. Burgess (eds) (2003) *Issues in Art and Design Education*, London: RoutledgeFalmer.

Burgess, L. (2007) 'Resource Based Learning', in N. Addison and L. Burgess (eds) (second edition) *Learning to Teach Art and Design in the Secondary School: A companion to school experience*, London: Routledge.

Burgess, L. and Gee, D. (2007) 'Curriculum Planning', in N. Addison and L. Burgess (eds) (second edition) *Learning to Teach Art and Design in the Secondary School: A companion to school experience*, London: Routledge.

Burgess, L. and Schofield, K. (2007) 'Issues in Craft and Design Education', in N. Addison and L. Burgess (eds) (2007) (second edition) *Learning to Teach Art and Design in the Secondary School: A companion to school experience*, London: Routledge.

Burgess, L. and Williamson, C. (2005) 'From Art and Design to Citizenship: The Role of Built Environment Education', in T. Brezlin and B. Dufour (eds) *Developing Citizens*, London: Hodder Murray.

Burke, C. and Grosvenor, I. (2003) *The School I'd Like: Children and young people's reflections on an education for the 21st century*, London: Routledge.

Butler, J. (1997) *The Psychic Life of Power*, Stanford, CA: Stanford University Press.

Cahan, S. and Kocur, Z. (eds) (1996) *Contemporary Art and Multicultural Education*, New York and London: Routledge.

Cameron, D. (2000) *Good to Talk?* London: Sage.

Carnell, E. and Lodge, C. (2002) *Supporting Effective Learning*, London: Paul Chapman Publishing.

Carroll, L. (1962 [1865]) *Alice's Adventures in Wonderland*, Harmondsworth: Penguin.

Chadwick, W. (1989) *Women, Art and Society*, London: Thames and Hudson.

Charman, H., Rose, K. and Wilson, G. (eds) (2006) *The Art Gallery Handbook: A resource for teachers*, London: Tate Publishing.

Chipp, H. B. (1968) *Theories of Modern Art*, Berkeley and Los Angeles, London: University of California Press.

Clark, T. J. (1999) *Farewell to an Idea: Episodes in a history of modernism*, New Haven, CT and London: Yale University Press.

Claxton, G. (1999) *Wise Up: The challenge of lifelong learning*, London: Bloomsbury.

Coldstream, W. (1960) *1st Report of the National Advisory Council on Art Education*, London: HMSO.

Collar, J. (2002) *Report of the Launch of the Feminist Theory and Research Website, Database and Register*, Liverpool: Institute for Feminist Theory and Research, University of Liverpool.

Cooke, B. and Kothari, U. (eds) (2001) *Participation: The new tyranny*, London: Zed Books.

Cowan, J. (2006) 'How Should I Assess Creativity', in N. Jackson, M. Oliver, M. Shaw and J. Wisdom (eds) *Developing Creativity in Higher Education*, London: Routledge.

Craft, A. (2006) 'Creativity in Schools', in N. Jackson, M. Oliver, M. Shaw and J. Wisdom (eds) *Developing Creativity in Higher Education*, London: Routledge.

Croce, B. (1901) *The aesthetic as the science of expression and of the linguistic in general*, tr. C. Lyas, Cambridge; New York: Cambridge University Press.

Cropley, A. J. (2001) *Creativity in Education and Learning: A guide for teachers and educators*, London: Kogan Page.

Crowther, P. (1993a) *Critical Aesthetics and Postmodernism*, Oxford: Clarendon Press.

Crowther, P. (1993b) *Art and Embodiment: From aesthetics to self-consciousness*, Oxford: Clarendon Press.

Csikszentmihalyi, M. (1996) *Creativity: Flow and the psychology of discovery and invention*, New York: Harper Perennial.

Cunliffe, L. (1999) 'Learning How to Learn: Art Education and the "Background"', *Journal of Art and Design Education*, 18(1): 115–121.

Cunliffe, L. (2005) 'Forms of Knowledge in Art Education and the Corollary of Authenticity in the Teaching and Assessment of Such Forms of Knowledge' *International Journal of Art and Design Education*, 24(2): 199–208.

Cunliffe, L (2008) 'A Case Study of an Extra-Curricular School Activity Designed to Promote Learning', *International Journal of Education Through Art*, 4(1): 91–105.

Dalton, P. (2001) *The Gendering of Art Education*, Buckingham: Open University Press.

Daniels, H. (ed.) (2005) (second edition) *An Introduction to Vygotsky*, London: Routledge.

Danto, A. (2000) 'Shirin Neshat', an interview in *Bomb*, 73: 60–7.

Dawtrey, L., Jackson, T., Masterson, M. and Meecham, P. (eds) (1996) *Critical Studies and Modern Art*, Milton Keynes: Open University Press.

DePalma, R. (2007) 'Civility, Complaint and Dialoguing with the Other', in M. Reiss, R. DePalma and E. Atkinson (eds) *Marginality and Difference in Education and Beyond*, Stoke on Trent: Trentham Books.

DCMS (1999) Policy Action Team 10. *Report on Social Exclusion*. Available at: <http://www.culture.gov.uk/reference_library/publications/4728.aspx> (accessed 26 November 2008).

DCMS (2005) *Understanding the Future: Museums and 21st century life*, London: DCMS.

DCMS (2008a) *Creative Industries.* Available at: <http://www.culture.gov.uk/3084. aspx> (accessed 12 June 2008).

DCMS (2008b) *Creative Britain New Talents for a New Economy – A strategy document for the creative industries.* Available at: <http://www.culture.gov.uk/Reference_library/ Publications/archive_2008/cepPub-new-talents.htm> (accessed 1 May 2008).

De Sausmarez, M. (1964) *Basic Design: The dynamics of visual form,* London: Studio Vista.

DES (2004) *A National Conversation about Personalised Learning.* Available at: <http://publications.teachernet.gov.uk/default.aspx?PageFunction=productd etails&PageMode=publications&ProductId=DfES+0919+2004> (accessed 26 November 2008).

Design Council (1980) *Design Education at Secondary Level,* London: Design Council.

Design Council (1987) *Design and Primary Education,* London: Design Council.

Design Council (2008) *Resources for Schools.* Available at: <http://www.designcouncil. org.uk/en/About-Design> (accessed 23 May 2008).

DCFS (2007) 'Community Cohesion' in *The Education and Inspections Act 2006.* Available at: <http://teachernet.gov.uk/wholeschool/Communitycohesion> (accessed 26 November 2008).

Dewey, J. (1915 s1899]) *The School and Society.* Chicago; London: University of Chicago Press.

Dewey, J. (1999 [1916]) *Democracy and Education,* New York: Free Press.

Dewey, J. (1980 [1934]) *Art as Experience,* New York: Perigree Books.

Dewulf, S. and Baillie, C. (1999) *How to Foster Creativity,* London: DfEE.

DFE (1991) *National Curriculum Art Order,* London: HMSO.

DfEE (1999) *National Curriculum Order for Art and Design,* London: HMSO.

DfES (2003) *Raising Standards and Tackling Workload: A national agreement,* London: DfES.

DfES (2006) *2020 Vision – Report of the Teaching and Learning in 2020 Review Group,* London: DfES.

DfES (2007) *Diversity and Citizenship: Curriculum Review.* Available at: <http:// publications.teachernet.gov.uk/eOrderingDownload/DfES_Diversity_&_ Citizenship.pdf> (accessed 26 November 2008).

Domasio, A. R. (1994) *Descartes' Error: Emotion, reason and the human brain,* New York: Putnam.

Downing, D. and Watson, R. (2004) *School Art, What's in it? Exploring visual art in secondary schools,* Slough: NFER.

Duncan, C. (1995) *Civilizing Rituals: Inside public art museums,* London: Routledge.

Duncum, P. (2005) 'Popular Visual Culture and Ten Kinds of Integration', in M. Stockrocki (ed.) *Interdisciplinary Art Education: Building bridges to connect disciplines and cultures,* Reston, VA: National Art Education Association.

Eagleton, T. (1983) *Literary Theory,* Oxford: Blackwell.

Eco, U. (2006 [1962]) 'The Poetics of the Open Work', in C. Bishop (ed.) *Participation,* London and Cambridge, MA: Whitechapel and MIT Press.

Efland, A. (1990) 'Art Education in the Twentieth Century', in D. Soucy and M. A. Stankiewicz (eds) *Framing the Past: Essays on art education,* Reston, VA: The Natrional Art Education Association.

Efland, A., Freedman, K. and Stuhr, P. (eds) (1996) *Postmodern Art Education: An approach to curriculum*, Reston, VA: The National Art Education Association.

Egan, K. (1992) *Imagination in Teaching and Learning*, London: Routledge.

Ehrenzweig, A. (1967) *The Hidden Order of Art*, London: Weidenfeld and Nicolson.

Eisner, E. (1968) *A Comparison of the Developmental Drawing Characteristics of Culturally Advantaged and Culturally Disadvantaged Children*, Washington: ERIC.

Eisner, E. (1972) *Educating Artistic Vision*, New York: Macmillan.

Eisner, E. (1985) *The Art of Educational Evaluation*, London and Philadelphia: Falmer Press.

Eisner, E. (1998) *The Kind of Schools We Need: Personal essays*, Portsmouth, NH: Heinemann.

Elkins, J. (2000) *What Painting Is*, New York, London: Routledge.

Ellsworth, E. (1997) *Teaching Positions: Difference, pedagogy, and the power of address*, New York: Teachers College Press.

Ellsworth, E. (1989) 'Why Doesn't this Feel Empowering? Working Through the Repressive Myths of Critical Pedagogy', *Harvard Educational Review* 59(3): 297–324.

Engage (2003) *The 'Get It Together' programme: 'A very different energy'*, London: Engage.

Enwezor, O. (curator) (2002) Dokumenta 11 [exhibition]. Kassel, Germany.

Falk, J. and Dierking, L. (2004) *The Museum Experience*, Washington DC: Whalesback Books.

Feldhusen, J. F. and Treffinger, D. J. (1980) *Creative Thinking and Problem Solving in Gifted Education*, Dubuque, IA: Kendall/Hunt.

Felshin, N. (ed.) (1995) *But is it Art? The Spirit of Art as Activism*, Seattle: Bay Press.

Fernie, E. (1995) *Art History and its Methods*. London: Phaidon.

Field, D. (1970) *Change in Art Education*. New York: Routledge, and Kegan Paul and Humanities Press.

Field, M. and Stow, D. (2002) 'Transforming Teaching and Learning Through Assessment', in C. Haynes (ed.) *Innovations in Interdisciplinary Teaching*, Westport, CT: American Council on Education/Oryx Press.

Fiske, J. (1989) *Understanding Popular Culture*, London: Routledge.

Foucault, M. (1977) *Discipline and Punish*, tr. A. Sheridan, New York: Vintage.

Franks, A. (2003) 'The Role of Language Within a Multimodal Curriculum', in N. Addison and L. Burgess (eds) *Issues in Art and Design Teaching*, London: RoutledgeFalmer.

Frayling, C. (2008) 'Then and Now', *A'N'D*, (29):9–10, Corsham: NSEAD.

Freedman, K. (2003) 'Recent Shifts in US Art Education' in N. Addison and L. Burgess (eds) *Issues in Art and Design Teaching*, London: RoutledgeFalmer.

Freire, P. (1985) *The Politics of Education: Culture, power and liberation*, tr. D. Macad, Boston: Bergin and Garvey.

Freire, P. (1972 [1968]) *Pedagogy of the Oppressed*, London: Penguin.

Freire, P. (1990 [1968]) *Pedagogy of the Oppressed*, New York: Continuum.

Freire, P. and Faundez, A. (1989) *Learning to Question. A Pedagogy of Liberation*, New York: Continuum.

Freire, P. and Macedo, D. (1999) 'Pedagogy, Culture, Language and Race: A dialogue', in J. Leach and B. Moon, (eds) *Learners and Pedagogy*, Milton Keynes: Open University Press.

Fry, R. (1909) 'An Essay in Aesthetics', in F. Frascina and C. Harrison (eds) (1982) *Art and Modernism*, London: Paul Chapman in association with the Open University.

Fry, R. (1920) 'Retrospect' From *Vision and Design* (1957) reproduced in E. Fernie, (1995) *Art History and its Methods*, London: Phaidon.

Fukuyama, F. (1989) *The End of History?* Washington: Irving Kristol.

Gablik, S. (1995) *Conversations Before the End of Time: Dialogues on art, life and spiritual renewal*, London and New York: Thames & Hudson.

Gardner, H. (1993) *Frames of Mind: The theory of multiple intelligences*, New York: Basic Books.

Gardner, H. (1999) *Intelligence Reframed: Multiple intelligences for the 21st century*, New York: Basic Books.

Gardner, J. (ed.) (2006) *Assessment and Learning*, London: Sage.

Georgaki, M. (2000) *'Can an understanding of art, craft and design as spheres of cultural production enable a more critical approach to the evaluation of studio practice?'*, Unpublished research report, London: ACHiS, Institute of Education, University of London.

Gergen, K. (1985) 'The Social Constructivist Movement in Social Psychology', *American Psychology* 40(3): 266–275.

Getz, I. and Lubart, T. I. (2000) 'An Emotional-Experiential Perspective on Creative Symbolic-Metaphorical Processes', *Consciousness and Emotion* (1): 282–312.

Gilbert, C. (2006) *2020 Vision: Report of the Teaching and Learning in 2020 Review Group*. Available at: <http://publications.teachernet.gov.uk/eOrderingDownload/6856-DfES-Teaching%20and%20Learning.pdf> (accessed 26 November 2008).

Gingell, J. (2006) 'The Visual Arts and Education', *IMPACT 13*, London: The Philosophy of Education Society of Great Britain.

Giroux, H. (1992) *Border Crossings: Cultural workers and the politics of education*, New York, London: Routledge.

Giroux, H. (1995) *Living Dangerously: Multiculturalism and the politics of difference*, New York: Peter Lang Publishing.

Giroux, H. (1997a) *Channel Surfing: Racism, the media and the destruction of today's youth*, New York: St. Martin's Griffin.

Giroux, H. (1997b) *Pedagogy and the Politics of Hope: Theory, culture and schooling*, Oxford: West View Press.

Giroux, H. (2005) (second edition) *Border Crossings: Cultural workers and the politics of education*, London: Routledge.

Giroux, H. and Mclaren, P. (eds) (1994) *Between Borders: Pedagogy and the politics of cultural studies*, New York: Routledge.

Goleman, D. (1996) *Emotional Intelligence: Why it can matter more than IQ*, London: Bloomsbury.

Goodman, N. (1984) *Of Mind and Other Matters*, Cambridge, MA and London: Harvard University Press.

Graham, D. and Tytler, D. (1993) *A Lesson for Us All: The making of the national curriculum*, London: Routledge.

Greco, M. and Stenner, P. (eds) (2008) *Emotions: A social science reader*, London: Routledge.

Greene, M. (1970) 'Imagination', in Smith. R. A. (ed.) *Aesthetic Concepts in Education*, Urbana, Chicago, London: University of Illinois Press.

Greene, M. (1995). *Releasing the Imagination: Essays on education, the arts, and social change*, San Francisco: Jossey-Bass Publishers.

Greene, M. (2001) *Variations on a Blue Guitar*, New York: Lincoln Center Institute.

Green, P. (1974) *Design Education: Problem solving and visual experience*, London: Batsford Ltd.

Gretton, T. (2003) 'Loaded Canons', in N. Addison and L. Burgess (eds) *Issues in Art and Design Teaching*, London: RoutledgeFalmer.

Gupta, S. (ed.) (1993) *Disrupted Borders: An intervention in definitions and boundaries*, London: Rivers Oram Press.

Hall, S. (1988) *The Hard Road to Renewal*, London: Verso.

Hall, S. (1997) *Representation*, London: Sage (in association with the Open University).

Hapgood, S. (1994) *Neo Dada*, New York: The American Federation of the Arts.

Harding, A. (2005) *Magic Moments: Collaboration between artists and young people*, London: Black Dog Publishing.

Hardy, T. (2003) 'The Trouble with Ruskin ...', *International Journal of Art and Design Education*, 22(3): 335–341.

Hargreaves, D. H. (1983) 'The Teaching of Art and the Art of Teaching: Towards an Alternative View of Aesthetic Learning', in M. Hammersly and A. Hargreaves (eds) *Curriculum Practice: Some sociological case studies*, London: Falmer.

Harrison, C. and Wood, P. (1992) *Art in Theory 1900–1990: An anthology of changing ideas*, Oxford: Blackwell.

Hebdidge, D. (1988) *Hiding in the Light*, London: Routledge.

Hein, G. (2001) 'The Museum and How People Learn', paper given at CECA (International Committee of Museum Educators), 15 October, Jerusalem.

Hickman, R. (ed.) (2005) *Critical Studies in Art and Design Education*, Bristol: Intellect.

HMI (2006) '*Emerging Good Practice in Promoting Creativity*'. Available at: <http://www.hmie.gov.uk/documents/publication/Emerging%20Good%20practice%20in%20Promoting%20Creativity.pdf> (accessed 26 November 2008).

Holdsworth, B. (2005) 'Marion Richardson', in M. Romans (ed.) *Histories of Art and Design Education: Collected essays*, Bristol: Intellect.

Holland, D., Lachicotte, W., Skinner, D. and Cain, C. (1998) *Identity and Agency in Cultural Worlds*, Cambridge, MA and London: Harvard University Press.

Holt, J. (1996) 'Art for Art's Sake', in L. Dawtrey, T. Jackson, M. Masterson and P. Meecham (eds) *Critical Studies and Modern Art*. Milton Keynes: Open University Press.

hooks, b. (1994) *Teaching to Transgress*. New York and London: Routledge.

hooks, b. (2003) *Teaching Community: A pedagogy of hope*, New York and London: Routledge.

Hooper-Greenhill, E. (2007) *Museums and Education: Purpose, pedagogy, performance*, London: Routledge.

Hughes, A. (1989) 'The Copy, the Parody and the Pastiche: Observations on Practical Approaches to Critical Studies', in D. Thistlewood (ed.) *Critical Studies in Art and Design Education*, Harlow: Longman.

Hughes, A. (1998) 'Reconceptualising the Art Curriculum', *Journal of Art and Design Education*, 17(1): 41–49.

Hughes, A. (1999), 'Art and Intention in Schools: Towards a New Paradigm', *Journal of Art and Design Education*, 18(1): 129–134.

Hulks, D. (2003) 'Measuring Artistic Performance: The Assessment Debate and Art Education', in N. Addison and L. Burgess (eds) *Issues in Art and Design Teaching*, London: RoutledgeFalmer.

Hutchinson, F. P. (1996) *Educating Beyond Violent Futures*, London: Routledge.

ICOM (International Council of Museums). Available at: <http://icom.museum/mission.html> (accessed 26 November 2008).

Illich, I. (1971) *Deschooling Society*, London: Penguin.

JanMohammed, A. R. (1994) 'Some Implications of Paulo Freire's Border Pedagogy', in H. Giroux, and P. Mclaren (eds) (1994) *Between Borders: Pedagogy and the politics of cultural studies*. New York: Routledge.

Jones, A. (ed.) (2003) *A Companion to Contemporary Art since 1945*, Oxford: Blackwell.

Jones, A. (2006) *Self/Image: Technology, representation and the contemporary subject*, London: Routledge.

Kanpol, B. (1994) *Critical Pedagogy: An introduction*, Westport, CT and London: Bergin & Garvey.

Kearney, R. (1998) (second edition) *Poetics of Imagining: Modern to postmodern*, Edinburgh: Edinburgh University Press.

Kester, G. (2004) *Conversation Pieces: Community and communication in modern art*, Berkley, Los Angeles, London: University of California Press.

Koestler, A. (1965) *The Act of Creation*, London: Hutchinson.

Lackey, L. (2005) 'Elementary Classroom Teachers, Arts Integration, and Socially Progressive Criteria', in M. Stokrocki (ed.) *Interdisciplinary Art Education: Building bridges to connect disciplines and cultures*, Reston, VA: NAEA.

Lacy, S. (ed.) (1995) *Mapping the Terrain: new public genre art*, Seattle: Bay Press.

Lambert, D. (2003) 'A Burden on the Memory or a Light in the Mind?' *Teaching Geography* 28(1): 4.

Lambert, D. and Balderstone, D. (2000) *Learning to Teach Geography*, London: RoutledgeFalmer.

Lave, J. and Wenger, E. (1991) *Situated Learning: Legitimate peripheral participation*, Cambridge: Cambridge University Press.

Ledda (2007). '*Personalised Politics: How "personalisation" devalues education and diminishes citizenship*'. Available at: <http://www.culturewars.org.uk/2007-06/personalised.htm> (accessed 26 November 2008).

Leppert, R. (1996) *Art and the Committed Eye: The cultural functions of images*, Boulder, CO and Oxford: Westview Press.

Livingstone, J. and Ploof, J. (eds) (2007) *The Object of Labour: Art, cloth, and cultural production*, Cambridge, MA: MIT Press.

Lindstrom, L. (2006) 'Creativity: What is it? Can you assess it? Can it be taught?', *International Journal of Art & Design Education*, (25)1, pp.53–56.

Lippard, L. (1997) *The Lure of the Local: Sense of place in a multi-centred society*, New York: The New Press.

Lowenfeld, V. (1947) *Creative and Mental Growth*, New York: Macmillan Co.

Lukács, G. (1971) *History and Class Consciousness: Studies in Marxist dialectics*, tr. R. Livingstone, London: Merlin Press.

Lynton, N. (1992) 'Harry Thubron: Teacher and Artist', in D. Thistlewood (ed) *Histories of Art and Design Education*, Harlow: Longman.

Macdonald, S. (1970) *The History and Philosophy of Art Education*, London: University of London Press.

Manzella, D. (1963) *Educationists and the Evisceration of the Visual Arts*, Scranton, PA: International Textbook Co.

Marx, K (1975) *Early Writings [of] Karl Marx*, Introduced by Lucio Colletti, tr. R. Livingstone and G. Benton, Harmondsworth: Penguin; New Left Review.

Maslow, A. H. (1962/3) 'The Creative Attitiude', San Jose, CA: Psycosynthesis Distribution. (Reprinted from *The Structurist* 3 (1963). Saskatchewan: University of Saskatchewan, 8th National Assembly of the Canadian Society for Education Through Art.)

Maslow, A. H. (1968) *Towards a Psychology of Being*, New York: Basic Books.

Mason, R. (1995) (second edition) *Art Education and Multiculturalism*, Corsham: NSEAD.

Mason, R. (2005) 'Meaning and Value of Home-Based Craft', *International Journal of Art and Design Education*, 24(3): 256–268.

Mason, R. and Iwano, M. (1995) *National Survey of Art and Design & Technology Curricula and Courses at Key Stages 3 and 4 in England and Wales*, London: University of Surrey, Roehampton.

Mason, R. and Steers, J. (2006) 'The Impact of Formal Assessment Procedures on Teaching and Learning in Art and Design in Secondary Schools', *International Journal of Art and Design Education*, 25(2): 119–133.

Matuga, J. (after 1994) 'New Pictures of the Art Room: Peer Interactions and Artistic Development', Indiana University School of Education. Available at: <http://web-pages.charter.net/schmolze1/vygotsky/> (accessed 26 November 2008).

Matthews, D. (2003) (second edition) *Drawing and Painting: Children and visual representation*. London: Paul Chapman.

Mayo, P. (2002) 'The Binds That Tie: Civility and Social Difference', *Educational Theory* 52, pp. 169–186.

McKay, G. (1996) *Senseless Acts of Beauty: Cultures of resistance since the 1960s*, London: Verso.

McNiff, J. and Whitehead, J. (2002) *Action Research: Principles and practice*, London: Routledge.

McRobbie, A. (1994) *Postmodernism and Popular Culture*, London: Routledge.

Meecham, P. and Sheldon, J. (2000) *A Critical Introduction to Modern Art*, London: Routledge.

Merleau-Ponty, M. (1964) 'Cezanne's Doubt', in *Sense and Non-Sense*, tr. P.A. Dreyfus, Evanston, IL: Northwestern University Press.

Merleau-Ponty, M. (1974 [1945]) *The Phenomenology of Perception*, tr. C. Smith, London: Routledge and Kegan Paul.

Mercer, K. (1999) 'Ethnicity and Internationality: New British Art and Diaspora-Based Blackness', *Third Text*, 49(winter): 51–62.

Mercer, N. (2002) 'Developing Dialogues', in G. Wells and G. Claxton (eds) *Learning For Life in the 21st Century: Sociocultural perspectives on the future of education*, Oxford: Blackwell.

Miliband, D. (2004) *Personalised Learning.* Available at: <http://www.standards.dfes.gov.uk/personalisedlearning/> (accessed 26 November 2008).

Miller, J. H. (1992) *Illustration*, Cambridge, MA: Harvard University Press.

Mitchell, S. E. (1996) 'Institutions, Individuals and Talk: The construction of identity in fine art', in *Journal of Art and Design Education*, 15(2): 143–154.

Mirzoeff, N. (ed.) (2002) (second edition) *The Visual Culture Reader*, New York, London: Routledge.

MLA (2001) (the then council for Museums, Archives and Libraries) *Renaissance in the Regions: A new vision for England's museums.* Available at: <www.mla.gov.uk/website/programmes/renaissance/ren_report> (accessed 26 November 2008).

Montessori, M. (1964 [1909]) *The Montessori Method*, New York: Schocken.

Moore, A. (1996) 'Responding to Bilingual Pupils in the Art Classroom', *Journal of Art and Design Education*, 15(2): 179–188.

Moore, A. (2004) *The Good Teacher: Dominant discourses in teaching and teacher education*, London: RoutledgeFalmer.

Moore, A. (ed.) (2006) *Schooling, Society and Curriculum*, London: Routledge.

Moss, G. (2005) *Literacy and Gender*, London: Routledge.

muf (2001) *This is What we Do: A muf manual*, London: Batsford.

NACCCE (1999) *All Our Futures: Creativity, culture and education*, a report from the National Advisory Committee on Creative and Cultural Education, London: DfEE.

National Advisory Committee on Creative and Cultural Education (NACCCE) (1999) *All Our Futures: Creativity, Culture and Education*, London: Department for Education and Employment (DfEE).

National Curriculum Online, '*Supporting Guidance on Assessment for Art and Design*'. Available at: <http://curriculum.qca.org.uk/key-stages-3-and-4/subjects/art-and-design/Supporting_guidance_on_assessment_for_art_and_design.aspx> (accessed 26 November 2008).

NCEE (2006) '*Tough Choices or Tough Times*'. Available at: <www.skillscommission.org/request_copy.htm> (accessed 26 November 2008).

Neitzsche, F. ([1872/86] 1999) *The Birth of Tragedy*, Cambridge: Cambridge University Press.

Ng, A. K. (2003) 'A Cultural Model of Creative and Conforming Behaviour', *Creativity Research Journal*, 15 (2&3): 393–430.

Nochlin, L. (1971) 'Why Have There Been No Great Women Artists?', *ARTnews*, 69(9): 22–39.

Noon, M. and Blyton, P. (1997) 'Emotion Work', in *The Realities of Work*, London: Macmillan.

Notes from Nowhere (eds) (2003) *We are Everywhere: The irresistible rise of global anti-capitalism*, London: Verso.

Ofsted (2004) *Ofsted Subject Reports 2002/03: Art and design in secondary schools*, London: TSO.

Ofsted (2005a) *The Annual Report of Her Majesty's Chief Inspector of Schools 2004/05*, London: TSO.

Ofsted (2005b) '*Ofsted Subject Reports 2003/04: Art & design in secondary schools*'. Available at: <http://live.ofsted.gov.uk/publications/annualreport0304/> (accessed 26 November 2008).

Osler, A. (2008) 'Citizenship Education and the Ajegbo Report: Re-imagining a

Cosmopolitan Nation', in J. Annette, H. Starkey and D. Kirwan (eds) *London Review of Education*, Special Issue: Education for Democratic Citizenship: diversity and national identity, 6(1): 11–25.

Paley, N. (1994) *Finding Art's Place*, London and New York: Routledge.

Papanek, V. (1994) *The Green Imperative*, London: Thames and Hudson.

Parker, R. and Pollock, G. (1981) *Old Mistresses*, London: Pandora.

Perry, L. (1987) 'The Educational Value of Creativity', *Journal of Art & Design Education*, (6)3: 285–296.

Pestalozzi, J. H. (1977 [1801]) *How Gertrude Teaches Her Children*, D. N. Robinson (ed.) Washington: University Publications of America.

Pevsner, N. (1940) *Academies of Art, Past and Present*. Edition (1973) New York: Da Capo Press.

Pijnappel, J. (ed.) (1994) *Art and Technology*. London: Academy Group Limited.

Piper, A. (2006 [1985]) *Notes on Funk, I–II*, in C. Bishop (ed.) *Participation*, London and Cambridge, MA: Whitechapel and MIT Press.

Piper, K. and Rodney D. (1988) 'Theory and Practice', in K. Owusu (ed.) *Storms of the Heart: An anthology of black arts and culture*, London: Camden.

Plowden, B. (1967) *The Plowden Report*. Available at: <http://www.dg.dial.pipex.com/documents/plowden.shtml>

Polanyi, M. (1966) *The Tacit Dimension*, New York: Doubleday & Co.

Pope, R. (2005) *Creativity: Theory, history, practice*, London, New York: Routledge.

Prentice, R. (1995) 'Learning to Teach: A Conversational Exchange' in R. Prentice (ed.) *Teaching Art and Design: Addressing Issues and Identifying Directions*, London: Cassell.

Prentice, R. (2007a) 'Making Connections Between Subject Knowledge and Pedagogy: The Role of Workshops' in N. Addison and L. Burgess (eds) (2007) (second edition) *Learning to Teach Art and Design in the Secondary School: A companion to school experience*, London: Routledge.

Prentice, R. (2007b) in conversation with author, Crete.

Putnam, J. (2001) *Art and Artifact: The museum as medium*, London: Thames & Hudson.

Puwar, N. (2004) *Space Invaders, Race, Gender, and Bodies Out of Place*, Oxford: Berg.

QCA (2004) *Assessment for Learning Guidance*. Available at: <www.qca.org.uk/qca_4334.aspx> (accessed 26 November 2008).

QCA (2007a) *National Curriculum*. Available at: <http://curriculum.qca.org.uk/key-stages-3-and-4> (accessed 15 June 2008).

QCA (2007b) *National Curriculum: Creativity and critical thinking*. Available at: <http://curriculum.qca.org.uk/key-stages-3-and-4/cross-curriculum-dimensions/creativitycriticalthinking/index.aspx?return=/key-stages-3-and-4/cross-curriculum-dimensions/index.aspx> (accessed 13 October 2008).

QCA (2007c) *Art and Design Key Stage 3*. Available at: <http://curriculum.qca.org.uk/key-stages-3-and-4/subjects/art-and-design/index.aspx?return=/key-stages-3-and-4/subjects/index.aspx> (accessed 13 October 2008).

QCA (2007d) *Design and Technology Key Stage 3*. Available at: <http://curriculum.qca.org.uk/key-stages-3-and-4/subjects/design-and-technology/index.aspx> (accessed 13 October 2008).

QCA (2007e) 'Art and Design, Personal Development and Every Child Matters'.

Available at: <http://curriculum.qca.org.uk/key-stages-3-and-4/subjects/art-and-design/art_and_design_personal_development_and_every_child_matters.aspx> (accessed 26 November 2008).

QCA (2008) 'Personal Learning and Thinking Skills'. Available at: <http://curriculum. qca.org.uk/key-stages-3-and-4/skills/plts/index.aspx> (accessed 26 November 2008).

Rayment, T. (ed.) (2007) *The Problem of Assessment*, Bristol: Intellect Books with NSEAD.

Read, H. (1989 [1935]) *The Green Child* (G. Greene Introduction), London: Robin Clark.

Read, H. (1937) *Art and Society*, London: Faber and Faber.

Read, H. (1943) *Education Through Art*, London: Faber and Faber.

Read, H. (1950) *Education for Peace*, London: Routledge and Keegan.

Reay, D. (2007) 'Unruly Places: Inner City Comprehensives, Middle Class Imaginaries and Working Class Children', *Urban Sudies* 44(7): 1191–1203.

Richardson, M. (1948) *Art and the Child*, London: University of London Press.

Roberts, P. (2006) *Nurturing Creativity in Young People*, London: Department of Culture, Media and Sport. Available at: <http://www.idea.gov.uk/idk/ aio/5720952> (accessed 23 May 2008).

Robinson, K. (ed.) (1982) *The Arts in Schools: Principles, practice and provision*, London: Calouste Gulbenkien Foundation.

Rogoff, I. (2000) *Terra Infirma: Geography's visual culture*, London: Routledge.

Romans, M. (ed.) *Histories of Art and Design Education: Collected essays*, Bristol: Intellect.

Ross, M. (1978) *The Creative Arts*, London: Heinemann.

Ross, M. (1984) *The Aesthetic Impulse*, London: Pergamon Press.

Rousseau, J. J. (1979 [1762]) *Emile*, tr. A. Bloom, Harmondsworth: Penguin.

Ruskin, J. (1857) (second edition) *The Elements of Drawing*, London: Smith, Elder, & Co.

Ruskin, J. (1903 [1849]) (Reprint of the 1880 edition) *The Seven Lamps of Architecture*, London: George Allen.

SCAA (1997) *Survey and Analysis of Published Resources for Art (5–19)*, London: SCAA.

Schachter, S. (1971) *Emotion, Obesity and Crime*. New York: Academic Press.

Schon, D. (1987) *Educating the Reflective Practitioner*, San Francisco: Jossey Bass.

Scruton, R. (1999) 'What Ever Happened to Reason?' *City Journal*. Available at: <http://www.city-journal.org/html/9_2_urbanities_what_ever.html> (accessed 13 October 2008).

Seabury, M. B. (2002) 'Writing in Interdisciplinary Courses. Coaching Integrative Thinking', in C. Haynes (ed.) *Innovations in Interdisciplinary Teaching*, Westport, CT: American Council on Education/Oryx Press.

Sennet, R. (2008) *The Craftsman*, London: Allen Lane.

Shohat, E. and Stam, R. (1995) 'The Politics of Multiculturalism in the Postmodern Age', edition: Art and Cultural Difference: Hybrids and clusters. *Art & Design*, London: Academy Group Ltd.

Simonton, D. (2005) 'Creativity', *New Scientist*, 29 October (Online). Available at URL: http://www.illumine.co.uk/blog/?p=297&preview=true (accessed 14 August 2009).

Skeggs, B. (2004) *Class, Self, Culture*, London: Routledge.

Skillset (2008) *The Diploma in Creative and Media*. Available at: <http://www.skillset.org/qualifications/diploma/> (accessed 15 June 2008).

Skinner, B. (1953) *Science and Human Behaviour*, New York: Macmillan.

Smith, D. G. (1999) *Interdisciplinary Essays in the Pedagon: Human Sciences, Pedagogy and Culture*, Counterpoints 15, New York: Peter Lang.

Smith, R. (ed) (1970) *Aesthetic Concepts and Education*, Chicago and London: University of Illinois Press.

Solomon-Godeau, A. (1997) *Male Trouble: A crisis in representation*, London: Thames and Hudson.

Spivak, G. (1988) 'Subaltern Studies: Deconstructing Historiography', in R. Guha and G. Spivak (eds) *Selected Subaltern Studies*, Oxford: Oxford University Press.

Stallabrass, J. (2006) *High Art Lite: The rise and fall of young British art*, London: Verso.

Steers, J. (2003) 'Art and Design in the UK: The Theory Gap', in N. Addison and L. Burgess (eds) *Issues in Art and Design Teaching*, London: RoutledgeFalmer.

Steiner, R. (1904) *Theosophy: An introduction to the supersensible knowledge of the world and the destination of man*, London: Rudolph Steiner Press.

Swafield, S. (2008) *Unlocking Assessment: Understanding for reflection and application*, London: Routledge.

Swift, J. (1992) 'Marion Richardson's Contribution to Art Teaching', in D. Thistlewood (ed.) *Histories of Art and Design Education*, Harlow: Longman.

Swift, J. (1995) 'Controlling The Masses: The Reinvention of a 'National' Curriculum', *Journal of Art and Design Education*, 14(2): 115–127.

Swift, J. and Steers, J. (1999), 'A Manifesto for Art in Schools', *Journal of Art and Design Education*, 18(1): 7–13.

Taylor, B. (ed.) (2006) *Inspiring Learning in Galleries*, London: Arts Council England and Engage.

Taylor, B. and van der Will, W. (eds) (1990) *The Nazification of Art: Art, design, music, architecture and film in the Third Reich*, Winchester: Winchester Press.

Taylor, R. (1986) *Educating for Art*, Harlow: Longman.

Taylor Webb, P. (2001) 'Reflection and Reflective Teaching: Ways to Improve Pedagogy or Ways to Remain Racist?', *Race, Ethnicity and Education* 4(3): 245–252.

Thistlewood, D. (1984) *Herbert Read: Formlessness and Form*, London: Routledge and Kegan Paul.

Thistlewood, D. (1988) 'The Early History of the NSEAD: the *Society of Art Masters* (1888–1909) and the *National Society of Art Masters* (1909–1944)', *Journal of Art and Design Education* 7(1): 37–64.

Thistlewood, D. (1989) *Critical Studies in Art and Design Education*, Harlow: Longman.

Thistlewood, D. (1992a) *Histories of Art and Design Education*, Harlow: Longman.

Thistlewood, D. (1992b) 'A Continuing Process: The New Creativity in British Art Education', in D. Thistlewood (ed.) *Histories of Art and Design Education*, Harlow: Longman.

Thistlewood, D. (1992c) 'The Formation of the NSEAD: A Dialectical Advance for British Art and Design Education', in D. Thistlewood (ed.) *Histories of Art and Design Education*, Harlow: Longman.

Thompson, D. W. (1992 [1917]) *On Growth and Form*, New York: Dover (reprint of 1942 second edition).

Torrance, E. (1970) 'Stimulating creativity', in Vernon, P. (ed) *Creativity*, Harmondsworth: Penguin.

Torrance, E. P and Myers, R. E. (1974) *Creative Learning and Teaching*, New York: Dodd, Mead and Company.

Torrance, E. P. (1981) 'Creative Teaching Makes a Difference', in J. C. Gowan, J. Khatena and E. P. Torrance (eds) (second edition) *Creativity: Its educational implications*, Dubuque, IA: Kendall/Hunt.

Townsend, J. H. (1993) 'The Materials of J.M.W. Turner: Pigments', *Studies in Conservation* 38(4): 231–254.

Trapese Collective (eds) (2007) *Do It Yourself: A handbook for changing our world*, London: Pluto.

Vasari, (1987 [1568 second edition]) 'Michelangelo Buonarotti of Florence, Painter, Sculptor and Architect (1475–1564)' in *Lives of the Artists*, tr. G. Bull, London: Penguin. Available at: <http://employees.oneonta.edu/farberas/arth/Arth213/michelangelo_vasari.html> (accessed 25 November 2008).

Vygotsky, L. (1978a [1935]). *Mind and Society: The development of higher psychological processes*, Cambridge, MA and London: Harvard University Press.

Vygotsky, L. (1978b [1935]) 'Interaction between Learning and Development', in *Mind and Society*, Cambridge MA and London: Harvard University Press.

Vygotsky, L. (1994 [1931]) 'Imagination and Creativity of the Adolescent', in R. Van der Veer and J. Valsiner (eds), *The Vygotsky Reader*, Oxford: Blackwell.

Vygotsky, L. (2004) 'Imagination and Creativity in Childhood', *Journal of Russian and East European Psychology* 42(1): 7–97.

Vygotsky, L. and Luria, A. R. (1994) 'Tool and Symbol in Child Development', in R. Van der Veer and J. Valsiner (eds.) *The Vygotsky Reader*, Oxford: Blackwell.

Wacquant, L. (2004) 'Following Bourdieu into the Field', *Ethnography* 5(4): 387–414.

Walker, J. (2003) *Learning to Paint: A British art student and art school, 1956–61*, London: Institute of Artology.

Warnock, M. (1976) *Imagination*, London: Faber and Faber.

Watkins, C. (2005a) 'Classrooms as Learning Communities: A Review of Literature', *London Review of Education* 3(1): 47–64.

Watkins, C. (2005b) *Classrooms as Learning Communities: What's in it for schools?*, London: Routledge.

Weintraub, L. (1996) *Art on the Edge and Over*, New York: Art Insights, Inc.

Wenger, E. (1990) *'Towards a Theory of Cultural Transparency: Elements of a social discourse of the visible and invisible'*. Available at: <www.ewenger.com/pub/pubdissertationdownload.htm> (accessed 21 November 2008).

Wenger, E. (1998) *Communities of Practice: Learning, meaning and identity*, Cambridge: Cambridge University Press.

Wentworth, J. and Davis, J. R. (2002) 'Enhancing Interdisciplinary Teaching Through Team-Teaching', in C. Haynes (ed.) *Innovations in Interdisciplinary Teaching*, Westport, CT: American Council on Education/Oryx Press.

White, J. (ed.) (2004) *Rethinking the School Curriculum: Values, aims and purposes*, London: RoutledgeFalmer.

Widdowson, J. and Lambert, D. (2006) 'Using Geography Textbooks', in D. Balderstone (ed.) *Secondary Geography Handbook*, Sheffield: Geographical Association.

Wiliam, D. (2007) 'Learning About Learning'. Available at: <www.ltscotland. org.uk/learningaboutlearning/aboutlal/biogs/biogdylanwiliam.asp> (accessed 21 November 2008).

Wilkins, C. (1999) 'Making Good Citizens: The Social and Political Attitudes of PGCE Students', *Oxford Review of Education*, 25(1 and 2): 217–230.

Willats, J. (1997) *Art and Representation*, Princeton, NJ: Princeton University Press.

Williams, R. (1965) *The Long Revolution*, Harmondsworth: Pelican.

Williams, R. (1983) *Writing in Society*, London: Verso.

Williams, R. (1988) *Keywords*, London: Fontana Press.

Willis, P. (1990) *Common Culture*, Milton Keynes: Open University Press.

Witkin, R. (1974) *The Intelligence of Feeling*, London: Heinemann.

Wolff, J. (1981) *The Social Production of Art*, London: Macmillan.

Yeomans, R. (2005) 'Basic Design and the Pedagogy of Richard Hamilton', in M. Romans (ed.) *Histories of Art and Design Education: Collected essays*, Bristol: Intellect.

Zizeck, S. (1989) *The Sublime Object of Ideology*, London: Verso.

Index

Abbs, Peter 56–8
Araeen, Rasheed 85–9
accountability 45, 69, 81, 94, 125
accuracy 13, 105–6
activism 136–8
advertising 10, 12, 36, 77, 106, 116
advocacy 14, 18–19, 72, 77
aesthetic(s) 9, 19–21, 27, 44, 46, 74,
    101, 104, 121, 132; contemplation
    126; dialogic 9, 137; disposition 118;
    experience 20, 44, 51–9; formalist 88;
    group 104; relational 9, 137, 146
affective 16, 34, 49, 54, 56, 60–2, 103,
    107–8; turn 23
agent(s) 52, 81, 126; of change 70, 73,
    77, 85, 125
agency 44, 71–4, 105, 114, 118, 125,
    12–9, 132–3
alienation 3, 15, 44, 80
Alys, Francis 84–5
anticipation 59, 63
anti-racist education 21–2
apprenticeships 36, 61
art 9–16; community 9; curriculum 21,
    26, 51, 69, 78, 119
art and design curriculum 28–31, 2–39,
    73, 77, 81
artisan 21, 34
art history 11–15, 21, 89, 118
Arnold, Matthew 15
artist(s) 8–12, 17–18, 45, 47, 55–67,
    7–92, 102–3, 105–6, 118, 120–1,
    125, 137–46
artist/teacher 85–92, 134, 152
Arts and Crafts Movement 12–15,
    19–20
assessment 31–5, 69, 93–110, 115;
    criteria 57, 66, 94, 101–8; formative

96, 103, 109–10; learning 35,
    93; negotiated 104, 107–8; 144;
    summative 107
assumption(s) 39, 45, 51–4, 62–3, 78,
    89, 129
attention 16, 34, 55, 57, 63, 98–9,
    109–10
audience 30, 57, 61–3, 77, 82–8, 10–3,
    109, 116, 127
authority 32–3, 69, 115, 123, 127

Basic Design 19–21, 26
Bauhaus 9, 19–20, 25–6
Beech, David 91–2
belief(s) 1–2, 7–10, 15, 39, 43–5, 73,
    105, 121, 130, 132, 137, 146
Bourdieu, Pierre 10–11, 52, 90–2,
    108–10, 114–15, 11–18, 123–5, 128
binary opposition(s) 88–9, 11–20, 131
Boccioni, Umberto 53
body 44, 46, 51–2, 55–6, 122–3; docile
    13, 60; sensations 52, 59, 99
border-crossing 77, 125, 132–3, 136, 146
bourgeoisie 9–11, 16, 117–18
Bourriaud, Nicholas 9, 137, 146
Brecht, Bertolt 61
Burbules, Nicholas 129–31
built environment 20, 72–8, 103–5

canon 117–18, 120, 131–3
capital 10, 108; academic 117, 128
capitalism 9, 11, 91, 128, 146
carnival 123
celebration 12, 130
class 2, 11–16, 22–3, 52, 61–62,
    95, 117–19, 122, 124, 128, 132;
    dominant 95–6, 117, 126–8, 131–32;
    oppressed 116; privilege 10

classrooms as ecosystems 68
challenge 12, 30, 34, 39, 45, 63, 68–70, 88, 103, 114, 141, 143, 147
chance 64, 100, 121–2
child-centred pedagogies 16–17
children 13, 15–21, 25–6, 34–5, 47, 49–53, 55, 68, 97–99, 134–5, 138–47; educated 17; innocence/ goodness 15
Christian iconography 120
cinema 12, 112; Iranian 112
citizens 37, 68, 70; productive 68, 125
citizenship 72–77, 134–147
Cizek, Franz 35
co-actors 145
co-constructivist learning theory 71
cognitive 20–1, 48, 59, 66, 89, 94–97, 133
Coldstream, William 21
Cole, Henry 23
collaboration, 65, 68–71, 78–92, 96, 99–102, 134–147
colour 95, 99–102, 105
common language 66
communication(s) 12, 15, 22, 46, 48, 63, 104–5; zones 135
communities 36, 66, 68–71, 95, 113, 136; diasporic 114
community 15, 39, 63; 101, 103, 115, 127, 132, 133; Cohesion (DCFS 2007) 73; local 104; of practice 61, 66, 67–8, 85, 91, 113; school 68–9, 72–7
confidence 31, 33, 34, 53, 60, 144
consensus 67, 69, 101, 113–14, 130
conservatism 9, 119, 133, 136
constraint(s) 45, 53, 68, 77, 85, 100–2, 120, 127
constructivism 48, 71, 94, 136
Cook, Ebenezer 16
consumerism 26, 117–18, 128
contemporary art 20, 22, 78, 82, 118, 125, 136, 141; artists 8, 12, 84–90, 138; galleries 125–7; practice 138
convention(s) 12, 15, 17–18, 21, 45, 53, 102–3, 106–7, 121, 129, 131
cosmopolitanism 130, 145, 147
craft(s) 12–15, 19–20, 24–8, 46, 53–6, 61, 96, 97, 104, 123–25, 128; people 8, 53, 136
craftsmanship 13–14, 61

creative 30–9, 67, 93–4, 97, 108, 113; environment 63–6; industries 28–9, 35–6, 113; and Media Diploma 38; models 16–19; partnerships 29, 126, 147; potential 43–66; practices 2, 8, 11, 20–1, 67, 101–3; thinking 37, 70
creativity 21–40, 43–66; conditions for 34, 43, 62–66, 67; free 17, 49; pseudo 17; and ordinariness 46–51; recommendations for 62–66
Critical Minds 67, 78–85, 91
critical 14, 60–1, 66, 73, 86–7, 144, 147; dialogue 74; pedagogy 113–33, thinking 30, 36–8, 57, 68, 78–9, 89–91; turn 21–22
critique 2, 9–10, 31, 46, 49, 61, 81, 87–90, 97, 106–7, 117–19, 131–3
crits 96–7
cross-curricular 26, 30, 35–7, 54, 65, 70, 72–3, 77, 134, 146
cultural: barriers 62; conflict 91; difference 130; diversity 70, 131; enrichment 13; excellence 47, 125, 133; identity 35, 44, 70, 74; politics 77, 127; practice 21, 45–50, 63–4, 68, 94, 117–18; power 133; production 13, 17, 19–20, 44, 56, 118, 124, 133; resources 48–9, 100–2, 118, 126, 133; situation 52, 94–7, 114, 116; studies 119, 131–3; theorist 123; tolerance 130; transformation 127; understanding 60–1, 70–1; values 90, 103, 119, 124–5, 133, 142
culture 1, 15, 35–6, 88, 117; academic 59; Athenian 121; children's 26; commercial 118, 120; consumerist 118, 128; cyber 56; of dependency 83; distort 130; dominant 132; Islamic 102; minority 131–2; popular 22, 118–19; visual 3, 17, 22, 76–7, 116, 131, 135–6; western 47
curators 78, 85, 89, 134, 137
curiosity 53, 59, 62, 67; epistomological 74–77
curriculum 7–8, 15–16, 21–39, 51, 53, 69–73, 77–78, 81–2, 85, 90–1, 96, 114, 119, 135, 143: instrumentalist 19; National 43, 46, 76, 94, 126, 130, 144, 146

Deconstructions: Zero to Infinity 67, 85–90
democracy 10, 22, 76, 113–14, 119
demonstration 96, 98–9
De Sausmarez, Maurice 20, 26
design 8–14, 24–40, 72–6, 97, 123–5, 137; Basic 19–21
desire 10, 50, 52–54, 59, 106, 117, 121, 128
Dewey, John 9, 48, 115
DePalma, Renee 69
dialectical 88–9
dialogue 23, 62, 66, 69, 71–2, 74, 76–8, 97, 99, 114, 116, 129–133; with materials 53, 56
dialogical practices 9, 43, 65, 67, 95–7, 101, 114, 119–20, 125, 129, 133
diaspora 102, 114, 133
dichotomy 3, 83
didactic 14–16, 18–19, 102
difference 8, 45–5, 65, 67–8, 72, 78, 114, 117–18, 123, 125–6, 128–133, 145–6
Discipline-Based Art Education 21
discomfort 60–1, 69, 140
discussion 54, 57, 70, 74–5, 78, 83, 89, 100–4, 107–8, 120, 129–33, 134–5, 142
disidentification 117, 124
dissemination 60, 81, 102
distanciation 61
distinction(s) 10–13, 131, 133; hierarchical 117–19, 123
diversity 44, 58, 60, 65, 70, 73, 91, 101, 103, 106, 130–2
doxa 69, 90
domestic(ation) 13, 16, 27, 106, 131
drawing(s) 13, 15–17, 19, 24–5, 28, 55, 100, 106, 121–3

eastern 60
education 7–23; formal 51, 71; informal 51, 71, 91; moral 13–16; problem-posing 30, 64, 115–16
embodiment 43–66, 93, 109, 117, 123, 126, 128, 142
emotion(s) 16, 23, 53, 56, 58–62, 66, 82, 103
empathy 49, 60–1
empowerment 128, 130, 133
enculturation 51–2

engaged pedagogy 44, 61, 69, 83, 119, 140
English: art education 12–23; culture 15; language 14, 22, 36; literature 14–15, 22; theorists 19–20, 115
environment 8, 12, 26, 37, 44, 46, 48, 50–2, 63, 135–147; built 20, 72–7; creative 57, 66; discursive 57, 129–33; learning 49, 62, 64–5, 78, 94–110; local 83–5; social 67–85, 116; workshop 61
environmental justice 136
epistemological curiosity 74–77
equality 132
equity 119, 131
ethics 14, 18, 137, 146
Eurocentric 19, 47, 87, 126; non-137
evaluation 35, 38, 57–60, 62, 93–111
evolutionary model of the child 17
examination(s) 28–32, 66, 70, 107–8, 128; -safe 45
experience(s) 2, 49–50, 90; aesthetic 51–62, everyday 47, 81, 108, 116, 119, 125, 127–29, 135; shared 68
experiment(ation) 9, 17, 20, 65, 100
expression(s) 15–17, 21, 25, 32, 46, 53, 55–6, 62, 63, 101, 117, 133; self- 8, 43, 45, 57, 72, 118
exploitative acts 32, 51, 102, 108
exploration 37, 51–4, 59, 64–5, 82
exquisite corpse 131

Fauves 99
feeling(s) 14, 45, 58–63, 80, 94, 102, 135, 141–2; tone 59
feminist 126, 129; pedagogy 71; perspectives 22
field(s): of academic enquiry 55; of practice 1–2, 9–10, 17, 19, 27, 51, 63–5, 125, 136–8; of perception 99; of possibility 99, 110; restricted 11, 20, 56, 86–7, 117–18; sensory 99; unified 52
finality 55
formal elements 20, 13, 105
formalism 17, 19, 26, 88, 101
Freire, Paulo 61, 74, 76, 105, 115–17, 142
Fry, Roger 14–17, 115
fulfillment 30, 44, 52, 60
funk 61

futures 22–23, 28–39, 56, 63, 66, 90, 96, 99, 103, 116, 143

galleries 22, 67, 71, 78–85, 91, 118, 125–27, 133
gender 2, 15, 17, 19, 22, 23, 68, 102, 117, 124, 128, 134; and power 69
genitalia 121
genius 12, 47
Georgiaki, Maria 123–5
Gilbert Report '20 20 Vision' 71, 91
global(ism) 23, 29, 35, 37, 46, 77–8, 87, 91; capital 10, 91; citizenship 133–47; dimensions 70; understanding 131
Goethe, Johann Wolfgang von 102
Greenberg, Clement 19
guild(s) 16–19

habit(uation) 33, 34, 49, 50, 52–3, 64, 74, 96–9, 108–9, 116, 117, 125
habitus 52
heurism 15, 44
hierarchy 11–12, 22, 47, 123
Higher Education 19–20, 21, 38, 145
history 44, 63, 90, 103, 115, 119, 131, 139, 141; art education 7–23, design education 24–28; industrial 141; of modernism 97, 126; personal 1; popular 118; rewriting 107; social 51
hooks, bell 69, 79, 119
Hooper Greenhill, Eileen 126

ICT 28, 38, 82, 105
idea(s) 25, 26, 30, 32–35, 37, 43–4, 54–6, 60, 64–5, 67, 73, 77, 82–3, 90, 91, 100, 103–4, 108, 135, 139, 144; emergent 65
ideal 18, 19, 123, 124, 130–31
identity 1, 35, 63, 68, 73–4, 91, 104, 107, 132, 145; European 59
identification 52, 61, 63, 100, 108, 131, 133, 143; dis- 117, 124
illustration 132
illegitimacy 120–2
imagination 10, 11, 15, 17, 30–1, 46–51, 56, 58, 65–7; and ICT 28; popular 8; prophetic 144
immediacy 52, 54
immersion 8, 45, 60, 63, 65, 97, 109
improvisation 100, 109
incubation 34, 64

individualism 97, 145, 146
industry 11–16, 19, 20, 24–5, 39, 45, 141
inclusion 10, 22, 106, 125, 126, 130, 137
Initial Teacher Education 77, 89
injustice 132, 135
inner-city 142–3
inspection(s) 28, 31, 35
Inspiring Learning in Galleries 67
installation 84, 85, 88, 109, 122–3
instrumental education 7, 16, 46, 113, 115
intention(al) 11, 48, 52, 54, 64, 109
interculturalism 60, 106, 118, 133, 139
interdisciplinary 65, 105, 119, 136–46
interest(s) 23, 30, 39, 55, 59, 62–4, 82–3, 93–4, 96, 99, 102–3, 106, 116, 143
interlocuter 128
Internet 98, 120, 134
interpretation 31, 55, 60, 76, 90, 107, 117, 128, 145; formalist 17, mis- 18
intervention 9, 26, 83, 85, 88, 91, 114, 119–23
interventionists, friendly 85
intuition 20, 64, 97
Iran 102–3

Jews 59
Judenplatz Holocaust Memorial 59
judgements 54, 106, 108
justice 71, 130, 135–6

Kaprow, Alan 91
Klee, Paul 20
knowledge 20, 34, 44, 48–53, 64, 76, 77, 102–3, 117–118, 129, 135, 142; abstracted 44; application of 38, 93, 101; construction 63–4, 95–98, 105, 147; craft 55; cultural 126; declarative 63, 95; domain-specific 107; local 142; /power 119, 130; prior 21, 54, 101; practical 45, 61, 93, 103, 108; procedural 63, 95–6; propositional 108–10; object of 76; self- 60, 126; technical 96; transferable 105

Lave, Jean and Wenger, Ettienne 68, 91–2
learning 95–9; and assessment 99–110, banking system of 105, 115;

collaborative 61 62–6, 65–110, 134–147; dialogic 65, 69–92, 114, 119–20, 129–133; social process 67–92, 133–147; dispositions 7, 52, 128; evidence of 28, 100–1, 107, 110, 126; experiential 22, 69, 77, 126, 142; objectives 32, 65, 105, 107, 109; outcomes 30, 44, 53, 57, 93, 107; personalised 72; situated 95, 107, 131; transmission 48, 83, 107
The Learning Impact Research Project 126
Leavis, Frank Raymond 14–15, 19
legitimacy 45, 56, 120–22
liberatory practices 134–147
local 22–3, 30, 37, 48, 68, 77, 103–4; campaigners 138; community 69, 137; environment 74, 83–4, 141–2, resources 8

mass- education 114–15; media 10, 12, 78, 87, 132; production 12, 20, 24
materials 38, 53, 55–6, 64–5, 74, 82, 104, 106, 109, 142
media 10, 20, 37–8; electronic 46
mediation 58, 95, 99; of language 52, 124
metacognition 66, 96–7
metaphor 68, 88, 142
Michelangelo's *David* 120–3
mimesis 47
Minimalism 87–8
model 31, 62–3, 79; pedagogic 2, 17, 20–4, 64, 83, 135, 141; research 78
modernism 9–21, 61, 97, 118, 126
Moholy-Nagy, Lazlo 20
moral(s) 32, 48, 65, 70–1, 130; education 13–16, 19; guidance 13; invert 123
Morris, William 12–14, 19
motivation 35, 62–3, 126
multiculturalism 21–22, 130
multimodal 137, 142
multimedia 10
museums 71, 78, 118, 120, 125–7
mutuality 68–71

Nazi 9, 59
Neshat, Shirin 102–3
neutrality 131
Nietzsche, Freidrich 9, 18

neurotic 18
norms 9, 54, 63, 93, 119, 125, 131, 141
NSEAD 70
nude sculpture 120

objective probabilities 109
Ofsted 28, 32
Op artists 99
oppression 114, 116
originality 57, 60, 117
other(s) 52, 60, 65, 131, 137; thinking 49, 90, 99, 117, 142

painting 12, 24–5, 28, 53–56, 95, 98, 101, 105
participation 9, 29, 61–2, 68, 83, 88, 92, 126–7, 142; civic 35, 48
partnerships 65, 70, 72, 78, 91, 125–7; creative 29, 51, 137
passionate attachments 1, 67, 86, 89
pastiche 21
pedagogy, Bauhaus 19–21, 26; creative 16–19, 43–66, critical 113–33; engaged 44, 61, 69, 119, 140; progressive 7–8, 15–17, 19, 67, 114–15, 127, 133, 140; traditional 2, 9, 15, 19, 48–9, 82–3, Victorian 12–16
perceptualism 21, 55, 83, 105
performance 54, 57, 85, 100–1, 139, 153
perspective, axonometric 106, 109
Personalised Learning 72
photography 99, 101
pictorial regime 19, 105
Piper, Adrian 61–2
Piper, Keith 145
Place Making 72–76
Plato 47, 108
pleasure 7, 60, 122
pluralism 130
primitivism 27
Prince's Foundation 67, 72–3
privilege 3, 59, 114, 118, 125, 129, 137
possibility(ies) 45–6, 49, 54, 57, 83, 99–100, 110, 113, 127–31, 133, 141, 144
postmodernism 22, 84, 126
power 10–11, 52–3, 69, 116–17, 125; relations 10, 71–2, 80, 119, 127–146; and representation 46

practical knowledge 45, 61, 95, 103, 108–110
problem-solving 30–4, 51, 64, 74, 95–6, 115–16
process 84, 88–9; creative 17, 33–4, 47–48, 56–8, cognitive 48, 59, 94, 97, 107; social 10, 71, 99
programme of study 27, 70, 96
progressive education 7–8, 15–17, 19, 67, 114–15, 127, 133, 140
Proust, Marcel 13
psychoanalysis, Jungian 28
public intellectual 147
purpose 14, 30, 38, 57, 63, 71, 93, 104, 107, 117, 127

Queen Victoria 121

race 68, 106, 124, 134
Read, Herbert 2, 9, 18–19, 25
reconciliation 130
recreational justifications 18
reflection 45, 54, 57–8, 74, 76, 89–92, 96–7, 100, 109, 140, 144–5
reflective practitioner 62, 89
reflexivity 3, 68, 85, 90, 92, 109
Rego, Paula 53–4
relevance 30, 73
representation 11, 46, 53, 55, 56, 63, 96, 102, 105–6, 116
research 54, 59, 71, 72, 89, 93, 108, 124; action 78; reports 2, 28, 31, 67, 74, 78, 85, 91, 104, 118, 119
resistance 54, 85, 103, 117–19, 123, 125–8, 131
resource(s) 2, 46, 53, 55, 56, 60, 64, 71, 77, 84, 118, 123, 133; justice 139, 143
review(s) 27, 34, 36, 39, 96
revolution 9, 27, 32, 102, 115–16, 140; cognitive 94
Richardson, Marion 15, 17–18, 25
Riley, Bridget 99
risk-taking 53, 65–6, 103–4, 108–9, 130, 140, 144, 146
Rodney, Donald 145
Romantic tradition 8, 10–11, 15–16, 47, 97, 145
Rousseau, Jean-Jacques 15–16, 25
rules 45, 53, 64–5, 75, 85, 103, 109, 115, 120, 130
Ruskin, John 13–16, 19

Schon, Donald 58, 100
school, art 9, 19, 28, 32, 45, 83, 93, 105–6, 114, 125, 135, 141; subjects 8, 13, 15, 25–7, 30–1, 34, 76, 135, 141, 143, 146
science 51, 58, 115, 136; domestic 27
sites of contestation 67, 69–70, 92
skill(s) 11, 13, 28–31, 36–9, 46, 51, 66, 69, 72, 75, 77, 78–85, 91, 93–4, 96–7, 99, 107, 123–4, 136, 137, 141, 144
social 63; change 36, 125; emancipation 115; situation 43–4, 48, 50–52, 57, 61, 65, 114–19, 127–38; harmony 35; interaction 94–5, 99, 123; norms 9, 54, 63, 119, 125, 131; practice 2, 8–22, 45, 77–92, 140–7; process 48; role; stability 35, 60
socially engaged 10, 44, 67, 69, 83, 87–8, 119
spectatorship 61, 125–6
status quo 22, 60, 70, 78
stimulus 34, 59, 60, 62–3
subject(s) 87, 116
subjectivity 87, 117
sustainability 12, 108, 116, 137
symbolic 10, 12, 53, 63, 93, 94, 100, 108, 123, 125–6; violence 114
synthesis 49, 64

tactile 37, 52–3, 124
taste 52
technical, assessment 103, competence 25, 45, 53, 99, 105, 107; knowledge 96; resources 108
Technical Manifesto of Futurist Sculpture 53
technological: change 29, 36–7; determinism 46
technology 11, 26–29, 37–8, 58, 140; digital 46, 99–101, 120, 144; hydro 139
Third Text 87
Thompson, D'Arcy 20
time 34, 54, 70, 78, 81, 91, 96, 99, 100, 104, 106, 125, 130, 141, 144, 146; and space 52, 64–5
tradition(s) 2, 11, 12, 19, 48, 51, 53, 55–6, 106, 113; craft 24; western 47
transformation 7, 10, 17, 48, 49, 54, 101, 116, 125–7, 131, 134
tokenism 137

totalitarian 18, 128
Turner, Joseph Mallard William 102

ukiyo-e artists 106
uniqueness 8, 10, 17, 50, 51, 71, 104,
  115, 145
universal(ism) 17, 19, 22, 34, 102, 115,
  126, 133
urban 9, 21, 45, 132, 138–42
USA 19, 20, 21, 46, 94, 114, 118–19,
  128, 132
utopia 18

value(s) 1, 15, 29, 30, 37, 45, 51, 54,
  57, 66, 70–5, 82, 83, 91, 101–2,
  108, 119, 124, 128–9, 131, 135;
  ecological 139; monetary 10–11,
  124; naturalised 119, 130; normative
  115, 123; of ordinary life 48; shared
  82–85, 104, 128; social 33, 52,
  70, 90, 95–6, 103, 106, 108, 136;
  universal 133; use 66

Victorian legacy 12–16, 19, 105
visceral arousal 59
visibility 59, 87, 130, 132
visual culture(s) 3, 17, 22, 76–7,
  116, 131, 135–6
visualisation 49
Vygotsky, Lev 49–50, 58, 94–99,
  107, 110

Wacquant, Loic 90
well-being 8
western 10, 12, 44, 47, 53, 60, 98,
  102, 108, 118, 119, 123
Whiteread, Rachel 59
Williams, Raymond 11–12, 47
women 16, 22, 102–3; teachers 16
word(s) 22, 63, 94, 122, 140
Workload Agreement 70
writing 82, 103, 139, 144

zone of proximal development
  96